Paul Naschy
Memoirs of a Wolfman

Paul Naschy
Memoirs of a Wolfman

Translated by Mike Hodges

Luminary Press
Baltimore, Maryland

ISBN 1-887664-38-6
Library of Congress Catalog Card Number 98-105416
Manufactured in the United States of America
Printed by King Printing, Lowell, MA
First Printing by Midnight Marquee, Press, Inc., 1997
Second Printing by Luminary Press, a division of Midnight Marquee Press, Inc.,
        November 2003

To Elvira —
my companion in success and failure,
my muse, star of my best film,
the story of my own life;
a wonderful picture
of lights and shadows,
made with the exclusive
subsidy of love and loyalty.

PREMIO ESPECIAL DE INTERPRETACION A PAUL NASCHY EN LA II CONVENCION DE CINE FANTASTICO DE PARIS

EL JOROBADO DE LA MORGUE

PAUL NASCHY   ROSSANA YANNY   VIC WINNER

con ALBERTO DALBES Y MARIA PERSHY

director JAVIER AGUIRRE   EASTMANCOLOR   productor EVA FILMS, S. L. (FRANCISCO LARA POLOP)

Table of Contents

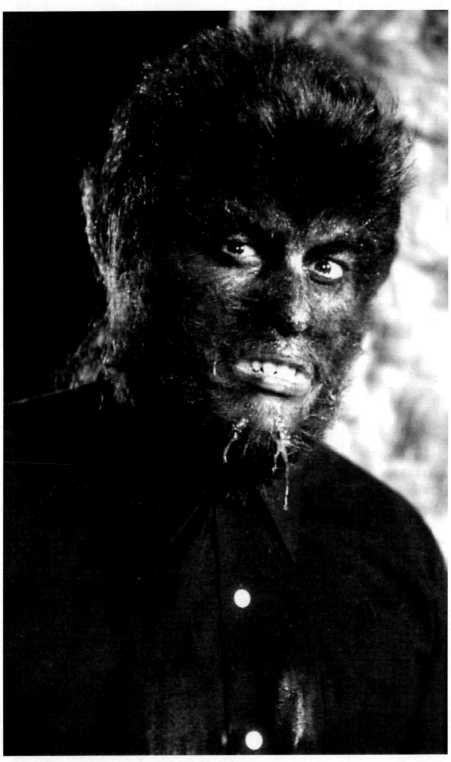

Paul Naschy

American Introduction

There has never been a filmmaker like Paul Naschy. Naschy's involvement in cinema spans 40 years and counting, with work as an actor, screenwriter, director and producer. He has molded his own vision under these assignments, and provided an unheard of spectrum of clues to his personality, passions and ethos.

Born Jacinto Molina in Madrid, Paul Naschy became known in the United States for films like *Frankenstein's Bloody Terror, The Werewolf vs. the Vampire Woman* (both edited for the American market) and a spattering of other movies released on double-bills that were all too frequently ignored by the critics or at most treated with ridicule and disdain. TV showings, pruning nudity and gore, made their vague impressions. Video releases provided a semblance of coherency to an appreciation of Naschy's work, but the prints used were generally inferior, cut in certain cases and presented full-frame, diluting the impact, as well as the physical and spiritual breadth of their creator's artistic vision.

A growing cadre of Naschy fans were still unfamiliar with most of his work, however, and knew little about the man himself. His best and most personal films—*El huerto del Frances* (*The Frenchman's Garden*), *El caminante* (*The Traveler*)—never saw release in the United States, either theatrically or on official video. His unique epic-scaled Wolfman film, *La bestia y la espada magica* (*The Beast and the Magic Sword*), a more noteworthy film than many better known works, has been made available only through illegal dupes whose poor quality obliterates the exacting detail so carefully crafted by the filmmakers. Practically unknown is a film short, *Hambre mortal* (*Mortal Hunger*), which offers an Oscar winning-type performance by Naschy that would stun his fans. Japanese-produced docudramas made by Naschy and starring him in a wide range of juicy roles, and indispensable for a complete picture of his vigorous talent, have never been seen in the United States, and were even ignored in Spain, Naschy's homeland.

But the times they are a-changing. Thanks to DVDs, genre specific publications and dedicated maverick researchers, respect for all varieties of European film is growing. Naturally, attention is being focused again on Naschy, and the focus this time around is serious and appreciative. Spain and Germany are releasing excellent prints on video and DVD; the United States promises to follow suit, though much is hampered by tightfisted rights holders with exorbitant monetary demands. The battle to view and make known Naschy's work still goes on.

The battle is worth it. If we just speak of the horror genre, Paul Naschy is a distinctive talent. Perhaps one shouldn't step on the carefully protected toes of the familiar horror "kings" of the past and present, but Naschy is their equal, and in terms of involvement in the genre—as screenwriter, director and producer—he outdistances every one of them. This is not a man who simply sits by the phone waiting for an agent to call.

Even now, Naschy continues to fight for horror fantasy. An English translation of Naschy's screenplay, *Los ojos del lobo* (*The Eyes of the Wolf*), the latest Waldemar Daninsky moon-blessed chiller, is being prepared for a possible co-production deal with the United States; Naschy is generating a film festival in Estepona, hoping to give a boost to the genres he so loves. Projects and opportunities, trials and triumphs still await this Romantic man of the cinema who consumes life with robustness and seeks continual release through the creative act.

This autobiography is Naschy's manifesto of will and dedication. It is also a great read, filled with engaging anecdotes, earthy asides, written with ease and intelligence, brimming with soul and a heart sometimes suffering, all the time passionate. (Accolades must go to British-born film historian Michael Hodges, now living and working in Spain, whose impeccable translation of Naschy's text offers a smooth conduit to the original and whose bracketed explanations illuminate but never intrude.)

If you are unfamiliar with Naschy, now is the time to become introduced to this living legend; if you are familiar with him, your understanding of the man will be fleshed out and made more rewarding. Either way, the evidence is clear. There has never been a filmmaker like Paul Naschy.

—Miroslaw Lipinski
Author, Translator,
Webmaster of *The Mark of Naschy*
(http://members.aol.com/eurosin/naschy.htm)

American and British theatrical or video release titles of Naschy films have frequently diverged from being translations of the original Spanish titles.   Below is a list of the most important of such titles and Spanish-titled films they represent.

Assignment Terror - Los monstruos del terror
Blood Moon - La noche de Walpurgis
The Craving - El retorno del hombre lobo
Crimson - Las ratas no duermen de noche
Curse of the Devil - El retorno de Walpurgis
The Devil's Possessed - El Mariscal del Infierno
Dracula Vs. Frankenstein - Los monstruos del terror
Frankenstein's Bloody Terror - La marca del hombre lobo
The Hanging Woman - La orgia de los muertos
House of Psychotic Women - Los ojos azules de la muneca rota
Human Beasts - El carnaval de las bestias
Night of the Howling Beast - La maldicion de la bestia
The People Who Own the Dark - Ultimo deseo
Return of the Zombies - La orgia de los muertos
Rue Morgue Massacres - El jorobado de la morgue
Vengeance of the Zombies - La rebelion de las muertas
The Werewolf Vs. The Vampire Woman - La noche de Walpurgis
Werewolf's Shadow - La noche de Walpurgis

Introduction to the Spanish Edition
by Luis Alberto de Cuenca

I've been an admirer of Paul Naschy for 30 years now, from the time I first began to appreciate his formidable film work right up to the present, when I'm fortunate enough to enjoy the friendship of the man himself. I'm afraid—and I choose the word advisedly, since "fear," "fright" and "terror" are always suitable terms to employ when speaking of Naschy—that this admiration will not be confined to the space of the last three decades; I'm sure I'll admire this great Madrid born actor 'til the end of my days.

It's a wonderful feeling when someone whom you admire asks you to write a few lines to preface his memoirs. It's indeed a piece of good fortune that Jacinto Molina, alias Paul Naschy, has got around to writing his memoirs and that Alberto Santos [the original Spanish publisher] has decided to publish them, with all his usual flair and style. Good fortune indeed that these memoirs are wonderfully well written and as compelling as the most gripping novel. But the height of good fortune is that the name of the admirer—in this case, myself—should be so closely bound, bibliographically, to the object of his admiration. An honor for which I have to thank the multi-talented creator of Waldemar Daninsky.

I write "multi-talented" because Paul Naschy's life has encompassed an amazing diversity of activities. His first achievement was to be born in the historic Calle Postas. His latest accomplishment, to date, has been the writing of these memoirs which you are now holding. In between, he's made more than 100 movies as an actor, and countless others as scriptwriter and director. And many other things besides, because as will be seen from Paul Naschy's totally enthralling autobiography, his film career is just one facet of his remarkably diverse personality.

Throughout these memoirs Paul, who is famous for having portrayed countless characters on screen, reveals many other aspects of his own persona, equally as fascinating as his interpretations of Dracula, the Wolf Man or Gilles de Rais. We'll meet the nephew devoted to two unforgettable characters, his uncles Jacinto and Emilio; the accomplished sportsman; the writer of Wild West novels; the father; the enthusiastic reader of horror-fantasy literature. So many other aspects of Jacinto Molina are displayed through the pages of this book, each one enriching the fictional creatures with human warmth and depth.

The full moon sometimes turns us into wolves. Paul Naschy knows more about that than most. But other times it casts its silvery light on the angels we once were. Between wolf and angel lie an infinity of intermediate states which Paul writes about with passion. Congratulations are due to Naschy fans; we've known and admired his splendid gallery of Masks—now we can get to know and admire the true face of Paul Naschy.

Paul Naschy

Preface:
A Stormy Life

I've been asked to write my autobiography. It's something I've been wanting to do and it didn't take me long to make up my mind.

Two days after this request I find myself sitting alone in my study facing the difficult challenge of looking back over my own life. I can't help feeling a certain reticence as well as the burden of responsibility which comes from having to be totally sincere, of removing the mask, limited only by the bounds of my own conscience.

This screenplay of my own existence won't be easy to write. The truth is that none of them ever are, though in this case the difficulties are greater, since trying to condense so many vitally important sequences into just over 300 pages is going to be a job and a half. Still, it won't be for want of determination on my part.

Along my own private time tunnel many events will unfold with their accompanying joys, sorrows, successes, failures, loyalties, betrayals, along with dramatic, comical and even bizarre situations.

Of course, this is a story that as yet has no end but which is undoubtedly jam packed with incident since, with 60 years behind me and even without having to exert my memory too much, I can obviously recall a great number of "battles" to relate.

Battles or skirmishes, some inflicting slight damage, others truly bloody, but at the end of the day battles all the same, because for me life is like a war that is fought day by day, month by month, year after year. In all this time we engage in stand offs and combats which only come to an end when we're finally reduced to a flatline on a monitor. Trying to be objective about one's own existence is no easy task. On the long and winding road too much has been left behind, things like innocence, naivete, affection, tears, friendships, hate, envy, love, sacrifice and even blood. Our passage leaves traces of what we could have been and what we finally are. A cascade of images, memories, and meaningful moments is reflected in my past and present; sometimes they're fleeting but all of them contribute to make up the fabric of my soul.

After this little preamble, I'll get on with my story. The readers will judge whether the publication of this book has been worthwhile.

Paul Naschy
November 1997
Madrid, Spain

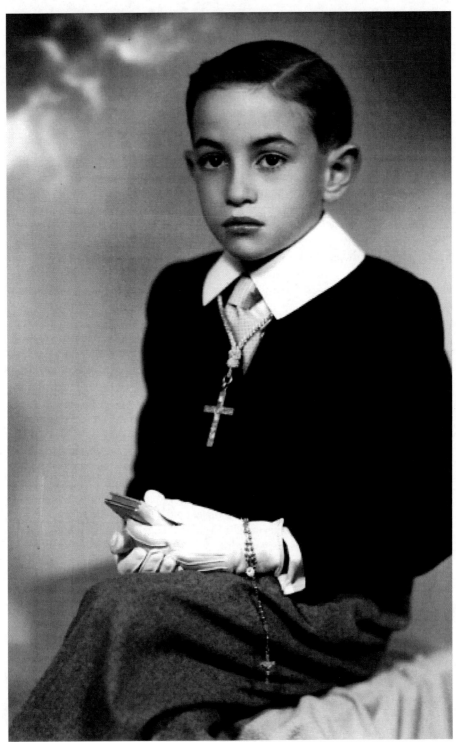

My First Communion photo

Paul Naschy

The Beginning

Six o'clock in the morning on the sixth of September 1934—these weren't good times for Spain. Something floating in the atmosphere forebodes a future full of fear and the air was almost palpably unwholesome. My father once told me that he'd looked at the sky that day at dusk and it had seemed to be steeped in blood. Well, such was the day I came into the world in the Calle Postas, close to the Plaza Mayor, in the very heart of Madrid. It was September 6 at six in the morning; it only needed one more six to complete the Satanic triad. I sure had a narrow escape.

My father, an athletic, good looking man, was a Basque, from Vitoria to be precise. He'd been a keen sportsman and started work at the age of 14. He started out as an errand boy for an antiques dealer and, once settled in Madrid, went into the fur and leather trade as a cutter. He started out as just another employee but he was talented, he had ambition and though it was a long, hard slog he became one of the very top craftsmen in his field.

My mother hailed from Asturias. She still possesses a remarkable natural intelligence and surprising vitality. My father's name was Enrique Molina Omaña and her name is Pilar Àlvarez.

Before going any further, let me tell you something about my paternal grandfather. He was a Catalonian, born in Reus; a great artist, an extraordinary sculptor and carver of religious effigies. Outstanding among his works are the lovers of the Cibeles [a monumental fountain in the center of Madrid], the figure of Christ of Suances church, destroyed in the Civil War [1936-39], the statue of President Madero in Mexico and the Monument to the Heroes of Numancia. He also carved countless Holy images for Easter-Holy Week processions. His name was Emilio. I remember him as an extremely pious man, full of kindness, with a noble face, clear blue eyes and a flowing white beard. To me he seemed an authentic patriarch and from my childish perspective I endowed him with an unreal, magical aura. He used to tell me fantastic tales about saints, angels and their eternal enemies, the terrifying demons of Hell. Of course, in his marvelous stories Good always triumphed over Evil.

This exceptional man announced his own death. In his own words, Destiny had

The little Jacinto Molina

My grandfather Emilio Molina Pages

decreed that his time was up and his friends the saints were waiting for him. Of course, none of us believed him— "grandfather's ramblings" we thought. In fact he passed away peacefully in his sleep that snowy white Christmas.

It all seems so distant... and yet he's so near, if I close my eyes I can see him clearly, whittling away with his razor sharp gouge in his old workshop. Shortly before his death he carved for me a figure of the tormented Christ on the cross.

But I've got ahead of myself by relating these memories of my grandfather, so I'll now return to the beginning of 1936.

In the summer of that terrible year my parents and I went to spend the holidays in Cantabria, to a little village called Mazcuerras. This village would later be renamed "Luzmela" in honor of the famous authoress Concha Espina and one of her works *The Little Girl of Luzmela*.

The setting sun used to paint the sky in ever bloodier tones and the dark clouds were an omen of the imminent outbreak of the Sinister Storm that was about to fall down and engulf Spain for three long years.

Finally the Apocalypse came. The cannons started to roar and the tanks clattered into action, their objective death and destruction. Spaniard killed Spaniard in a war of bloody fratricide. The Civil War had begun.

Although it seems unbelievable, given my tender age, I can clearly remember a great many things. From the balcony of our summer residence I saw a man's head blown off by a shell and saw how the headless body took a few steps before collapsing in a macabre, twitching heap. I remember the zigzagging of the legendary "ratas" (as we called the Republican fighter planes) as they took on the old Fiat biplanes of Franco's Air Force. I'll never forget the lines of tracer bullets spewing forth from the machine guns, nor the trails of grayish smoke as the stricken planes went down.

One day as my young mother was carrying me in her arms along the glass fronted corridor a burst of machine gun fire shattered the heavy glass panes to smithereens. My mother was quick to throw herself to the floor and we survived.

Opposite the house there was a little square with a fountain and a crumbling stone cross. Many unfortunates were executed by firing squad at this place and I remember seeing the rigid, shattered corpses like puppets with broken strings. And other things,

My father Enrique—when I was a mere infant my father used a motorcycle to escape a political death sentence.

such as the time a bomb dropped close to the well in the patio of our house. It was a pure miracle that my mother, my aunt Milagros, my little cousin Sara and I weren't killed.

Even now, as I recall these events in the company of my mother, she still expresses her amazement: How can it be that I am able to remember things that happened when I was little more than two years old? I still don't know the answer. Perhaps my mother herself, although she doesn't remember it, told me all about those happenings. Maybe other people, over the years, have told me about those tragic events. Or perhaps I've stored away in my memory fragments of conversations overheard from friends and relatives. I don't know, but those chilling images will be with me until the end of my days. Such are the mysterious workings of the human brain.

But allow me to give a brief summary of the situation. My parents and I spent that fateful summer in the holiday home belonging to aunt Milagros, my mother's eldest sister. She was married to Prudencio Gonzalez, a landowner of aristocratic descent. They had two children of my age, Enrique and Sarita.

My father, who was not much more than a boy, was accused by someone in the village of being a devout churchgoer and having right wing sympathies. This was a treacherous lie because my progenitor was in fact a simple working man of humble background and completely uninterested in politics. In that place, at that time, such an accusation meant the death sentence. So he was to be executed together with the village priest, the schoolmaster and the mayor. Fortunately, however, a friendly militia man who had a motorcycle hidden in a haystack warned my father, who made his getaway that very night. He entrusted to my aunt the protection and custody of his family. However the escape went awry when somebody alerted a militia patrol and they went after my father, machine gunning him as he sped on his motorbike across the old Roman bridge. Man and machine plunged into the depths of the river and his pursuers gave him up for dead. It was left to the distressed Prudencio to break the news to my mother—at only 18 years of age she was a widow. It seemed that a tragedy had been played out.

The young woman now had to bring up her son as best she could in the face of adversity. Luckily a kind hearted militia man did all he could to help her out. He even suggested that I should be evacuated to the Soviet Union. My mother almost agreed to this suggestion but in the end she couldn't bear to be parted from her son.

One evil day the naked corpses of the mayor, the priest, the town hall secretary and the schoolmaster appeared hanging from meathooks in the butcher's shop. Their dripping blood was caught in metal pans. It was like one of Goya's gruesome engravings brought to life.

But my father hadn't been killed in that spectacular fall from the bridge and under cover of night was able to make good his escape. After many misadventures, including a spell working in a circus, he managed to reach Valencia. There, God only knows how, he enrolled as a crewman on a converted merchant ship which was about to set off on a mission which he never explained to me.

Food was in short supply aboard the vessel and the crew often went hungry. But Enrique Molina made himself popular due to his skill at fishing, as well as for being a good cook. The ship was berthed at the dockside in Valencia while it was being armed. The latrines which were situated on deck were provided with screens to hide the users from the indiscreet gaze of their crewmates but there were no screens on the side facing the port. Naturally when the crew went to answer the call of nature, their exposed backsides were clearly visible from the dockside. The vessel soon became known as *El Barco de los Culos* (The Ship of Asses).

My father struck up friendships with several of the crew, three of them in particular—a political commissar known as Paco "El Botas," a schoolmaster and Socialist Party militant called, if memory serves me right, Julián Castro, and a veteran Communist who had spent a lot of time in Russia. Each of them in their own way were a great help to their shipmates: Enrique with his fishing, Paco El Botas, who had "some experience with aspirins," assisting the ship's doctor, and the Communist entertaining the crew with his virtuoso balalaika playing.

Julián Castro spoke proudly of his father, a printer who had worked with Pablo Iglesias [founder of the Partido Socialista Obrero Español—Spanish Socialist Workers' Party] on *El Socialista* and *La Nueva Era* [Socialist Party newspapers]. My father was surprised to see that the combat hardened Communist veteran always wore on his chest a medallion with the image of the Virgin del Carmen which his mother had given him before he left for Russia.

After the war, Enrique ran into both Paco El Botas and the schoolmaster. They had just come out of concentration camps and were looking for work. My father got them jobs in his fur and leather workshop. Sadly, the Virgin del Carmen vet had been executed by firing squad. Both Paco El Botas and the schoolmaster remained true to their ideals and used to organize meetings with their comrades in some warehouses which my father owned in Chamartín. Luckily no one ever found out about these little clandestine gatherings.

I've just remembered an amusing anecdote. Paco El Botas, the schoolmaster and my father were in the habit of going away with their ladies to spend the weekends in the mountains, usually to a place known as La Pedriza. One fine day they were sitting down peacefully eating Spanish *tortillas* washed down with a measure of good red wine when, all at once, the three men leapt to their feet, feeling an excruciating jab in the backside. They'd all been well and truly stung by scorpions. There could be no doubt that they had been shipmates on the Ship of Asses.

When the new gun had been fitted, the vessel set sail. However, once at sea they came under attack from Admiral Cervera's flagship. After an exchange of broadsides the Republican vessel surrendered and the whole ship's company, including my father, were taken prisoner.

After a few days in prison they were made to form up in a courtyard. A captain of Franco's Army began to call out the names of a number of prisoners whom he ordered to stand to one side. One of the named men didn't answer and my father had the idea of answering in his place. Unfortunately, or rather, fortunately, his nervousness and inexperience gave him away. The captain looked him up and down and asked him if he was really the man whose name he'd called out. My father couldn't bear it and confessed that he was not. The officer smiled and asked what his real name was. The frightened young man replied "My name is Enrique Molina Omaña." The captain ordered him to follow and led my father to a large square near the docks where he showed him a pile of bullet riddled corpses. "There are the men on the list. You can thank God, my lad, that you're such a bad liar."

It turned out that having taken note of my father's name, the captain passed it on to Admiral Cervera, who summoned my father to his office. It was a truly amazing coincidence: The admiral was a close friend of Emilio Molina the sculptor, my grandfather.

After several other episodes, which I know nothing about, my father, after undergoing a crash course, was sent to the front as a tank crewman. He fought on several fronts, including Irun and Teruel. He saw many comrades killed and was himself wounded in the leg. Once recovered he returned to the front and became involved in another episode which could have had a most dramatic outcome. Following a tough battle, the Republican forces who had been defending a strategic position were finally overcome and the troops with whom my father was fighting took numerous prisoners. Several men abandoned their trenches with their hands aloft. Perched on the turret of his tank my father watched the scene, and imagine his surprise on seeing that among the defeated troops was none other than his brother Angel. The youngest of the nine Molinas had run away from home to join the Republican army. When he left home his

With my cousin Sarita in Mazcuerras

only baggage had been a loaf of bread, a string of cured sausages and a bottle of "firewater." He was still a child, but at the same time he was already an experienced veteran. Destiny, as unpredictable as ever, had taken a surprising turn, ending up with one man taking his own brother prisoner.

Many years later my uncle Angel told me that my father had said to him, "Thank God it was us who took you prisoner because behind us the Moors are coming." ["Los Moros"—"The Moors" was the popular name for the North African troops recruited from the colony of Spanish Morocco.] "He was quite right," added my uncle, "because the Moors didn't take prisoners, they just slit their throats." Needless to say, for Angel Molina the war ended that day.

Shortly after this my father managed to get a posting to Cantabria. The idea was to reach Mazcuerras and recover his wife and child. The bloody Civil War was entering its final stages.

The fighting was tough and in some places resistance was fierce but finally Enrique Molina made it to the village.

In a twist of fate, the militia leader who had supplied the Molina family with the means of subsistence was killed in the bitter fighting to capture the village, which in some places was hand to hand.

It was the middle of the night when the tall, strong Basque arrived at the summer house. Armed to the teeth, with several days' stubble and wearing a filthy, torn uniform he was a disturbing, threatening creature. The battle hardened soldier crossed the bedroom threshold and took his wife in his arms in an emotional embrace. The child, by contrast, let out a cry of terror and rushed to hide under the bed. This huge, blackened soldier was undoubtedly a monster in the eyes of the little Jacinto Molina, his first ever monster. The last screams and sounds of the dying battle drifted in from outside.

The phantasmagorical image of my father striding across that semi-darkened bedroom will always remain engraved in my mind.

To close this chapter, I'll narrate something which happened to me in the 1960s and which is related to the tragic events of my early childhood.

I was spending a few days with a friend in Santander, and on a sudden impulse I decided to pay a visit to Mazcuerras. I think we arrived on a Friday, at dusk, and we found accommodation in a small rustic guesthouse. After a good supper we went to bed, but I was too excited to sleep. I heard the cock crow early in the morning and got up in a state of some nervousness. I was served breakfast in a dining room full of

My father is in the center of the photograph.

heavy oak furniture—a large cup of milky coffee and big slices of locally produced bread and honey. It was here that I met the owner's father and his small talk unexpectedly began to bring back certain episodes from my past. Roque, for that was his name, must have been in his 60s, he was thin and wiry and his small, dark eyes sparkled beneath his thick gray eyebrows. He knocked back two glasses of "firewater" (a habit which, he said, kept him strong as an ox). He told me a lot of things, for instance, that his father had been executed by Franco's troops. He also told me about a ship which used to berth at the dockside in Santander. Many of those sentenced to summary execution by local "peoples' tribunals" would be weighted down with great stones tied around their necks and thrown overboard. It was, in his own words, a filthy trick.

Later he told me that when Santander had fallen to Franco's forces, a couple of divers went down at the spot and were horrified to discover a forest of cadavers rising from the depths, many of them still floating in the murky waters on the end of their ropes. According to Roque, one of the divers went out of his mind.

A little later the quaint old Republican and I went on a tour of the village; my friend was still sleeping like a log. It was astonishing; in spite of a few changes I recognized it perfectly: the little square, the old fountain, the crumbling stone cross and even the summer house with its long blue painted wooden verandah. The place was just as I remembered it. As in a flashback the long distant images came rushing back: the shelling, the dark heaps of corpses, the chatter of machine guns, the indistinct shadows of times long gone by. I didn't want to see any more, despite the kind offer of the hotelier to show me the rest of Luzmela or Mazcuerras.

That same afternoon, after lunch, we returned to Santander. My friend was unaware of my wanderings and I didn't feel like talking about it. I think it was Baudelaire who said, "Attempting to explain the incomprehensible often leads to confusion and, on occasion, to madness."

My Encounter with Gothic

For reasons unknown to me and which my family never explained, my father left the front for good and was transferred to Burgos, as Colonel Pastrana's aide-de-camp. This peculiar officer was, I believe, Chief of the VI Military Region, as well as a handsome and charismatic man, with a well earned reputation as a Don Juan. He used to wear expensive uniforms, designed partly by himself, rode a lively white horse and used spurs made of gold. I saw him on more than one occasion, but here my memories are much less distinct.

We lived in army accommodation and my parents had engaged a Fräulein, half-Prussian and half-Austrian, to educate me and teach me German. Her name was Maria Ronge and I remember her as a sweet little grandmother, strict but gentle at the same time.

It was at this time that, on a walk around the old Castillian city, I discovered the extraordinary Cathedral; its French inspired design lends it a totally unique appearance to my mind. The Cathedral impressed me greatly, as did the *Casa del Cordon*, San Esteban's Arch, The Hospice of San Juan and the Portico of Santa Maria. They all evoked the chivalry of the Middle Ages, with the image of the legendary El Cid to the fore. Incidentally, for a long time I had been trying to visualize what Rodrigo Diaz de Bivar actually looked like. Many years later, and thanks to the producer Samuel Bronston, I met his alter ego—that's to say Charlton Heston. My imagination was well satisfied and apparently so was that of the film's historical consultant, the great academic Menéndez Pidal.

Maria Ronge

A lot of things grabbed my attention and left a lasting impression on me, especially the stone and alabaster tombs of constables, warriors and bishops. As I observed the recumbent, immobile figures I felt a shiver run down my spine to think that they might suddenly come to life. Little did I know that the same idea had occurred—many, many years previously—to the great Gustavo Adolfo Bécquer.

Once settled in Burgos, my father, now a leading furrier, entered a partnership with Colonel Pastrana and together they set up a leather tannery in the village of Castañares. We left the army accommodation and went to live in a beautiful chalet. Things were going well, Enrique Molina had become the most fashionable furrier in Burgos. As well as the tannery he opened a large cutting shop and a retail store. The war was over and a new era had begun, although we didn't know whether things would turn out for better or for worse.

Meanwhile I went for walks along the Paseo del Espolón, played with other children, learned German and, in the company of Maria Ronge, visited the ancient monuments and buildings which so impressed me. Though I was still unaware of it, I had discovered something that would be a constant in my life—Gothic. For me Gothic came to be synonymous with ancient mysteries, cryptic messages, witchcraft, obscure necromancers, living gargoyles and enigmatic alchemists searching for the Philosopher's Stone.

I remember the weird, grotesque image of the well known *Flycatcher*, the figure which surmounts the Cathedral's clockface. I used to stand and gape at this sinister figure opening and shutting its mouth as the chimes marked the hour. I found the reverberating peals strangely disturbing.

These first encounters with Gothic cathedrals held a mysterious appeal for me. I was especially captivated by the sight of the sepulchers; the ogives and rose windows through which the faint, suggestive daylight penetrated to reveal tormented Christs, grieving Virgins, angels, saints and demons; the ancient altars; the Holy images, some naïve and some almost terrifying; the high vaulted ceilings, the engravings and the paintings. I was seduced by the whole style of this architecture rising up in search of God but always accompanied by the omnipresence of the malign.

In his book *The Mystery of Cathedrals*, Fulcanelli speaks of esoteric alchemical messages addressed to initiates, hinting at impenetrable mysteries. Whether or not these theories are correct, I immediately fell under the spell of these medieval temples, veritable Christian pyramids erected through the faith of men.

Then something unexpected occurred. The *Pastrana affair* blew up, and the officer was accused of banditry and corruption by some of his comrades at arms. He was even said to have a huge cache of booty, the fruits of extortion and looting, hidden in an underground warehouse. He was tried and sentenced to a long term in prison.

My father, who had already left the army, was bound to the officer not only by business ties but also by bonds of friendship. He took the decision to hand over the greater part of his personal patrimony, which he had worked so hard to obtain, to the family of the disgraced Colonel. It became inevitable that we should go back to Madrid in search of new horizons.

I must point out that the case of Pastrana was by no means exceptional among the victors of the tragic conflict; revenge and back-stabbing were the order of the day thanks to sordid personal ambition taking priority over loyalty and ideology.

Eventually we left Burgos. My sister Lourdes had been born in the fine old Castillian city and was then two years old. So the Molina clan consisted of five members, including fräulein Maria Ronge.

Obviously my father was keen to set off on a new tack and get away from an environment which he now found unpleasant. I left behind a lot of things that had constituted important moments during my early years. Above all, I lost the fascinating Gothic mystery of a city where time seemed to have stood still.

Some years later the gallant Colonel with the golden spurs passed away in his prison cell and, as if ordained by some inexorable destiny, he died in the arms of the only friend who never abandoned him: Enrique Molina.

Years of Initiation

We returned to Madrid around 1941. My father established his new fur and leather shop in the Calle Mayor, a stone's throw from the Puerta del Sol, one of the capital's most important thoroughfares. He rented a modest flat in the Calle Andrés Mellado and we prepared to start a new life.

Madrid in those days had very little in common with how it is today. It was a fairly quiet, almost provincial town, full of peaceful little squares and possessing an almost 19th century atmosphere. I remember the old trams, El Retiro park with its characteristic biscuit vendors, the street photographers and the uniformed maids flirting with the soldiers. I was taken for walks, usually to the Parque del Oeste and Rosales. In the mornings I was woken by the trilling of the birds in the trees along the boulevard and I became accustomed to the knife grinders' whistle and the almost guttural cries of the rag and bone men. At night I would hear the nightwatchmen striking their sticks on the ground when some night owl called for their services. These men, nearly always Galicians [from the northwest Spanish region of Galicia] in their peaked caps, long coats and carrying their characteristic short truncheons, made the night safer and the sight of them will always be remembered fondly by anyone who knew them.

These were hard times and we lacked almost everything. It was the age of ration cards, old gazogene fueled cars [gazogene—mixture of benzene and alcohol], wireless radios, millet bread, chicken stock and, above all, black marketeering. It wasn't so easy to get potatoes so instead we roasted *boniatos* [type of sweet potato, known in Central America as batata] which I was very fond of.

The happy and confident atmosphere of the city gave rise to a flourishing café society, with informal debates being held in the city's classic old cafés with their red velvet sofas and gold painted wainscots. To these *temples* of knowledge people went to talk, to exchange points of view, to argue, even to conspire in hushed tones and tell jokes about Franco and his family. There were debates for all tastes: about literature, bullfighting and sports; soccer was already the great national passion.

The weather was as extreme as the character of the Spanish people of that generation: you froze in winter and stewed in summer. The blizzards were near apocalyptic and semi-paralyzed the city. When that happened I was glad because I got to miss school. I would snuggle under the sheets and daydream, thinking that when I grew up I'd like to be El Zorro or Robin Hood.

I must also say something about the checkpoints which were set up on all the roads into Madrid in an effort to stop contraband and black market goods coming into the city. In the villages it was possible to obtain from the villagers items like white bread, cooking oil, butter, meat etc., products which were strictly controlled by the severe rationing system. Little by little the checkpoints relaxed their vigilance. I recall one night driving back from the northern sierra with the trunk of my father's car bursting with provisions. As often before, we ran the risk of being searched and although that's what happened on this occasion, a payment in kind to the customs officers made good our misdemeanor. In exchange for a string of cured sausages, a loaf of bread and a bottle of oil we took home several packets of chicken stock cubes as well as a packet of select ready rubbed tobacco and several books of cigarette papers. Many years after these anachronistic checkpoints had been taken down came the age of the honey vendors, villagers who would come into town selling honey and other country produce from door to door. Every time one of them called at our home my mouth watered in anticipation of the coming treat.

My uncle Jacinto told me how one night at one of the checkpoints there had been a Chicago–type Roaring '20s shoot out. A gang of Italians had been out committing a robbery but they were surprised by the Customs men. Although the guards gunned down all the Italian crooks, two cops were shot in the course of the battle.

Jacinto used to tell me about the exploits of real-life gangsters while he rolled cigarettes with the aid of a strange looking little machine. He loved to narrate the adventures of Alfonso Capone, Colosimo, Johnny Torrio or Lucky Luciano. His idol, however, was John Dillinger, public enemy number one, who had been caught "all because of some woman" while coming out of a cinema. Jacinto's favorite movie gangster was George Raft because, he said, he had more class than Edward G. Robinson, James Cagney, Paul Muni and Richard Widmark put together. One day the Italian bandit Salvatore Giuliano was gunned down and my uncle brought me a newspaper cutting showing him lying in a pool of blood. I remember vividly the image of the shattered body.

At that time the Second World War was at its height and everything German was in fashion; on the advice of the dear fräulein I was sent to a German school. We saw documentaries by Steinhoff, Ruttman and especially Riefenstahl. A sense of iron discipline was drummed into us and we did a lot of hard physical exercise. We sang military anthems and our lives ran to a strict timetable.

One day as soon as I arrived at school I became aware that something extraordinary was going on. Along with the other pupils I was herded into the Assembly Hall and then all was revealed: Adolf Hitler, the charismatic Führer, creator of the Third Reich, the thousand year empire, was dead. A large portrait adorned with black ribbons presided over the room. A blonde-haired, blue eyed lady teacher gave the command and we all sang "Deutschland, Deutschland über alles, über alles in der Welt." The eyes of the young and outwardly tough teacher were full of tears. Later I found out that the Führer had committed suicide together with Eva Braun in his bunker in Berlin, while the *Red devils* of the Soviet Army were advancing from house to house, annihilating the last of the SS and Wehrmacht forces.

The amazing Nazi paraphernalia, theatrical in the extreme and worthy of the most excessive Wagnerian opera, held a perverse fascination for me. The spectacular parades, the standards that were a hybrid of ancient Roman symbols and those of the ferocious Attila, the battle anthems, the flaming torches and red flags, the stormtroopers, looking like they were made of steel, the devastating, unstoppable war machine, all this possessed the essential appeal of pure evil. The black uniforms of the bloodthirsty SS, the Iron Crosses, the skulls of the Totenkopf, the leather jackboots and, above all, the diabolical, esoteric symbolism of the runes, sublimated by the thousand year old swastika, transformed the Third Reich into a Satanic Empire, as sinisterly appealing as it was ruthlessly lethal.

I remember that the magazine *Signal* used to be delivered to my house. We would see pictures of deadly dive bombing Stukas, of Panzers spitting fire and of unstoppable armies fighting in snow, desert, moorlands, always implacable, always invincible. Nazi propaganda led us to believe that Field Marshall Rommel, *The Desert Fox*, was greater than Napoleon or Marco Vipsanio Agripa and that Adolf Hitler was more talented than Frederick II of Prussia himself. On the other hand, as something of a curiosity, the Führer was said to feel a fascination for deep underground caves and to be particularly fond of wolves (which would explain his misanthropic nature). So much so that between 1919 and 1920 when he was acting as an army informer he employed the pseudonym *Wolf*. When the French requested the armistice in 1940, he named the Belgian HQ responsible for the operation *Wolfschlucht (Wolf Ravine)*. He named his HQ in Winnica, Ukraine *Wolfmensch* (Wolfman) and the one in Rastenberg, East Prussia, he called *Wolfschanze* (*Wolf's Redoubt*).

According to the reports of his physician, Dr. Eisler, Adolf Hitler suffered bouts of lycanthropy when there was a full moon; he would rage and foam at the mouth, his features would change to the point of becoming unrecognizable and he even went so far as to chew the carpets in his office. At daybreak the attacks passed off and he would make delirious decisions leading to acts of death and destruction.

He also had a well known penchant for researching Catharist secrets as well as a burning desire to find the Holy Grail. He consulted astrologers and believed in sorcery. The Bohemian corporal, the failed Art student, was a monster without equal in world history.

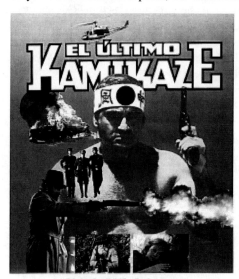

ACONITO FILMS, S. A. Presenta a
PAUL NASCHY como "EL KAMIKAZE" con
IRAN EORY • MANUEL TEJADA • Artista invitado GUILLERMO MURRAY como Yamaff
con la colaboración especial de JOSE BODALO y JULIA SALY como Silvia
Director de fotografía JULIO BURGOS. Producciones ejecutivas MASURAO TAKEDA
JULIA SALY. Productor delegado AUGUSTO BOUE
Un FILM de JACINTO MOLINA
DISTRIBUIDO POR CINEMA INTERNATIONAL CORPORATION

But all this I discovered much later, when I learned to my horror that behind the whole epic episode lay the unparalleled atrocities of the Nazi death camps. This world of horrors, the whole tapestry of torture, pain and death revolted me to the point of nausea, but I must admit its symbolism of leather and steel, of arcane lore halfway between black and red magic left its mark on me like a white hot firebrand. The horror of it I found totally abominable, but I couldn't help being influenced from an aesthetic point of view by the whole devilish, theatrical packaging. This is why, years later, I came up with films like the emblematic *El caminante*, *Los crimenes de Petiot*, and especially *El ultimo Kamikaze*. It's plain to see that those old, traumatic and sinister memories have been indelibly burned into my subconscious.

Childhood memories of Nazi horrors influenced *El caminante*.

From the standpoint of adulthood I can comprehend the reason for various obsessions which have affected my life and influenced my modest *oeuvre*: Nazism which I've just explained and Gothic, as mentioned in the previous pages.

To continue with my story, it was about this time that a string of circumstances came about which led to my acquiring a somewhat *ad hoc* classical education. My father bought the Espasa Encyclopedia and a highly suggestive new world opened up before the child who had a thirst for knowledge which regular school subjects couldn't satisfy. I dabbled in the history of such attractive, hermetic civilizations as that of the Ancient Egyptians; I learned about mysterious, age-old tombs, grave robbers, scheming archaeologists, ancestral curses. I was especially fascinated by the discovery of Tutankhamon's tomb.

Reading the epic exploits of Hernán Cortés and Pizarro totally enthralled me. I got hooked on the history of Ancient Rome and learned all about gladiatorial combats, the cruelty and madness of Nero or Caligula and I immersed myself in the study of biographies of a host of famous people. In short, the Espasa Encyclopedia was both a great fountain of knowledge and a source of pleasure for me in those days.

My family's kilometer ticket c. 1945-1946

Paul Naschy

Two Uncles, One Destiny

The title of this chapter sounds a bit like a film title [this refers to the title under which *Butch Cassidy and the Sundance Kid* was released in Spain, *Dos Hombres y Un Destino—Two Men, One Destiny*] but it's perfectly suited to what I am about to relate.

Shortly after arriving in Madrid I met my uncle Jacinto, about whom I have already spoken. My mother's youngest brother was godfather at my christening and he persuaded my parents to name me after him, in spite of the fact that they would rather have named me Enrique. My godmother was one of my father's sisters, Juana, who married an aeronautical engineer and emigrated Down Under, never to return. Incidentally, I was baptized in Santa Cruz church, close by to what is now the Ministry of Foreign Affairs.

My uncle Jacinto was thin, frail and I never really knew what he did for a living. I do know that he spent some time in Valladolid and in that in Madrid's Calle de la Paz he opened a chocolate parlor which proved a failure. In any event, in his company I lived through a number of experiences which still glisten in my memory.

One grayish, gloomy day he took me to the University Campus, or rather to what little remained of it. All around was desolation and ruins: half-demolished, bullet-riddled walls, twisted and rusting metal structures, trenches, bomb craters, machine gun emplacements and all the dramatic debris of a long and terribly bloody battle. Walking through that scene of death wasn't a very sensible thing to do, seeing that unexploded bombs were lying all over the place. But then again, my sickly uncle Jacinto wasn't exactly noted for being sensible.

At one point he stopped to pick up a stick and, rummaging among some thick bushes, he unearthed a skull, with some hair and dried flesh still attached. My own hair stood on end; for the first time in my life I saw how ugly and horrible death can be. He threw the thing into a ditch and we carried on walking. My legs had turned to jelly. A few meters further on, sticking out of a pile of rubble, we came across the bones of a leg still clad in a moldy leather boot. Seeing these human remains made a terrible impression on me. After all, what had happened in Cantabria now seemed distant and dream like, whereas this was here-and-now and brutally real. (Up until then the most frightening thing I had ever experienced had been watching *Snow White* with my mother in the Palacio de La Música cinema. When Walt Disney's wicked witch appeared on the screen, I literally wet my pants).

We continued our stroll through the ruins of the University Campus. The sky took on a reddish tone and was suddenly filled with huge rain clouds, looking blacker than the Devil's soul. All at once it started pouring down, mighty thunder claps boomed all around and forked lightning flashed and flickered, looking like so many fiery snakes. Uncle Jacinto took me by the hand and we ran in search of shelter.

By now it was raining furiously and we ended up taking cover inside a pill box. It was pitch dark beneath the concrete roof. Looking out through the opening I watched the wall of water coming down and it occurred to me that through that sinister slit, one day not so long ago, the weapons brandished by unknown combatants had been spitting out fire and death. We had had a tense few moments but now my uncle was smiling. After a little while the storm ended and we came out of the little bunker. We walked through a wasteland of mud and, after arriving home, soaked to the skin, I fell ill.

I whiled away the time during my long convalescence by reading fairy tales and comics. Some of those children's stories were really scary. Take *Little Red Riding Hood* for instance, where the hunter rips open the wolf's belly and fills it with stones. Or the tale of *Hänsel and Gretel*, fattened up by the wicked witch so she could, after roasting them in the oven, devour their flesh in an unmistakable act of cannibalism. And above all there was the story of *Bluebeard*, the inveterate male chauvinist whose terrifying taste for necrophilia led him to make a collection of the corpses of his imprudent wives. However, he got his just desserts when his last wife's avenging brothers turned up at the castle and decapitated him, throwing his severed, bloodied head off the battlements.

On the other hand, I remember with fond nostalgia the unforgettable cartoon strips about *Pinocho y Chapete* and *Pipo y Pipa*, excellently drawn in a modern, flowing style by the great Salvador Bartolozzi (who died in Mexico in 1950).

Apart from fairy tales, whenever I was bedridden—which was pretty often as I suffered a lot from bouts of illness—I amused myself by reading comics. I couldn't get enough of titles like *El Guerrero del Antifaz* (*The Masked Warrior*), *Roberto Alcázar y Pedrín, Juan Centella, Tarzan* and, above all, *El Hombre Enmascarado* (*The Masked Man*) [*The Phantom*]. I was captivated by this crime fighter whose noble mission was handed down from generation to generation. His throne in the heart of the jungle was adorned with human skulls and nobody knew of his secret except for a tribe of faithful pygmies. On the frequent occasions when the *Spirit-That-Walks* let loose with his cudgel, he used to leave the mark of a skull stamped on the villain's face.

My favorite graphic artists were Alex Raymond and Milton Caniff. I was addicted to the comic books *Cuto*, drawn by the extraordinary Blasco, *TBO* and, particularly, *Pulgarcito*. I spent many happy hours with characters like Don Furcio Buscabollos, the reporter Tribulete, the Gilda sisters and El Loco Carioco, but my favorite of all was the ever-hungry Carpanta whose greatest ambition was to get his jaws round a big, juicy roast chicken. It was of course a dream shared by many Spaniards in those days, not just in the comics. I'll come back to the wonderful world of comics later on, but now let me return to the story of uncle Jacinto.

My mother's brother used to have lunch and dinner with us every day (we were living in Calle Alberto Aguilera) and he would run errands and do odd jobs for my father who paid him a small wage to help him get by. My uncle was never in the best of health because he suffered from poor circulation. Sometimes his ankles got so swollen that he could hardly walk. He used to take me to the stop where I caught the school bus. This was in Calle Rodríguez San Pedro and on many an occasion we crossed paths with the famous author Wenceslao Fenández Flórez. I don't know how or why, but it seems that Don Wenceslao was an acquaintance of my uncle's and many mornings he'd stand and chat with us a while. If I remember rightly, the writer was then living in the Casa de las Flores, the last word in urban architecture at that time.

Whenever the subject of my uncle's health cropped up, the author shook his head in a characteristic way he had and advised, "Go easy on the spicy food, Jacinto. I know you overdo it a bit and that's terribly bad for you." On taking his leave, Don Wenceslao always told me the same thing, with slight variations: "My boy, study hard at school, but above all, read. Real culture can only be acquired through reading." And off he went.

Uncle Jacinto was very proud of the deference with which such an eminent character treated him.

One day my uncle made me a gift of a paperback book which I seem to remember was called *Anthology of Spanish Poetry*. According to him, the best poet of them all was Espronceda. Later he also presented me with a paperback copy of *Legends* by Gustavo Adolfo Bécquer. I must admit that at

My uncle Jacinto Alvarez

that time I preferred reading works by Stevenson, Salgari, Mark Twain, Cooper or Jules Verne. After a time my tastes would change.

My flamboyant and sometimes mysterious uncle was in the habit of going for walks in cemeteries and occasionally he'd take me along. I well remember those melancholy wanderings among gravestones, crosses, pantheons and funereal monuments. He would stop before the oldest graves, which were often cracked and covered in moss, and speak to me of the people who were buried there: Once they had belonged to the land of the living, they had loved, experienced joy, suffered, hated, but now they were no more than dead meat, rotting under ground. He wondered if there was anything on the other side of death and I was aware that it troubled him. One grayish autumn day, with the cypress trees silhouetted against a dull, leaden sky, he said something to me that I've never forgotten: "Nephew... apart from being a great writer, Larra had balls. One day he got out of the wrong side of bed and blew his brains out with a pistol. I guess he was really pissed off." After he'd spoken these words we carried on walking in silence. The only sounds were the crackling of the piles of yellow leaves underfoot and the mournful cries of a blackbird.

A few years later uncle Jacinto entered a convent. I remember going to visit him in his modest cell and he presented me with two 16th century books. One of them was a cookery book.

In 1959 my uncle died of a perforated intestine in the Hospital Provincial de Madrid. He was scarcely past his 40s. This taciturn man left an indelible mark on me, especially through his strange passion for the macabre which would have an influence on my future career.

My uncle Emilio

Someone else who had a great deal to do with my artistic vocation was my father's older brother Emilio. He was a tall thin man with a pinched face and thick white, almost silver, hair. My father's family comprised nine siblings—six brothers and three sisters. Three of the brothers would make their living in the fur and leather trade: José; Enrique, that is my father, who specialized in *Haute Coûture*; and Luis who worked as a designer. They set up large factories and workshops for tanning, dyeing and tailoring the garments.

Another of my uncles, Ricardo, I knew less well. He had a bake shop, very renowned in its day, called Anakar. My father went into partnership with him and imported from Germany the most modern and sophisticated machinery then available. For reasons which I never found out about Luis, an intelligent man who had already made a fortune, reputedly being something of a financial wizard, ousted my father from the partnership. He associated with Ricardo himself and together they set up a chain of grocery shops which was highly successful. I saw the whole affair at close quarters and know how much my father suffered over it. He even fell ill through worry because, as my mother was to tell me years later, the operation had been rather shady.

Luis' elder son, José Luis, went on to be a big noise in the leather and fur trade, establishing the company which bore his name, an internationally prestigious firm whose customers were members of the élite. I must add that it was my father who taught José Luis his trade, although it's also true that my cousin was an exceptional designer, whose undoubted creative talents led to his association with none other than the great Balenciaga.

José Luis' younger brother, my cousin Rodolfo, was for a long time my inseparable companion, sharing in my dreams and adventures. We were the terror of the fairgrounds because we would clean out every rifle range with our unerring accuracy. We were also fond of fighting and, together with our other cousins, we had some monumental battles. We used to come out of it all with black eyes and bleeding noses. I was an out-and-out slugger, Rodolfo was the one with the fancy footwork; false modesty apart, my killer right hook caused absolute carnage.

Thanks to the mischievous Rodolfo I saw a naked woman for the first time, which, in those days, was both a terrible sin and a big thrill. My cousin drilled a spy hole in the maid's bathroom. She was a buxom country lass and as soon as she went in we rushed to the door like a couple of hungry vultures to get an eyeful of sex. Watching her take a shower was the height of forbidden pleasure. The sight of her well endowed (*very* well endowed) body gave us more than a passing thrill. It's my belief that the girl knew perfectly well that she was being watched by two youthful peeping toms and made a show of it for our benefit.

In Rodolfo's company I had many other, slightly morbid, experiences. One day I was shocked when he showed me four shrunken human heads. One of them was a white man's. Rodolfo's father, my uncle Luis, was an avid collector and apart from some strange and even macabre items, like the four shrunken heads, he possessed paintings by some of the great artists like Veronés or Picasso. His spacious study was graced by valuable furniture crafted by my uncle Àngel, and sculptures carved by my grandfather in hard woods. It sometimes seemed to me to be not just a room, but rather an entire evocative, enigmatic world which always offered up something new and mysterious.

Luis also collected letters written by famous characters from the past and he even came by the occasional document of great historical value. I remember one letter from Robespierre himself, ordering a number of executions by guillotine. At the bottom of the list of names was the signature and seal of Citizen Maximilien de Robespierre. I was so impressed by this document that I made a note of the date: August 17, 1792. My uncle Luís had made a great fortune which allowed him to bid in all the major auctions. I learned that during the war he had stayed in Madrid and worked for the Republican Army. His factory had produced, among other garments, the leather flying helmets and flying jackets worn by the pilots of the "Red" Air Force.

Unfortunately my cousin Rodolfo died before his 19th birthday as a result of heart failure. His premature death was a hard blow for me to take.

Now I come once more to my Uncle Emilio who was an important figure in my life. He was a great artist—sculptor, graphic artist and decorator—and he specialized in lacquered objects. You couldn't have distinguished his folding screens and furniture from the real things made in Peking or Shanghai. But apart from being an artist and a Bohemian, he was also a first class participant in the typical "tertulias," those informal debates about almost any topic under the sun which sprang up spontaneously when a group of "intellectuals" happened to meet in one of the capital's plush cafés. Here he often rubbed shoulders with important and well known figures of the time. He was also a great bullfighting aficionado and enjoyed the friendship of Manuel Rodríguez *Manolete* [one of the most famous Spanish matadors of all time], among others. He subscribed to the bullfighting magazine *Ruedo* and went to watch all the big *corridas* [bullfights].

He also had an unusual friend whom the bullfighting fraternity nicknamed "El Tagarnina," a midget who wore his hair greased back and smoked huge cigars which were bigger than he was. This character was an authority on everything to do with bullfighting and knew all about the lives and times of every one of its exponents past and present and spoke of them as if they had all been personal friends of his. His knowledge of the subject by far surpassed all the information contained in the numerous volumes of Cossío, the greatest encyclopedia of bullfighting ever published.

I'll never forget his account of the death in the bullring of the matador Granero. "El Tagarnina" had of course been present when the tragedy happened. "It was horrible, a total shambles," he recalled, eyes shining with emotion. "The beast speared him in the eye with one of its horns and a jet of blood came spurting out and soaked the

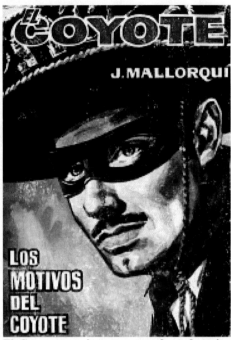
El Coyote soon became one of my favorite characters.

wooden fence around the bullring. Some people fainted and I must admit even I felt pretty sick myself, and I've seen it all. Poor old Granero, he was a pal, I used to go visit him a lot in Valencia. It sure was a stroke of bad luck."

He also used to boast that he was going to write the definitive history of bullfighting and with the profits he'd buy a flashy car with a uniformed chauffeur to drive him around.

It was 1944 and I wasn't yet 10 years old. From time to time my uncle would take me to his "tertulias" [get-togethers], which my mother frowned on since she thought they were a waste of time when I should be studying. In actual fact I was delighted to be able to go along and meet—and above all, listen to—a lot of important people. I still think I was privileged to have my life enriched in this way.

One day my uncle Emilio came to visit me. I was confined to bed with one of my frequent bouts of illness. He brought me a novel about the adventures of a masked crime fighter who made the villains tremble with fear, a character known as "El Coyote." At the time I was really keen on "El Zorro" and I remember that one Christmas I had as a present a Zorro costume, complete with a sword which had a rubber stamp on the end in the form of the letter 'Z'. I used to dress up and act out imaginary duels in front of my wardrobe mirror. That's why my uncle knew I'd be thrilled by this book by José Mallorquí. He was right and I was soon hooked on "El Coyote" too.

This same day Emilio told me that Tagarnino, the sentimental and bullfight loving midget, had died from a stroke. But he quickly consoled me by saying that the very same night his closest friends were going to honor him with a really good wake with the best food and liquors. Since he'd died without a penny to his name they'd had a whip round to give him a proper funeral, even going so far as to hire a brass band from Vallecas to accompany the funeral cortege with *pasodobles* which would have pleased the deceased man.

As regards what Emilio did during the war, I don't know a great deal. The only information I could glean was supplied by Basilio, one of my father's employees. He informed me that my uncle had been a commander in the Republican Army, seeing action on several fronts, and Basilio himself had served under him as a sergeant. He recounted an episode which filled me with admiration for my uncle. The column under Emilio Molina's command was returning from participating in some tough operations on the front at Extremadura and after long weeks of hard combat the men were tired and hungry. They were approaching a small village where they were to obtain provisions and take some rest when, close to the little cemetery, they spotted a group of militia men shepherding a group of men whose hands were tied above their heads.

This sinister platoon forced the prisoners to keep walking by brutally thrusting the barrels of their rifles into them. By now they were quite close to the wall of the grave-yard. On seeing this, my uncle ordered the trucks to pull up and jumped from his vehicle, followed by Basilio and several privates. When they saw the column the militia men came to a standstill. The commander addressed the man who appeared to be in charge, asking him where they were taking the prisoners. The villainous looking fellow replied that the prisoners were fascists and they were being "taken for a walk." [This was the standard euphemism used by both sides to mean that the prisoners were to be executed by firing squad.] Several corpses were already lying before the bullet riddled cemetery wall, rotting under the intense heat with clouds of flies buzzing around them.

The Republican officer inquired what crimes they had committed and which court had tried them. The militia leader repeated that they were fascists and that he didn't have to explain himself to anybody. Emilio Molina ordered him to release them at once because he wouldn't stand for unarmed men being shot in his presence. There followed several moments of unbearable tension as the safety catches of Mauser machine pistols were clicked off. As Basilio told it, for a few seconds which seemed an eternity, the black shadow of Death hovered poised over that cemetery. The only sounds were the moaning of the wind and the plaintive cries of a flock of ravens. Even the terrified fascists had frozen in their tracks. Regular troops and militia men stood facing each other as if they were waxwork figures. A machine gun was trained on the scene from the cab of one of the trucks.

The commander, without a second thought, drew his Astra pistol from its holster and pressed the cold muzzle to the militia leader's forehead. The surly tough guy backed down. Once the tension had been broken, my uncle barked out an order, pointing to the swollen cadavers of the executed prisoners. "You're going to bury them right now. As for the other prisoners, they're coming with me." It seemed for an instant as if the militia chief was going to rebel but the commander took a firmer grip on his pistol and shortly afterwards the platoon of murderers were digging graves for the dead men. My uncle commanded them: "You bastards know who they were. Mark the graves with stones and have the common decency to inform their families."

Basilio, a half-bald redhead, added, "Those fascists who were being 'taken for a walk' were nearly all hired laborers. Only two among them had any land and cattle. Believe me lad, it was a fucking shitty war. We were slogging it out up at the front, we didn't have anything to do with those rearguard ambush affairs. Anyhow, your uncle saved the lives of those poor devils by taking them with him to Badajoz."

As I listened in rapt attention the figure of my uncle Emilio took on epic proportions in my mind. Basilio went on to tell me more and concluded by saying that my uncle, who appeared to be so refined, had "more balls than (General) Espartero's horse" because he had once dared to confront Campesino, and it sure took balls to do that.

My uncle Emilio was a man of left wing sympathies, generous, sensitive with an easygoing nature and he remained true to his ideals until the end, when he died in poverty.

Jose Gutierréz Solana

All these testimonies from both sides lead me to the conclusion that the Spanish cinema has never even come close to making a film which reflects the reality of the Civil War, free from twisted, biased interpretations.

Let me continue where I left off, with the death of El Tagarnina. Uncle Emilio took me to his *tertulias* quite often. He told me about the important people we rubbed shoulders with and he even wrote down their names in a little notebook which I still possess. He often said to me: "Nephew, take a good look, the history of Spain is unfolding before your very eyes."

Of course, Emilio Molina had his own personal criteria as regards the importance of those people in the history of our country. I know that on various occasions I was in the presence of Jardiel Poncela, Miguel Mihúra and a very thin, pencil-faced Camilo Jose Cela [this writer received a Nobel Prize for Literature in the 1990s]. Some years later I became acquainted with Cela's *La familia de Pascual Duarte* which really made an impression on me at the time. Later on I saw the film version and felt that it didn't do justice to the splendid novel. What's more I left the cinema sickened by the scene in which the protagonist kills a dog for real on screen. I'd never have allowed anything like that.

At the beginning of 1945 my uncle presented me with two books about art, the first about Jose Gutierréz Solana, a good friend of his, and the other about the eccentric Salvador Dalí. I liked the works of both, but Solana's marked me for life.

Those incredible paintings seemed to be taken from a museum of horrors: the bullfights, the gaudy carnivals, the *danse macabre* of skeletons, the bloody Christs, the wretched beggars, the processions, the posers, pimps and whores; the whole murky world of larger than life characters and deep rooted customs were transformed into something fantastic. Goya, Zurbarán, Brueghel and El Bosco were blended and filtered through the privileged mind of Solana, to be regurgitated without contemplations.

The paintings reflect Solana's travels round hamlets and villages, constituting a sort of dark chronicle of deepest Spain. The motifs of his works run the gamut from crime, catastrophes and executions, to archeological museums and waxworks, as well as fairground freaks that not even Tod Browning could have envisaged. Nightmares fermented along with the slow digestion of garlic sausage, thick pork chops and fried eggs washed down with heavy red wine. In short, José Gutiérrez Solana, born in Madrid of half Cantabrian, half Mexican descent, really got under my skin and touched the deepest recesses of my soul.

I have a vivid recollection of one day when I was 10 years old. I was in my room, Madrid was covered in snow after a heavy blizzard and I was leafing through the illustrated pages of the book. One by one the paintings passed before my avid gaze: *My Uncle, In the Tribunal of Terror, The Return of the Emmigrant, Death by Garroting, The Singer of Crimes, Claudia's Girls, Procession of the Scapularies, The Burial of The Sardine, The Chorus Girls, The Meatwagon, The Ossary* and the hideous *Chinese Torture*. I kept looking at them over and over again with a mixture of horror and wonder.

A few weeks later, uncle Emilio sprang a great surprise on me: We were going to visit Don José in his new home on the Paseo Ramón y Cajal, close by the Pantheon of Illustrious Men. (Previously Gutiérrez Solana had lived with his crazy mother and two brothers in the Calle Santa Feliciana.) When we set out it was cold enough to freeze the ideas in your head. We caught one of those creaky old trams and I was so nervous that I kept asking my patient uncle all kinds of daft questions about the man we were going to visit.

Solana's Procession of Death

José Gutiérrez Solana employed a flamboyant maid whose true vocation was that of acrobat. She opened the heavy front door of the painter's house, greeted us and, without prior warning, treated us to a superb display, throwing a series of somersaults all the way down the long corridor with skirt and petticoat flying in all directions and revealing her skinny legs clad in black and brown striped stockings. The artist's dog, a true philosopher, watched indifferently from its corner. Once the magnificent floor show was over, the servant led us to Don José's study.

I wasn't at all disappointed by the artist's house. It was like a musty old museum, crammed full of dark old furniture. There were clocks everywhere. Tall clocks, short clocks, oblong clocks. French clocks, Italian clocks, cuckoo clocks. There were even clocks encased in glass panels. There were also a number of paintings to be seen, most of them the work of the artist himself, and others that had were faded with age. I saw all kinds of minerals, brought back from overseas, shells and even fossils. But what impressed me most were the automatons. The house was full of them. I remember especially a couple of Chinamen which Solana told me moved automatically to make coffee. I also saw a human skull and other objects whose use I couldn't even try to fathom out.

Solana himself was an imposing figure. He was a very tall man with a round face, graying close cropped hair and penetrating yet benevolent blue eyes. He wore a faded corduroy suit, waistcoat and a dark tie. If I remember rightly the collar of his shirt was somewhat creased. Soon the two men, who knew each other very well, were chatting away. The painter mentioned that his brother Manuel had been taken to a psychiatric hospital after suffering a fit of madness. They talked of old times and shared anecdotes, speaking about Ramón Gómez de la Serna who was then in Paris, about the Café Levante and the Bar Pombo. Don José made a remark about Valle-Inclán [the famous playwright] who was always pestering him and talked of Picasso, whom he'd met at a gallery in Paris where he'd had an exhibition. His comment was a curious one: "Picasso can see into one's paintings but one can't see into Picasso's paintings."

Solana spoke about the whooping cough which he had contracted at the age of 45 and which had left him in bad shape. Well, the whooping cough and the wine, cognac and spicy cured pork sausages. While he told us this he chain smoked one cigarette after another and I recall his memorable phrase: "If one weren't a painter, one would be a famous criminal." The artist kept an old dog, Canelo, which had never set foot outside the flat. Whenever it was time for Solana to take his siesta, he would remove the dog from where it was sleeping and take its place himself because, he said, "Only the dog knows which is the coolest place in the house."

Regarding women, the artist was like the primitive and forthright cave dwellers of Altamira. He often said, "One doesn't paint nudes, one paints naked broads."

He talked about many notable people and he once referred to Juan Ramón Jiménez as "a mad doctor." He agreed with Murillo's famous phrase about Valdés Leal: "To look at a painting by Valdés Leal you need to cover your nose with a handkerchief." Evidently he didn't regard his own macabre creations from the same perspective.

This artistic genius, son of emigrants with Cantabrian and Mexican blood coursing through his veins but as much a native of Madrid as his fellow citizens, always had the *mot juste* which he delivered like so many pearls of wisdom: "Pictures should be painted, not talked about" or "Goya is the most modern of painters because he is the most painterly."

About nine o'clock my uncle and I left. I clearly remember the huge figure of the artist, like a friendly ogre, outlined against the yellowish light of the hallway. Clocks were whirring and chiming all over the place. It's more than likely that at that very moment, in the hidden depths of my subconscious, the embryo of *El huerto del Francés* was taking shape. When I was back in the street again I felt that, at the tender age of 10, I had known something of the oft-misunderstood mystery of the true creator. That was the advantage of having an uncle like mine, an artist who was equally capable of carving an effigy of the Virgin of Lourdes, illustrating a pack of erotic playing cards or inventing someone like José Gutiérrez Solana. Because the truth is, apart from meeting Solana in person one dark winter evening, I learned a lot about him thanks to the little notebook in which Emilio Molina took down the sayings, anecdotes and thoughts of the unique artist.

Solana died in June 1945. The gossips said he died from eating an enormous cake which he had spent several days painting as part of a still life study.

It should be evident that my father's elder brother had a lot to do with my artistic vocation. On Sunday mornings he used to take me to visit museums: El Prado, the Archeological Museum, the Natural History Museum, the Lázaro Galdiano, the Army Museum—above all, by his side I learned a lot about art. He knew how much paint-

After a visit to Solana, the embryo of *El huerto del Francés* took shape.

ings were worth and boasted that he had discovered an authentic Lucas in a friend's loft. Apart from this, I always loved drawing from an early age. My first efforts were of ships, planes and strange looking submarines with many cannons and funnels. As I got older I started on animals, especially lions, tigers and elephants. I went through a phase when I was obsessed with scorpions and snakes. Later on as my technique improved I progressed to drawing armor, battles—in particular Napoleonic ones—and my great specialty was in depicting gladiatorial combats. Before embarking on these drawings I did research on the types of weapons used by the combatants as well as their armor, tactics, fighting styles and training. This was followed by a period of Wild West drawings and gangster shoot outs. Paradoxically, I took a long time to start on doing horror pictures.

But back to my uncle. Besides giving me a fairly comprehensive view of Velázquez, Goya, El Bosco, El Españoleto, El Greco, Fray Angélico, Zurbarán, Murillo, Durero, Vermeer de Delft and Mantenga, he also taught me about modern art and he was always giving me books on Juan Gris, Picasso, Dalí, Utrillo, Van Gogh, Renoir, Gauguin,

Modigliani, Rosseau El Aduanero, Toulouse-Lautrec or Chagall. This list shows how dedicated he was to his teachings. He also interested me in sculpture, architecture and archeology. Emilio Molina was quite a Humanist. Between him and the Espasa Encyclopedia I acquired what I consider a fairly impressive basic cultural education.

Now I'm going to relate an episode involving my uncle which shows how tough life really was in the post war years. This occurred in the early '50s. As already mentioned, Emilio Molina was a great bullfight fan and one day he took me to one of the typical narrow streets near the Puerta Del Sol, swarming with shady types—pimps, whores and ticket touts offering tickets for the major *corridas*. My uncle sat down on a bootblack's stool to have his shoes shined. This bootblack, whom my uncle knew well, was known as El Zancajos. The street was full of bars with zinc-topped counters and tiled walls, serving cheap wine and *tapas*. I remember that everything smelled of fried food.

My uncle had already bought his tickets, after a lot of haggling and, as was his custom now, having his shoes cleaned in the street. He struck up a curious conversation with Zancajos. "So, Zancajos, how's life treating you?" The shoe shiner applied his chamois skillfully and with a yellowish, dogged end hanging from his lips replied: "I get enough work to get by, but only just. And now with this new guy in power (Franco) us old Republicans are gonna get a rough ride. God damn the fuckin' Generalisimo!" My uncle with a sly smile replied: "Well, neither you nor I will see the back of the Generalisimo, Zancajos." "And why's that? Is the bastard immortal or something?" My uncle answered sardonically, "That's what they say, Zancajos, that's what they say. Like his Moorish guards say, he's indestructible."

The conversation was interrupted at this point by a commotion in the street. Two men who looked like Gypsies had started a fight over something. One of them, a small, wiry fellow called Lanchares, pulled out a huge knife and took a couple of swipes at the other chap which, had they found their mark, would have finished him off. People were shouting and running all over the place but the Gypsy with the knife, eyes bulging and foaming at the mouth, was determined to drive his blade into his opponent. Suddenly, when it all looked likely to end in a good deal of bloodshed, an old boy in a hat came out of one of the bars and started thrashing the shit out of the knife wielding Gypsy with a fearsome looking walking stick. It ended as suddenly as it had begun. The thug with the knife fell to his knees sniveling while blow after blow rained down on him. The old boy kept up the thrashing till his arm grew weary. Surprisingly, not a single cop had appeared on the scene.

The tough, stick swinging patriarch was called Antonio Silva and I got to know him after the violent incident narrated above. Don Antonio had first been a tinker, then a fairground stallholder and later a livestock dealer (he claimed that his skill at selling broken down donkeys was second to none; today he could probably have been a successful politician) and finally he became a bullfighter. He considered himself number one but was dogged by bad luck and a bull's horn punctured one of his lungs. After this he could only take part in the *corridas* as a matador's alternate. He spent many years as a black market spiv and made a small fortune. Later he was awarded the patriarch's stick, and what a stick it was! It had an enormous silver handle in the shape of a howling wolfhound's head.

Don Antonio knew that my uncle was a sculptor and he commissioned a bronze bust; he wanted it to be like the busts of Julius Caesar, with laurels and all. My uncle accepted the commission and started work in a studio he owned in Cava Baja. Don Antonio paid in advance, handing over bags full of silver coins. Unfortunately the bust was never finished because Don Antonio was murdered. One night in the Plaza de las Visitillas an unknown assailant smashed his skull in with the heavy silver handled stick. The crime was never solved but the criminal underworld believed it had been the revenge of the sinister Lanchares.

Getting back to the walk with my uncle, now with shiny bright shoes, we made our way towards the Plaza Mayor. There was a street market there that my uncle adored and I loved walking around it. I'll never forget the stalls selling habits and religious curios, the second hand bookstalls, the candle sellers, silversmiths and other delightful shops, many of which thankfully still exist. One day under the Cuchilleros Arch we met the famous Domingo Ortega. When the maestro had gone my uncle remarked: "Domingo is the most learned matador of them all. He reads Blasco Ibañez, Miguel Hernández and even Azorín. I tell you, nephew, he's very well read."

The Field of Skulls

For this part of my memoirs I have to return to the years 1945 and 1946. After the German school closed, my parents sent me to San Fernando, a school run by Piarist clergymen. This was a rather out of the way place, situated in an undeveloped area with very few buildings around. Not far away there was an expanse of wasteground (with a little fog it could have been used as a location for *The Hound of the Baskervilles*) which had once been a cemetery, now almost totally cleared to make way for building. Property developers don't respect even the dead. Along with the other kids, I saw workmen taking away human remains. This wasteground was known as "The Field of Skulls," but before I relate the experiences I had there, let me say something about the Piarist school.

The clergymen had clear ideas about education going hand in hand with strict discipline, and they used to hit us a lot, especially padre Juan de Dios, the headmaster. This *brother*, a competent cigar smoker, was fat and ruddy and he submitted us to refined tortures by pinching us, hitting us with rulers, smashing his knuckles down on our heads and slapping us round the face. Another expert in corporal punishment was padre Maximiliano, who specialized in blows to the back of the neck. Still, it must be admitted that we pupils were practically all budding delinquents. Arguably the only way to domesticate such "fauna" was through the energetic application of physical correctives. Heaven help anyone who went to padre Juan de Dios with trendy pedagogical theories!

In those days we spent the breaks playing marbles, trading cards with photos of our favorite sportsmen and, of course, playing soccer. I remember my favorite soccer star was Gorostiza, *Bala Roja* (the Red Bullet). Practically from birth I was a supporter of Atlético de Aviación [this team was originally made up of ex-pilots from Franco's air force, hence the name, later renamed Atlético de Madrid].

I'll never forget the legendary line up of Domingo, Riera, Aparicio, Lozano, Silva, Múgica, Juncosa, Hernández, Ben Barek, Carlson and Escudero. It happened that my aunt Milagros (the one from Mazcuerras) had opened a guest house in the Calle Buen Suceso. Several of the players lodged there, including my idol Silva, so I was able to meet them in person. I also used to see them in one of the old bars in the Calle Princesa, called El 51. It goes without saying that I always wore the Atlético insignia on my lapels.

An uncle of mine, this time on my mother's side, used to take me to the old Metropolitano Stadium to see the matches. Pepe, which was this relative's name, wasn't very tall but he was quite good looking and he sported the little clipped moustache which was then in fashion. He was quite a poser and was always bragging to his pals about how many whores he'd had. He used to pick them up at Chicote's Cocktail Bar. Pepe Alvarez learned the furrier's trade with my father and then went and set himself up in Burgos.

The famous Madrid soccer team, Atlético de Aviación, of which I was an avid supporter.

Some of my schoolmates used to take photos of naked women to school and charge us money to look at them. Many initiated the practice of masturbation, thanks to these pictures. One of the priests, whose name I've forgotten, used to lead us in spiritual exercises, for which he constructed a most lugubrious and appropriate set—a table draped with a black cloth, a candle and a skull. With precise elocution he lectured us on the world, the flesh and the Devil. He became especially exalted when speaking about the sixth commandment: Women were highly dangerous and lusting after them would lead us straight to the eternal flames of Hell. The truth is, he was a fine, convincing actor and he ranted and raved against self abuse. Masturbation would lead irrevocably to Old Nick's hothouse, as well as driving us mad. The comical thing about it is that some years later I found out that this character got a shop girl pregnant, and had hung up his habit to go and live in sin with the girl.

Those were the times of *paloluz* [In the post-war years candy was a luxury item. *Paloluz* was the name given to a type of sweet tasting root which Spanish children used to suck like a lollipop], licorice and trading cards: Swapping them was quite an art and of course some cards just never turned up in the packets. I remember particularly one animal collection and the hardest card to get hold of was one with a picture of a Death's Head moth (The Sinister even accompanied me in my hobbies).

At school it was the survival of the fittest. You held your place in the most primitive fashion, by slugging it out with your fists and your feet and if need be hitting below the belt. But it was all done following a process, a kind of ritual. A challenge was given and the two parties waited to fight it out after class. I was one of the ones who had to mark territory day by day. Although I don't recall how many fights I had, how many times I had my eyes blackened or my nose bloodied, I was strong, my reflexes were fast and I had my share of spite. What's more I had my killer right hook.

But I had to put up with a real pain in the ass by the name of Burgaleta, whom I saw many years later on TV, when he was a big noise with the Department of Transport or some such. The scraps I had with this animal were on an epic scale, and both of us always came off badly. Luckily, one day I gave him such a thrashing that he never bothered me again. I sometimes think that the disgusting cod liver oil that my mother used to force down my throat must have given me extra strength.

The worst thing about these contests was the waiting till classes were over. The last thing on one's mind was trigonometry, natural history or religion. All I could think about, and dread, was the fight that I had coming after school. The last thing I saw as I left was the great crucifix which presided over the classroom, flanked by portraits of (the dictators) Franco and Jose Antonio (Primo de Rivera).

The Field of Skulls was an obligatory meeting point where the schoolboy gangs engaged in huge rumbles. We used to fight hammer and tongs and chuck stones at each other, and we all accepted as a matter of course that we were going to get roughed up.

One day I found myself in a pretty extreme situation. It was spring and several of us had come from school and we were waiting for some other friends to join us for a soccer match. Then a group of boys came towards us. We knew them by sight and always avoided them because they looked mean. They came from a nearby shanty town. We had with us a leather soccerball, a good one. One of the newcomers, who looked like the ringleader, came swaggering up to us and tried to take the ball off us. I knew that this bully was at least three years older than me, but he didn't look very tough. I blocked his way and the lad whipped out a knife. By the look on his face I knew he wouldn't think twice about stabbing me. Without hesitation I snatched up a stone and smashed it in his mouth. The ruffian dropped his knife and started spitting blood; I'm sure he must have lost several teeth. We hotfooted it off under a hail of stones.

Some time later I witnessed a tragic event which upset me badly. On our days off from school I used to go cycling with a group of friends. We hired the bikes from a shop owned by Berrendero, the great cycling champion. One day four or five of us went for a ride. We were in the habit of racing down the steep slopes of the Parque del Oeste as fast as we could go. But that day tragedy was waiting for one of my companions who crashed into one of the trees that lined the road. It was a head-on collision and death was instantaneous. I'll always carry in my mind the image of the twisted body lying immobile among the piles of fallen leaves. His eyes were glassy and blood trickled from the corner of his mouth. It was horrible.

Meanwhile my father had become a prestigious furrier, being the first to organize fashion shows in the Palace Hotel. Renowned actresses showed off his creations on the catwalk. He became friendly with many famous showbiz names such as José Nieto and Nani Fernández, Sara Montiel, Alfredo Mayo, Guillermo Marín, the impresario Muñoz Lusarreta, the film director Antonio Román and the excellent actor Antonio Casal.

Later on, when he was established at number 16 in the Calle Princesa, a long list of famous stars who were in the country on business or holiday visited his premises, including Sofía Loren, Charlton Heston, Gina Lollobrigida, Stephen Boyd, Frank Sinatra and Cary Grant. My parents also enjoyed lasting friendships with other notable characters like the bullfighter Jacinto Guerrero, the popular variety starlet Celia Gámez, the

My father and his cousin pose with actress Sara Montiel.

dancer and choreographer Luisillo, Santiago Bernabéu, the noted poet Rafael de Léon, the great concert pianist José Cubiles, the Bienvenida brothers, Lucero Tena and many others.

The extraordinary actor and movie director Indio Fernández was such a curious character that he warrants a paragraph of his own. This Mexican with decidedly indigenous features, was constantly traveling to Madrid to visit us and to have my father craft the holsters of his revolvers from specially textured leather. Indio had the reputation of being quick on the draw and as sure a shot as Jesse James or Billy the Kid. He had blown away more than one rival. Maybe this was legend, maybe it was true, but what was certain were the colossal drinking bouts he used to indulge in on his visits to Madrid. He was quite a character. Once he was rumored to have killed a promising leading man in a duel, the son of actor Pedro Armendáriz. I had a look at his revolvers, which were highly polished and had mother-of-pearl butts. Although these duels usually ended with Indio paying a fine, one day he actually ended up in prison. However, he was very soon released. He wasn't a national institution for nothing.

This photo of me was taken in Lozoya in 1949.

Paul Naschy

When the Lights Go Out

In 1942 my father bought a plot of land in the Sierra outside Madrid. It was one kilometer from Lozoya village and 11 kilometers from the monastery of El Paular (at that time in ruins, today a luxury hotel run by monks). The place was known locally as Snake Hill. Stony and inhospitable, it was crisscrossed by trenches and other remains that bore witness to the fierce fighting which had taken place there. It was quite common to come across helmets, spent cartridge cases and even rusty old weapons. One day I found a half buried revolver and a helmet belonging to a member of the International Brigades. My father brought in the builders to start work. They used dynamite to blow up stubborn outcrops of rock and sink well shafts. It took years of hard work but eventually a wonderful country house was completed, standing in its own extensive grounds, and christened "La Granja."

Here I spent some unforgettable times throughout my life. This was where I had my sexual awakening, where I dreamed up all sorts of stories, where I lived out my fantasies and where I also suffered. I had some extremely happy times and also times of great sorrow. To a great extent my personality was forged here, and my artistic vocation as well.

I must relate two events which made a deep impact on me. One night in the month of February when the moon was full, I was coming back from the village after spending the evening with a lovely girl, Mariuca, who I was going out with at the time. The bluish moonlight conferred an unreal, phantasmagorical quality to the surrounding countryside. I had almost reached our gate when a terrifying growl drew me up short. Then I spotted it: an enormous wolf with hackles raised and eyes glowing like carbuncles in the darkness. It watched me menacingly, paralyzed with fear for what seemed like an eternity. Just when I was expecting the worst the wolf turned and sloped off, disappearing into the night. In those days there were still wolves roaming the Sierra and hunger had driven this one down to devour the carcasses of some sheep which had died nearby. Maybe Waldemar Daninsky was born at that very moment.

The other event occurred when I was driving back with my father after a day's hunting. The commander of the Civil Guard post made us pull in at the side of the potholed road. The sergeant, who was a good friend of my father's, informed us that they had surprised Rojo Terrinches in an ambush and he'd been killed in the ensuing gunfight. Rojo Terrinches was the most bloodthirsty member of the Resistance still at large in the Sierra. One of the Civil Guards had also been killed. I saw the two corpses, a frightful sight lying in a pool of blood. Once more I was face to face with death.

Let's leave Lozoya for the time being and go in search of movie magic, a magic which comes alive when the lights go out. I have a vague idea that grandfather Emilio was the first to take me to the pictures. I don't remember the name of the film but I recall a scene in which a deep sea diver, looking like a huge robot, went down in search of a sunken vessel.

The Adventures of Captain Marvel **with Tom Tyler guaranteed thrills.**

But it was my mother who was mainly responsible for my movie mania. She would take me to cinemas with names like Calatrava, Argüelles, Urquijo or Actualidades, to see those incredibly gripping serials which always finished with a cliffhanger ending. Of course, to find out what happened next you had to wait several suspense-filled days for the next installment. I remember classic titles like *The Drums of Fu Manchu*, in which the sinister mandarin was played by Henry Brandon.

Another unforgettable serial was *Mysterious Doctor Satan*, released in Spain in three installments: "Mysterious Doctor Satan," "The Human Tank" and "The Lurking Death." I was knocked out by the incredible robot which fired death rays from its claws and was directed through remote control by doctor Thomas Scott. Alone against the evil minions stood the masked hero known as The Cobra, in reality good guy Bob Wayne who confronted Dr. Satan repeatedly in a long-running series of adventures. Finally Bob unmasked Dr. Satan and destroyed the mechanical monster.

I also remember *The Adventures of Captain Marvel* in two installments: "The Golden Scorpion" and "The Lenses of Death." Captain Marvel, played by cowboy actor Tom Tyler, could fly through the sky and was able to perform all kinds of amazing feats after saying the magic word "Shazam!" His mortal enemy was a hooded villain who possessed a lethal weapon in the shape of a great scorpion and which could disintegrate solid rock when the lenses in its claws were aligned. The most amazing adventures were guaranteed in the company of Captain Marvel.

Over the years I saw *Los crimenes del duende*, *Nioka* (aka *Perils of the Jungle*), *The Death Ray* starring Rin-Tin-Tin and *The Clutching Hand* (aka *The New York Mysteries*).

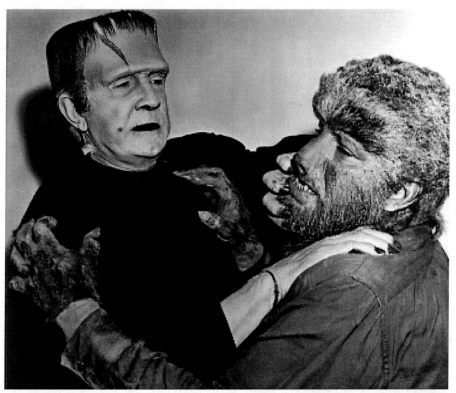

Bela Lugosi and Lon Chaney, Jr. in *Frankenstein Meets the Wolf Man* held an irresistible attraction for me.

But the best was yet to come: my encounter with Lawrence Talbot (Lon Chaney, Jr.). The film *Frankenstein Meets the Wolf Man* opened at Madrid's Capitol cinema, but since children weren't allowed in to see it, all I could do was to stand outside the cinema and stare. It held an irresistible attraction for me.

My chance to see the film came when it was re-released on a double bill at a cinema near my home. The lights went out and the magic began. Suddenly I was immersed in the spellbinding story which led up to the amazing, spectacular and quasi-surreal scenes in which the tormented lycanthrope slugs it out with Dr. Frankenstein's monstrous creature. After the film had finished I went out into the street in a trance. I didn't even remember to thank my good friend the usher for letting me in and running the risk of getting into trouble with the inspectors, who in those days were pretty strict.

That very night I sat down to draw the two terrifying characters locked in their brutal combat. From that day on Larry Talbot was my hero: After all, he was a good man whose only desire was to find a cure to free him from his need to kill. The stunning transformations brought on by the full moon really made an impact on me. I even recall that, on one occasion when my mother asked me what I wanted to be when I grew up, I replied, "A werewolf." You should have seen the look on her face!

Lon Chaney, Jr. could never have imagined how his performance as the troubled Larry Talbot would change the destiny of a young Spanish boy: When the lights go out

My drawing of the climatic finale of *Frankenstein Meets the Wolf Man.*

anything can happen. Sandokan, El Zorro and Robin Hood had lost their special place in my heart to be replaced by this nightmarish creature.

In those days we were highly fortunate that the cinemas still ran double bills, matinee performances and, above all, re-releases.

My father also contributed to my initiation to the seventh art. In our home in Calle Andrés Mellado he used to project 16mm films of cartoons and silent comedy classics: Chaplin, Harold Lloyd, Buster Keaton (who never really appealed to me), Laurel and Hardy and my favorite, Larry Semon, with his pasty face and outlandish costumes.

Naturally, Westerns were a staple of the double bills and the kids cheered on the courageous cowboys played by the likes of Ken Maynard, Tom Mix and Tom Tyler as they galloped after the baddies. What's more, continuous performances allowed us to see the same film several times over at the same showing. I established my own personal record for repeated viewings with the film *The Four Feathers.*

I have fond memories of a host of classic titles: *El Zorro, Captain Blood, The Charge of The Light Brigade, They Died with Their Boots On, Dodge City, Kim of India, Robin Hood, Ivanhoe, Winchester 73* and *Broken Arrow,* among many others. My favorite characters were always the villains and I remember how impressed I was by Claude Rains and Basil Rathbone, the latter in his roles as an expert swordsman. Later, other splendidly perverse villains made their appearance, like Jack Palance and Richard Widmark. Ah, let me not forget the inimitable Dan Duryea. Those guys really were mean mothers!

Other memories from those golden days include the comics I've already mentioned, the short and sometimes terrifying tales of Calleja (*The Castle of No-Return, John the Fearless,* etc.) and above all the ghost stories our housemaid Alejandra used to tell me. I remember a phrase that used to keep me awake at nights, it went something like: "From my coffin you took the plaque, now I'm coming to get it back!" What with school, movie serials and horror stories, time went rushing by.

We often made trips to Burgos and we spent the summers in La Toja. [La Toja is a small island off the coast of Galicia in northwest Spain. Its Spa waters, casino and golf course as well as its outstanding natural beauty make it a top holiday destination for well-to-do people from all over Spain.] I had already mastered the German language and I started learning French.

I cherish the memories of the Christmases of those years, when all the family was together—parents, uncles, brothers and sisters, cousins. My uncle Ricardo, who was in those days head man at the Patisserie Embassy, used to supply our gatherings with his cakes, tarts and exquisite *turrones*. [*Turrones* are traditional Spanish candy bars made variously with nuts, raisins, chocolate, wafer biscuits, caramel, etc., and eaten only at Christmas.] He was a past master at making these sweets and often traveled to America to supervise the making of this delicious confectionery. Inevitably, every year my father, who, by the way, people said looked like John Wayne, would perform a recital of improvised poetry. We all laughed and applauded his efforts and invariably we all ended up singing "Desde Córdoba a Sevilla..." (a kind of post war Spanish equivalent of "Row, Row, Row Your Boat, Gently Down The Stream").

Putting up the Christmas Nativity decorations was quite a ritual and, as I recall, my uncle Jacinto took the task quite seriously, constructing a magnificent Herod's Castle, windmills with revolving sails, rivers made of tinfoil and enormous figurines of the Three Wise Men. It was quite a surprising paradox that such a macabre and sinister man should be so gifted at putting up Christmas decorations.

At the time of the Nuremberg trials I shuddered on seeing a picture of the executioner, American sergeant John O. Woods, holding up the thick rope he would use to hang the Nazi top brass who were sentenced to death. Marshall Goering, who had been a comrade in arms of the legendary Red Baron in the First World War, committed suicide with cyanide in his cell. Among those hanged were Von Ribbentrop, SS General Kietel, racist theorist Rosenberg and Streicher. The demi-gods who had turned Europe into a Hell ended up swinging from the hangman's rope. The photographs of the corpses of these hated individuals were published in every part of the globe. Had Valdés Leal or Solana been alive they would have had a fine source of inspiration. The victors, Roosevelt, Churchill and Stalin, posed together for the press photographers, looking well pleased with themselves. A new world order was born.

Some time later "Joe" Stalin proved that even the insane Hitler could be surpassed.

For me, the boy Jacinto Molina Àlvarez, life carried on. In the Field of Skulls the bodies of two girls who had been raped and murdered were found. By some horrendous twist of fate it turned out that one of the murderers was the Gypsy boy whose teeth I'd smashed in with a stone. When I saw his picture in the papers I couldn't believe it.

Meanwhile two things happened which resulted in a big change in my life. The first was the death of a schoolmate who fell down the stairs after being assaulted by padre Maximiliano. The other took place when a lad whose surname was De la Morena sold me a caliber 6.35 pistol and a revolver, this latter with three bullets in it. I locked myself in my bedroom and could think of nothing better than to fire the revolver inside the room. The projectile embedded itself in the wall and my mother got the fright of her life. My parents, somewhat dissatisfied with the atmosphere at that school, took me out of San Fernando and enrolled me in Ramón de Maeztu High School. It was the end of an era for me.

Uncle Jacinto threw the pistol over a cliff and the revolver ended up being melted down over the gas stove in our kitchen. That shot I fired in my room had brought something to an end, as if it had been a real suicide, although, on writing these memoirs I get the impression that the shot didn't really hit the mark at all.

With my mother in La Toja

Paul Naschy

First Masks

The first car my father ever had was a Balilla, followed by a Topolino, then a Citröen and, finally, a black Mercedes. These cars reflected his ascent up the social scale. I remember a journey we made to Granada in the Topolino. There were five of us crammed in the little car: my parents, my sister, my widowed grandmother and myself. As if that wasn't enough we also took the dog, a fox terrier named Ninoska. The journey was quite an odyssey. We had to contend with the engine overheating and all sorts of breakdowns and incidents, making frequent stops at roadside workmen's huts. Eventually we made it to Granada and the first thing we did was to have our photo taken outside the Alhambra dressed in Moorish costumes. On our homeward journey we were very upset when the dog ran into the road and was hit by a car.

María Ronge no longer lived with us but she still gave me private classes and she used to come with us when we went on holiday to La Toja. During those summers my father, a keen hunter and fisherman, used to engage the services of a veteran mariner. His boat, a type of craft peculiar to that coast of Galicia, had high bows and a square stern and the keel was sealed with a thick layer of black pitch, making it very safe and seaworthy. We used to go out in it every day, hunting sea birds and fishing for conger eels. One day when we heaved one up into the boat the slippery creature thrashed about so much that it broke the skipper's arm and dealt me a terrific blow with its tail. The critter almost smashed up the boat and we had a job to chop it up with an ax. All three of us got pretty roughed up in the struggle. Needless to say I've never eaten conger eel since.

I look back on those summers spent in Galicia with fondness and a certain melancholy nostalgia. The mealtimes in the Gran Hotel accompanied by the soft music of the resident pianist, the little shell covered church, the decadent Spa resort, redolent of the 19th century, the beautiful scenery and unspoiled beaches all inspired in me the comforting sensation that the bad days were over and I was headed only for happy times. However, 1948 was my last summer on the island of La Toja.

I started my classes at Ramón de Meaztu High School, leaving behind the Field of Skulls, San Fernando Piarist School, rumbles, trading cards and a whole little world that was quickly vanishing.

My new high school was for the élite, rivaled only by a school called Pilar High. It provided all round, quite advanced teaching for its day. Sport was given prominence and the teachers, most of whom were university dons, were very liberal. However they were also very demanding and getting passing grades was far from easy. Those pupils who failed to measure up to the high standards were made to leave. I soon made a mark as a sportsman. On the athletics field I was a very good sprinter, and a good javelin thrower and shot-putter. On the soccer pitch I stood out for my speed. Some years later the school's headmaster went on to found Estudiantes, one of the most successful of all Spanish league basketball teams.

My school companions from the Ramón de Meaztu High School

Among other things I was renowned for my drawings and the caricatures made of the teaching staff. I have fond memories of my tutor and Latin teacher, Señor Pantoja, a great admirer of my works who used to pin these caricatures up on the noticeboards. Another member of staff I held in high esteem was Don Domingo, the German master who conducted his classes in the magnificent school library. Here I also had the chance to familiarize myself with the works of poets like Rubén Darío, Juan Ramón Jiménez, Lorca, Emilio Carrere, Machado and Marquina, among many others. Naturally the great Gustavo Adolfo Bécquer was, and still is, one of my idols; a love of the Romantics is a characteristic weakness of mine.

I used to spend a lot of time reading in that library. Pio Baroja, Valle-Inclán, Palacio Valdés, Stefan Zweig, Blasco Ibañez, Galdós, Graham Greene, Unamuno and a host of others fueled the fires of my literary passion. Such was my hunger for literature that I devoured everything, whatever the style or tendencies of the authors. I re-encountered Concha Espina, *Lady of Luzmela* and I tackled such writers as Ortega y Gasset and Eugenio d'Ors. Incidentally, I was captivated by the baroque illustrations of Sáenz de Tejada. The school library was, in addition to the already mentioned Espasa Encyclopedia, a source of fundamental knowledge for which I'll be eternally grateful.

I got on reasonably well with my classmates among whom I recall Fernando Moneo who sat next to me—now, sadly, deceased—and Carlos Rodríguez Jiménez, a doctor of medicine whose friendship I still enjoy to this day. Although you still had to mark your territory, I was respected for defending mine with wolf-like ferocity. One day a certain Baleriola tried to overstep the mark; he found himself on the receiving end of my killer right hook and went crashing through a window.

My outings with uncle Emilio, though a little less frequent, continued and in his company I visited all kinds of exhibitions and cultural events. The *tertulias* were now becoming decadent and for some reason I didn't much enjoy the ones we attended at the Café Gijón. One day my uncle took me to the theatre, as I recall it was the month of November, and once again there was a performance of José Zorrilla's *Tenorio*. [Zorrilla's play *Don Juan Tenorio*, recounting the exploits of the archetypal lady-killer was written entirely in verse and became a Spanish institution with new adaptations traditionally being staged in November each year.] On this occasion there was a notable novelty; the sets and costumes were the work of Salvador Dalí. This version was directed by Luis Escobar and Huberto Pérez de la Ossa. The surrealist concept dreamed up by the genius of Cadaqués was greeted in the main with excellent reviews. However one voice of protest was heard to shout out from the gallery of the María Guerrero theatre: "An atheist Don Juan!" I don't suppose I was the only one to be surprised at this outburst.

Afterwards Uncle Emilio introduced me to Luis Escobar, the leading players Luis Prendes and Elvira Noriega and, of course, to Salvador Dalí (years later I would work with both Escobar and Prendes). Dalí struck me as quite a character, as canny as they come and always playing the part people expected of him. His curious discourse touched on subjects as diverse as deep sea diving and rhinos and he also expressed his admiration for Vermeer de Delft. Once outside, my uncle remarked that besides his undisputed genius, the Catalonian painter was first and foremost interested in making money.

In 1951 and, needless to say, thanks to my uncle, I met a truly exceptional man. I refer to Jacinto Benavente. Uncle Emilio knew him from way back when they both used to go to the *tertulias* at the Café Hungría. The Nobel prize winner received us in his bedroom; apparently he'd fallen into the habit of writing in bed. He was a delicate looking man with tortoise shell rimmed spectacles, and his pointed white beard gave him the air of a faun or a satyr. His penetrating eyes sparkled behind his glasses, reflecting his privileged intellect. During the conversation the name of Valle-Inclán inevitably cropped up. Benavente praised him to the skies and justified Valle-Inclán's bad temper and angry outbursts as being the reactions of a shy man who was fed up of all the gossip, impertinence and nonsense written about him by second rate hacks.

> Look, Molina, do you think that anybody as intelligent as Don Ramón would ever say that Cervantes was a bad writer and Velázquez a lousy painter? For God's sake, in private he held exactly the opposite opinion. The problem is that some observers take a very superficial point of view, seeing Valle as a kind of Cyrano de Bergerac, a quarrelsome braggart with a venomous sarcastic streak. Well, far from it, I tell you that Don Ramón was in the same class as Michelangelo or Benvenuto Cellini... Once, in Lisbon, a journalist asked me who I considered to be the greatest Spanish novelist. I answered without the slightest hesitation: "Pio Baroja." He found that strange and he inevitably went on to ask, "What about

Nobel prize winner Jacinto Benavente

Valle-Inclán?" I answered that I don't count
Valle-Inclán as a novelist because Don Ramón
is much more than a novelist, he's an all
rounder.

In the course of the conversation the Nobel prize winner expressed his dislike of
the writer of erotic stories *El Caballero Audaz.* They also spoke about ballet, because
my uncle was crazy about it and he boasted that in Paris he'd met Nijinsky, Pavlova,
Tammanova and even Diaghilev. Benavente admitted that his true vocation was that of
actor but he'd remained a simple writer.

As the evening drew to an end we said our farewells. Before we left the writer
asked me, "What about you, young man? What would you like to do for a living?" I
replied somewhat tepidly that I wanted to be a surveyor. A mischievous spark lit up his
eyes and he responded, "That's fine, my lad, you'll be doing something really useful."
As we went out I thought to myself that I'd never forget the ironic and worldly wise
look on the face of the little faun.

Among the characters in this gallery of curious people with whom my uncle was
acquainted, I can't fail to mention a certain Mexican, whose name escapes me and
whom I met on the afternoon of my selection to take part in the Olympic Games in
Tokyo. He was an old poet and painter who had returned from exile in Mexico. His
face was covered in deep wrinkles and he had long flowing snow-white hair although
the top of his head was completely bald. This man was a die hard Trotskyist and he told

us about the murder of Leon Trotsky. He had been one of Trotsky's bodyguards at the time when Ramón Mercader smashed his skull in with an ice pick. He spoke of the affair with the utmost vehemence:

> There was nothing we could do because the bastard gained access to the house by an underhand trick. He was a sly one and he got close to Leon by seducing his secretary. That swine Stalin always had it in for him, he had him thrown out of France on trumped up charges of murdering Kirov, he tried to murder him several times and on that godawful day Mercader pulled it off. I tell you Emilio, Papa Stalin was a bigger son of bitch than Hitler and Mussolini put together. What can you expect from a failed priest? If I could get my hands on Mercader and his mother I'd blow their damned brains out with my Colt 45.

His political leanings were the cause of the antagonism between him and his compatriot, the painter Diego Rivera. "Rivera was a Stalinist and I used to shout out 'Viva Hernán Cortes' just to piss him off. Then I'd raise my arm and sing 'The International.' One day when Diego was painting a mural he chucked a pot of paint at me. He hit me too, but the bugger fell off his ladder." He laughed out loud as he narrated these events. He seemed to me quite a surreal character, but with my uncle anything was possible.

During the conversation with this Mexican I also found out that Emilio and my father had known Buenaventura Durruti in their youth. Years later I tried to make a film about the famous anarchist who was shot dead in Madrid in mysterious circumstances, but I couldn't interest any backers.

Incidentally, the absurd term subgenre, utilized by certain self important film critics, brings to mind another anecdote to do with uncle Emilio and which also provides me with the chance to say something about the concept of kitsch.

One afternoon long ago I accompanied my uncle to a reunion of intellectuals in honor of the prestigious art critic José Camón Aznar. I remember that among those present were many important friends and acquaintances of my uncle's. During the event a weird little man came up to us. He was about 50, with a thin face, long, curly graying hair, large nose and bug eyes. My uncle introduced him with the words "This is Orteguita."

This individual talked 10 to the dozen and fancied himself as an authority on every topic under the sun, from the flora of the Amazon to metaphysical paintings. I was told that he could turn his hand from being an art critic, to commentating on bullfights to reviewing theatre plays. He wrote about architecture, agriculture, even about D.I.Y. if need be. His main claim to fame was that his father, an old general in the catering corps, had slept with the spy Mata-Hari. He used to bore everyone stiff with this Mata-Hari clap trap.

At one point this fellow Orteguita, who wrote under different pseudonyms, started talking about the great painter from Córdoba, Julio Romero de Torres. "Romero de Torres is a subpainter. He's only fit to illustrate calendars." Uncle Emilio didn't like that one little bit. Not only did he admire the Andalusian painter but he'd also been a good friend of his as a young man. Orteguita looked at my uncle with a smug self righteous expression on his face, being, like all those who lack real talent, totally sure of himself and his opinions. He was smoking a large pipe and blowing the foul smelling smoke into my uncle's face.

Emilio Molina looked at the know-it-all with distaste and delivered a shattering put-down: "Orteguita, you're the missing link between man and ape. You know as much about art as I do about breeding earthworms." The critic went cherry red and blew a disrespectful cloud of smoke straight into Emilio's face whose reaction was to snatch the pipe from the man's mouth and throw it to the floor. Orteguita screamed: "You fucking Red! You've broken my pipe! My great-grandfather's meerschaum pipe! I'm going to write an article that'll put you out of circulation for good, you'll never sell another sculpture in your life! I should have expected something like that from somebody who never wears a hat!"

It all seemed Kafkesque to me. I didn't know then what meerschaum was, and the bit about hats was explained to me later on. [This is a reference to a well known advertisement which was popular during the Franco regime. It claimed that only Communists went out without a hat, thus encouraging upstanding citizens to continue purchasing headgear at a time of falling sales.] What nobody realized was that Camón Aznar had overheard the argument and unexpectedly butted in. "Calm down Orteguita. What's the big deal? Was the pipe given to the old man by the Kaiser or something? Come on, take it easy. Go and get to work on the hors d'oeuvres, that's what you're best at." Orteguita went off with a pained look on his face.

My uncle and I left and went downtown to have a beer. Night had fallen and the plaza was full of cheap hookers and shady characters. More than once they offered us their merchandise.

My uncle started to tell me about Romero de Torres.

> He could paint Andalusian women better than anyone. Dark haired, dusky maidens with wonderful firm round tits, more sensual than anything by Mezquita, Bilbao or even Morcillo. You see he was a great one for symbolism—naked women in weird landscapes surrounded by nuns, beds, guitars, dogs, shoes, coffins and even severed heads.

Still chatting away we headed for the Puerta del Sol. My uncle continued:

> The ladies were very fond of him and he was always ready to oblige them. He screwed practically all of his models. He certainly cut a dash in his cape and smart *cordobés* hat. It

La nieta de la Trini (1950) by **Romero de Torres**

was an uphill struggle, but he eventually got
the recognition he deserved: medals, exhibitions, tributes....He ended up doing portraits
of the most important ladies and Valle, who
liked him a lot, took him to all the *tertulias* in
Madrid. Benavente liked him too. He was a
gentleman, but a gentleman with talent. It's a
funny thing that this man who used to read
Lenin and Trotsky, should end up on the
banknotes of the Franco regime.

We had passed Puerta del Sol and were now in Calle Callao. My uncle kept talking:

He lived fast and he died fast too. I don't think
he lived to see his 60th birthday. As well as
oil paintings he did poster work and even book
covers for the novels of Manuel Machado or
that good for nothing Caballero Audaz. He
worked on a film called *La Malcasada* with
appearances by Valle, Azorín, Millán Astray,
Rusiñol, Francisco Franco and even his dog
Pacheco. The dog became nearly as famous
as its master. The artist's admirers included
King Alfonso, Pérez Galdós, the Quintero
brothers, Pardo Bazán, Pérez de la Ayala and
even Ramón Gomez de la Serna who was a

fanatic of Solana's work. A year before his death from bronchitis—and other things—I visited him at his home in Córdoba. We talked about many things and he told me that he'd really wanted to be a singer of flamenco. He was a truly great artist, but then along comes that dickhead Orteguita and calls him a subpainter only fit to paint calendars.

I have set down this paragraph about Romero de Torres because this episode gave me pause for thought. Today in the world of films there are a lot of Orteguitas, in fact too many. For many modern art critics Romero de Torres is a kitsch painter and since my movies have also been labeled as kitsch it's a subject which appeals to me.

In the '60s, kitsch sensitivities, along with camp and pop, revolutionized the world of culture. The tide of kitsch reclaimed characters and resurrected forms which had been lost in time. But it also brought equivocation and confusion. It cut short possibilities, mercilessly curtailed greatness, created a perverse typecasting and had a rather paralyzing effect. In short, a certain decoration, a certain object, a certain character, a certain film could be wonderfully kitsch or horribly kitsch, just like types of cholesterol which may be good or bad.

For many it was highly pleasing, for others despicable, almost scatological. I've come to the conclusion that my dog Lon is lovably kitsch, like all the world's dogs which is what makes them almost human. As I understand it this word can embrace everything from the sublime to the grotesque. The intransigent Hermann Broch goes some way to clarifying the issue. Among other things he says:

> Kitsch doesn't only mean marbled coffins, wedding cakes, red satin shoes, ashtrays shaped like snails, Eiffel Tower paperweights, garden gnomes, pantheons, piggy banks, golden statues with painted genitals, tinted picture post cards, etc. Kitsch can also apply to Goethe, Wagner, Walter Scott, Moreau, the Symbolists, the pre-Raphaelites, the ancient Egyptians who painted their huge temples in bright colors, the ancient Greeks who did the same, the legendary film director D.W. Griffith, and anything you like. Kitsch is a part Bourgeois, part Non-Conformist invention which seeks to reconcile aesthetic virtues with the love of decoration (the great cathedrals were originally multi-colored, could they be considered kitsch?), but this tendency also combines Puritanism with sex. In short, not to put too fine a point on it, the merging of Heaven and Hell.

My movies may be kitsch: I accept that in the sense of "a guilty pleasure." I see myself as a Gothic-Expressionist. To quote K. Edschmid, writing in 1921:

> The Expressionist artist does not look, he sees;
> he does not tell, he lives; he does not repro-
> duce, he recreates, he does not find, he seeks.

It's not easy to get to grips with the kitsch issue. A few days ago I was talking about this with my admired friend Luis Alberto de Cuenca. We had seen Steven Spielberg's *Jurassic Park: The Lost World* and after chewing the fat a while the kitsch question cropped up. I believe that both the great American director and his dinosaurs are kitsch to some extent.

In the '50s I saw a host of legendary American "B" movies. Many of them were true masterpieces. I'll always remember emblematic titles like *The Day The Earth Stood Still*—kindly aliens, flying saucers and a spectacular metal robot with an excellent Michael Rennie as Klaatu accompanied by Patricia Neal; *The Thing From Another World*—with an alien to make your hair stand on end, finally destroyed by electrocution; *The Five Thousand Fingers of Dr. T*; *Creature from the Black Lagoon*; *The Quatermass Xperiment* and many others too numerous to mention.

Apart from my cinemania, these were the years when I began to take an interest in girls. The best way to meet them was at parties. At first we all remained quite formal but little by little as the music played on (usually romantic tunes), and after downing several glasses of the inevitable punch which we lads used to make as strong as possible, things started to get more lively. Sometimes we held our partners so close while dancing cheek to cheek that we almost quivered in ecstasy.

Up till that time my experience of sex had been exciting but quite limited. I'd only got as far as a bit of kissing and clumsy fondling, and that was pretty daring. A young housemaid named Isabel had started to reveal to me certain secret pleasures, but it was all very rushed because we had to take advantage of when there was no one at home and we were rather nervous. The girl was always warning me that if her boyfriend, who was a Civil Guard, ever found out he'd kill us both. One day she disappeared and I never knew any more about her. I wonder if she ever married the Civil Guard? Anyhow, she had offered me a piece of mouth watering cake which I wouldn't get to devour until a few years later.

Let's go now to a party which turned out to be very special. It was in the spring of 1952 and organized by a classmate who came from a very well off family. There I met two gorgeous sisters, Cristina and Maria José. They were the daughters of a well known diplomat and had traveled all over the world. One of them was studying in Switzerland and the other in the U.S. In those days this made them a bit different and consequently even more desirable. I spent part of the evening dancing with Cristina who proved to be very, very liberated. Then I danced with María José and believe me, romantic music had never sounded so good. I reckon that I've seldom been the object of such envy as I was that evening.

The sisters told me they'd come to Madrid to have some of their qualifications validated; their parents were away at their respective postings. When the party was over we swapped phone numbers. There was something akin to animal magnetism about our farewell; their eyes seemed to hold the promise of something mysterious, seductive and perhaps even perverse. Naturally, at the age of 18, I had already been out with several girls but I'd never got beyond a bit of snogging and fondling. I don't think I was prepared for what I was shortly to experience.

A few days went by and I heard the phone ring. I picked it up and my heart skipped a beat; Cristina was inviting me over to have a drink and hear some music at her place. Both nervous and excited I took a tube train and was soon at the house of the enigmatic sisters. Cristina let me in. She looked stunningly attractive in a tight blouse and a short skirt which showed off her shapely legs. The subdued lighting created a most appropriate atmosphere. We drank a few fairly stiff *cubalibres* which gave me a measure of Dutch courage which I desperately needed. We started kissing and I was transported to a dimension which I had never known existed. We didn't stay long in the lounge but soon made our way to the bedroom. That afternoon I learned a lot—maybe too much.

After this first encounter a few days went by. I became obsessed by the experience. I phoned Cristina several times but there was no reply.

When I least expected it she phoned me again. That very evening I rushed over to their apartment. But when I arrived I was surprised to find both sisters there. Cristina and María José were looking really attractive and sensual. I noted a disturbing, almost morbid atmosphere which nevertheless appealed to me. Once again the lights were dimmed, the music warm and suggestive. I had quite a few drinks and presently we started dancing in a close embrace; I was drifting further and further from reality. When night fell we dined, bathed in flickering, unreal candlelight. Half drunk, I saw among the shadows projected by the candles that María José was offering me a drink made with some kind of herbs which were supposed to induce a tremendous feeling of well being. I drained the cup and the three of us entered the bedroom. Cristina lit some josticks which gave off a peculiar scent, like a mixture of incense and bergamot, while speaking these words: "Sometimes love is a ritual, a unique ritual."

The memory of what went on that night became lost among the fumes of my alcoholic stupor and a succession of hazy, dreamlike images.

When I woke up late the next morning I was alone. My back hurt and after seeing my own blood on the sheets I discovered that it was covered in deep scratches. I couldn't remember what had happened the previous night, but in spite of my confusion I knew that I'd be coming back again.

I continued to visit them for some weeks more, living on the borderline between fascination and fear, as if I had been the victim of a pair of vampires. It's likely that the memory of this experience provided me, many years later, with the inspiration for the scenes of the werewolf women who possessed Waldemar Daninsky in *La Maldición de la Bestía* [*Night of the Howling Beast*, US], like a kind of belated attempt at exorcism. I sometimes think of María José's deck of Egyptian Tarot cards and how her predictions were reflected in many of the events in my life.

As I've already mentioned, drawing and painting were my greatest hobbies, together with my love of sport. I harbored a secret wish to become a professional comic book artist. I was greatly influenced by Alex Raymond and his marvelous heroes *Flash Gordon*, *Jungle Jim* and *Rip Kirby* and by Harold Foster's *Tarzan* and *Prince Valiant*, not forgetting Lee Falk, creator of *The Masked Man* and *Mandrake* and Milton Caniff's

Terry and the Pirates. I'm certain that the language of comic strips had a great influence on my films, and it even taught me how to set up scenes. For example I first became aware of what a subjective shot was like when I saw one of Milton Caniff's panels which showed a scene as viewed through the eyes of one of the characters. It was as if a movie camera had been placed inside the character's head.

I can also remember, off the cuff, *The Little Eagle, The Stone Man, The Cub, Diego Valor, Captain Thunder* and *Dracula.* I was especially fond of *Inspector Dan.* Of the splendid Spanish

This *Flash Gordon* illustration by Alex Raymond helped influence my career choice.

comic book artists I'll always remember Esteban Maroto, Emilio Freixas, Jésus Blasco, Adolfo Buylla, José González, Jaime Brocal, Remohí, Victor de la Fuente and Juan Arranz, among others. I also read Tintin and Asterix.

In fact I did draw a number of strips and then went on to illustrate various books. However the most important work of this type I ever managed to do was in the field of illustrating record covers. I'll come to that presently.

1951 was the year I finished my secondary education after passing the dreaded final exams. It was a great moment. On the last day of classes the kindly Señor Pantoja asked us all what profession we hoped to follow. We each answered him in turn, and it doesn't take a great deal of imagination to guess the replies. There were numerous would-be engineers, architects, lawyers, doctors, diplomats and even biologists. When it came to my turn I replied straight-away that I wanted to be a film director. This caused such a stunned silence that had I said I wanted to be an actor they'd have had me carted off to the funny farm. This ambition, dictated to me by my subconscious, lasted but a few seconds and I quickly rectified, mumbling something about wanting to become a surveyor. A sigh of relief went up around the room, although from that moment on I was marked as the black sheep of the class. All the other lads wanted to become men of means. I was starting to hide behind a mask.

On Love, Death... and other issues

Writing about my own life is turning out to be harder than persuading Marlon Brando to go on a diet. That's why, by repeated use of flashbacks, I keep going backward and forward at my own convenience, as if traveling in a time machine.

So it is that now I'm going to write about three films which, for different reasons, represent crucial moments in the development of my passion for the cinema. For those countless self important film critics who are continually turning out encyclopedias, books, articles and such these titles may not be among the films they idolize, but these are my memoirs. The films in question are *Gilda, Duel In The Sun* and *The Third Man*.

When I saw *Gilda* for the first time, I felt like I was committing a mortal sin. But, since the great advantage of the Catholic religion is having the chance to confess, I thought I'd be able to atone for it later on, even though the penance may have been a bit stiff. I don't know how I managed to slip into the Argüelles cinema to see that sinful and incredibly arousing picture. It was a memorable experience, as unique as the strip-tease performed by the fabulous Margarita Carmen Cansino (Rita Hayworth) who, as she slowly peeled off that long black glove, oozed more sex and more sensuality than Sharon Stone (including the famous leg crossing scene in *Basic Instinct*), Kim Basinger or any other femme fatale in cinema history. When she sang *Amor mío* it really struck a chord in the hearts and minds of the audience. And the slap in the face she got from Glenn Ford was a real show stopper. Good old Glenn should have retired from movies after that; he'd had his finest hour.

Duel In The Sun is an epic western charged with a perverse eroticism. The terrific Gregory Peck was never meaner or more attractive, exuding rugged virility, mesmerizing malevolence and total self assurance; moreover he was as perfectly suited to blazing away with six-shooters as Charlton Heston was to wielding the mighty sword of El Cid. It was evident that the only possible climax was for the wonderful Perla Chávez to shoot him down in a hail of lead, only to end up dying by his side under the merciless sun of Cabeza del Indio. And let's not forget Lionel Barrymore, who from his wheelchair brought to this story of love and death his own brand of greatness. I saw the film 14 times.

So we come to *The Third Man*. Orson Welles was never as menacing nor Alida Valli as vulnerable and beautiful as in this picture, and a whole generation would be forever haunted by Anton Karas' zither music.

Naturally there were other important films but I'll come to those later. After this little digression which has given me a bit of a break I'll now get back to the realities of my past.

The story continues as I prepared to commence my studies to become a surveyor, although I really wasn't at all interested in the profession. Naturally, following on from my vampiric experiences with Cristina and María José, I had a number of girlfriends. Once I was doing my Clutching Hand act (to quote one of my favorite serials) with a rather straight-laced lass in the Parque del Oeste when the park keeper spotted us. I had to pay a fine of 400 pesetas for indecent behavior. The poor girl turned as red as a beet and nearly died of shame.

And then Isabel appeared in my life (if I'd met her today I'd naturally have renamed her Elisabeta).

Isabel was a good-looking girl; she was tall, with a well-rounded figure and she was reading Philosophy at the university. We got on well and soon started going out. We went dancing, we took walks in the historic parts of Madrid, we sat out on café terraces and above all we talked, we talked a lot. Isabel was surprisingly gentle, full of tenderness and very well educated. She liked giving me books as presents, especially books of poetry and, of all the poets, she most admired the work of Juan Ramón Jiménez. One day she told me the strange story of a young and beautiful sculptress whose unrequited love for Juan Ramón had driven her to suicide. She spoke of that distant tragedy with such passion that I suspected that it was something of an obsession with her.

She admitted that she could easily comprehend the desperate action of the sculptress, since to die for true love was the height of selflessness, the ultimate act of sacrifice for a loved one.

In Isabel's company I visited the cities of Segovia, Àvila, Toledo, Cuenca and, in particular, Sigüenza. Isabel was captivated by this town. She knew all about its history and its monuments and was strangely attracted by the fabulous statue of the courtier Don Martín Vázquez de Arce: "Had I known him, I'm sure I would have loved him with all my soul," she told me. She was so fascinated by the personalities and pomp of past times that on one occasion she even told me that I'd have made a fine lansquenet, a warrior-swordsman, and that I'd undoubtedly been born in the wrong century. Our peculiar love affair grew ever more stormy, ever more obsessive.

One day she presented me with a collection of extremely old penny dreadful-type books about celebrated Spanish bandits. They recounted the intrepid exploits of such outlaws as José María El Tempranillo, Los Niños de Écija, El Barquero, Diego Corrientes, El Cristo, Luis Candelas, Frasco Antonio and El Pernales. These periodicals were published in Madrid's Calle Valverde and priced at 20 centimes (of one peseta). I reproduce here a quaint example of the advertising blurb which was printed on the back cover:

> On sale throughout Spain, the true and most interesting story of the famous bandit El Pernales. The full story is published in one volume and among its pages the reader will encounter all of the graphic scenes which gave rise to the popular and tragic legend of the celebrated horseman. In the next issue, Luis Candelas.

This collection of antique printed matter, which I still possess, later played an important part in a certain affair which would involve film directors Vicente Aranda and Eloy de la Iglesia.

I still possess this booklet on the celebrated Pernales bandits.

One day while out walking with Isabel in Madrid's Retiro Park I suffered an epileptic fit. It was like a warning bell going off inside me. Isabel was getting more possessive by the day and was starting to smother me. I couldn't stand it any longer and started going out with another girl. Isabel's reaction to our breaking up was like something out of a cheap romantic novel; she screamed, she shouted, she begged and she pleaded with great tears filling her eyes. In spite of all this we had one last date in Paseo de Rosales where we spent the afternoon sitting together by a book vendor's stall. She presented me with the last two books she would ever give me; one by Rimbaud and the other a book of short stories by Apollinaire. The sky turned red with the coming of twilight and by the time we stood up to leave the sun had gone down completely. As she walked away I watched her go with mixed feelings of sorrow and relief.

Many years went by and I never knew any more about her. Then suddenly I heard the news; Isabel had committed suicide, leaping through a window to die like a shattered doll on the hard concrete of the patio far below. I was reminded of the courtier of Sigüenza and of the beautiful young sculptress who secretly loved Juan Ramón Jiménez. The ode to passion had fallen silent for ever.

One day in October 1957 I decided to kill a little time by playing a few games in the Boulevard Bowling Alley. I had given up studying to be a surveyor and was just starting a degree course in architecture. A friend happened to introduce me to a certain José María Jarabo Pérez-Morris. Jarabo seemed to be a pleasant, elegant and apparently very popular fellow. He was smartly dressed and his athletic bearing was the result of his being a dedicated practitioner of judo. His good looks and charming manner drove women wild. And he was great at bowling.

So I started to hang out with Jarabo. He was quite a lot older than me and I was really impressed when he took me to nightclubs like the Pasapoga, the Florida or the Villaromana. Being with him I got to know a lot of pretty girls, some of them were go-go girls and others were "on the game." There was an exotic dancer named, if I remember correctly, Naima Cherki. When it came to belly dancing she was in a class of her own.

Whenever we went out Jarabo drank heavily and then he used to take me into his confidence. He came from the town of Cuenca and had got married in Puerto Rico. "When I said, 'I do,' I was well pissed. You can only do a stupid thing like that when you're drunk." He told me about his mother who was Puerto Rican and a devoted

With my family at a dinner on New Year's Eve

follower of the "Virgin of the Tight Fist"—she hated spending money. He lived in a guest house in Calle Orense, although he liked to change his abode fairly often. He boasted about his important trading company and import-export business. He had worked for a time in the United States but decided that the lifestyle in "that country of dickheads" wasn't for him. Later on I found out that he'd been expelled because of some illegitimate activities to do with drugs.

He was obsessed by firearms and confessed that he usually carried a gun. One night in the toilets of a bar he showed me the pistol he was carrying. "It's an FN caliber 7.65. With this little beauty I can drill a hole through a 25 peseta piece at 50 meters." For some reason, something about this loud-mouthed weirdo appealed to me.

One day he took me out for dinner to a place called El Lar Gallego to celebrate the arrival of his girlfriend, a good-looking and likable English woman called Beryl Jones. That night, as was customary in Jarabo, he had too much to drink and had an argument with the waiter whom he accused of staring at Beryl in a lecherous manner. When we came out of the restaurant I left the couple and went home.

Two weeks later Jarabo phoned to invite me out. Beryl had gone back to London and he felt like going on a bender. He'd made a date with two air stewardess sisters for drinks and, I felt sure, for something else besides. We met up in the Café California. By the time I arrived he was pretty tanked up, having already downed three or four whiskeys.

The stewardesses' flat was modern and quite tastefully decorated. As I remember, hanging on the wall of the lounge were posters of Elvis Presley and Ché Guevara; it only needed one of Mao and they'd have had the complete set of what was considered vogue wall hangings in those days.

Things got warmed up pretty fast, the booze was taking effect and Jarabo proposed snorting a few lines of coke to get us even more in the mood. I didn't want to, but Jarabo and the two girls went ahead. Soon my friend and his partner went off into one of the bedrooms. Having overcome my initial reticence I got cracking with my stewardess, Marisa. When we were well and truly at it we heard a shout of rage and Jarabo and his half naked companion burst into the room. The man was beside himself and kept hitting the stewardess, shouting, "Don't try it on with me, you slut! Tell that Bolivian bastard to hand over the dough." I tried to break it up but the lumbering brute turned his dark, bloodshot eyes on me and in a flash I seemed to be staring once again into the eyes of that menacing wolf I'd seen in Lozoya. Jarabo was a predator too, but much more dangerous than a wolf because he was human. I didn't think twice, I just got the hell out of there.

I heard more of Jarabo in the summer of 1958, but this time through the press and television, which was just becoming popular in Spain at that time. The news was steeped in blood.

José María Jarabo Pérez-Morris went on trial on January 29, 1959, on four charges of robbery and homicide with the aggravating circumstance of malice aforethought, two charges of illegal possession of firearms, two charges of using false identities (one of which was Jaime Martín Balmaseda), one charge of forgery and one charge of defiling cadavers. On February 10th he was convicted and sentenced to death.

I think it's worth taking a look at the events which led up to Jarabo being put on trial.

The brutal orgy of blood began on July 19, 1958, a Saturday, between nine and 10 p.m. Jarabo called at the house of Emilio Fernández Díaz, co-proprietor, together with Félix López Robledo, of the pawnbroker's shop Jusfer. Jarabo had previously had a row with López about the return of a diamond ring belonging to his English girlfriend, Beryl Martin Jones, which he wanted to sell or pawn again for 50,000 pesetas. Beryl was now married and discretion was essential.

My old friend murdered both of the pawnbrokers as well as Emilio's maid, Paulina Ramos, and his wife, María de los Desamparados Alonso Bravo. He stabbed Paulina to death and ripped off her knickers to make it look like a sexually motivated attack and shot the others point blank through the head. The massacre left the floor and walls dripping with blood and brains. Jarabo spent the night drinking anisette in the Fernández home surrounded by the three corpses. Afterwards he went to López' office and did away with him. All this slaughter just because he couldn't recover the Englishwoman's ring.

Hardly 24 hours had elapsed before he was arrested. It seems incredible that such a cold, calculating killer should make such a blunder as taking his blood-stained suit to the dry cleaner's. The owners of the establishment called the police at once.

It was a spectacular trial which dragged on for several weeks. It was said that since Jarabo came from an important family he'd never face execution. Due to the five head injuries he'd received as a result of fights and traffic accidents, the psychiatrists called by the defense and by the prosecution argued over the true extent of his psychosis. On top of that, he'd also undergone treatment in Puerto Rico for syphilis. One of the private prosecutors, Nuñez Maturana, quoted Schneider's phrase: "The best treatment for a ruthless psychopath is the gallows."

Eventually Jarabo was sentenced to death by garroting. The evening prior to the execution the prisoner asked for six cigars and a bottle of whisky. He was only allowed a quick swig. Jarabo kept amazingly calm throughout and in his final declaration he lamented the horrible deaths he had caused. "I don't know whether I'm a psychopath or not. I don't know and I don't care. All I know is that I've been responsible for four deaths."

The lad who had been a pupil at the élite Pilar High School, who could have had it all, had ended up achieving nothing but death and horror.

Jarabo entered the death chamber at dawn on July 4, 1959. His garroting proved to be a revolting, Dantesque spectacle. Thanks to his immense strength and the thickness of his great muscular neck he took 20 minutes to die. Someone hidden in a locker filmed the murderer's demise with a super 8mm camera. I've seen the film, which still exists.

For me the whole affair was a terrible, morbid nightmare which I lived day by day via television, radio and the press. It was like looking at one of those bloodthirsty true-crime fairground posters with the barker pointing with his cane at each picture in turn and reciting the dreadful deeds of one of the most ruthless serial killers in the black annals of crime in Spain. It was a devilish frieze combining death, lust, sadism, greed and degradation, a crazy blend of Valdés Leal, Solana and Goya with the cosmopolitan and mundane world of those unique times. It all left a lasting impression on me. (Only Juan Andrés Aldige, the Frenchman, would surpass Jarabo's crimes, but I'll come to him later on.) That look he'd given me in the stewardesses' home, like a venomous, hypnotic, lethal serpent, would undoubtedly have an influence on the future film performances which were to become a fundamental part of my life.

The Year Marilyn Monroe Died

When our summers on the island of La Toja came to an end, my parents chose Suances in Cantabria as the place to spend part of the summer holidays and we vacationed there for more than six years. In those days summer holidays lasted a long time and we'd spend a month at the seaside and another month at our country house in Lozoya del Valle. They were happy years on the whole, since my father had prospered and had gone from being just a simple employee to enjoying quite an elevated social standing. The fur and leather business was doing well and apart from the factory and retail shop, he set up a tanning shop in the neighborhood of Chamartín.

I remember something about the factory which is both quite amusing and demonstrated, to some extent, my father's personality. He was very keen on animals and in the factory he kept a parrot, which swore like a trooper, a young leopard, an obscene monkey which used to leap on top of any woman within range and a genet (a type of wild cat). One day the genet escaped from its cage and went on the rampage through all the chicken houses in the neighborhood, leaving a trail of carnage and slaughter in its wake. Eventually the leopard, the monkey and the genet ended up in the zoo in the Parque del Retiro and my father gave the parrot to uncle Emilio. Dogs we always had, both at home and at our country house, but dogs are different; they're so faithful, affectionate and intelligent they end up becoming members of the family.

I had some good times in Suances and those summers spent on the beach and at Lozoya marked my passage from childhood to adolescence. In Cantabria I learned to dance and to play chess and I had a lovely girlfriend there called Carmen, who wore her hair in long plaits. I can remember the beautiful sunsets over Playa de los Locos, the two of us locked in a tender embrace and savoring the sweet kisses of first love. Suances was also where I first met Carlos Saura who was then studying to be an engineer although he admitted to me that his real interests were photography and cinema.

It was during those summer vacations that I first began to take part in athletics. Together with José María de Hoz (later president of the Spanish Athletics Federation) I practiced javelin throwing and sprinting on the cinder tracks of Torrelavega.

We used to stay at the Hotel Acacio and I would go dancing at a sort of open air club which bore the strange name Uchupi. In a cinema in Torrelavega I saw *High Noon* with a brilliant Gary Cooper, an unforgettable song sung by Frankie Lane and Lon Chaney, Jr. as the cowardly sheriff. I loved Westerns. Some years later I drew the sleeve for the record which Columbia issued of Frankie Lane's famous song.

Now I turn to a story which started out with all the joy of a wonderful love affair only to end up once more in tragedy and death.

September was the month when the village of Lozoya del Valle celebrated its annual *fiestas*. There were fairground attractions, dancing in the village plaza, bullfights and all the other events which were characteristic of these village festivities. One evening at the dance I spotted a gorgeous girl with very long light brown hair; I may

As Fu Manchu at a costume party in Suances

say, without fear of exaggeration, that she was the most beautiful woman I have ever seen in my life. Overcoming my natural shyness I went up and asked her for a dance. The village band were playing out of tune *pasodobles* under the light of paper lanterns. It was an unforgettable evening. Mariuca was the name of this girl with honey-colored eyes.

So began a long and idyllic relationship. Mariuca was tender, intelligent and passionate. One day she introduced me to her family. They owned a chalet near the marsh and the local people called them "the Handsome Family." The father was a good-looking man, but he had a disturbing presence. Once I heard him say, "If any man so much as goes near my daughter I'll kill him." So we met in secret. I used to put on my hunting togs and we would meet in out of the way places, hiding ourselves among the lush vegetation. Her father was a constant threat and she was afraid of him. Sometimes he looked at me in such an odd way that I instinctively smelled danger.

The tragedy occurred one evening in June. I took Mariuca home. Little did I know that that goodnight kiss would be our last. The following day I phoned her as usual but there was no reply. It didn't take me long to find out the tragic news; it was all over the papers in bold headlines. My girlfriend's father had been cleaning his shotgun while his son was inspecting his own weapon—they were planning to shoot partridges the following day. All of a sudden, for no apparent reason, the father shot his son in the back, killing him instantly. Mariuca and her mother rushed to see what had happened and froze in terror. Fearing for their own lives, both women turned and fled. The

With Carlos Saura at my parents' estate

murderer locked himself in an upstairs room, throwing furniture and other objects out of the window. The police arrived on the scene and ordered him to open the door. The man put the barrel of the gun in his mouth and pulled the trigger. Blood, brains and fragments of bone were plastered all over the walls and ceiling. It was a dreadful sight.

Mariuca and her mother went away to San Sebastian to stay at an aunt's house. We kept in touch by phone for a while but one day I decided not to call her any more. I've often thought that I abandoned her in the midst of that horrific tragedy by hiding myself away in Lozoya. Gradually her phone calls became less and less frequent until they stopped altogether. I've always regretted it.

The years went by. Then one day, as I was driving over the bridge at Lozoya on my way to our house, I spotted a figure standing by the side of the road. Through the side window I could make out the beautiful face of a girl who looked at me with honey-colored eyes—eyes clouded by sorrow and reproach. A wave of pity and shame swept over me but I didn't stop; soon Mariuca's silhouette faded away into the distance. I never saw her again. That was in 1962, the year Marilyn Monroe died.

At the time of my relationship with Mariuca the embryo of my modest *oeuvre* was starting to take shape. I began reading the works of authors of weird tales like Stoker, Maupassant, Poe, Lovecraft, Le Fanu—horror, in particular horror fantasy, started to take a hold of my soul. I was fascinated by the decadent romanticism of these authors'

Paul Naschy

tales which contrasted with the Gorgons and Chimeras of long dead artists like Hieronymus Bosch and the medieval gargoyles and futurism of Marinetti. I enjoyed the stories of Bradbury and Bloch as much as the works of Boris Vian and the cryptic theatre plays of Ionesco. It seemed to me that beyond our fast moving world of ever advancing, omnipresent technology there had to be something more.

Around this time my father struck up a friendship with Morcillo, the famous painter from Granada for whom he even set up a studio in Calle Mayor. My progenitor also lent a helping hand, on Morcillo's recommendation, to one of the artist's disciples, Emilio Roda. I was then seriously considering taking up painting for a living and Emilio taught me a lot. The models, who posed semi-naked for him, were also used by a young photographer who was destined to make a name for himself: Carlos Saura. One fine day Roda, whom I considered to be extraordinarily talented, left Madrid and I never knew any more about him. I remember that little studio with nostalgia, for when Emilio wasn't around, Mariuca and I used to meet there in secret. How often we watched the sunsets from that studio gallery.

Now it's time to say something about my experiences in the army. I could have enlisted in the University Militia but I preferred to wait and be called up for National Service. I was posted to the Communications Corps stationed at El Pardo. To adapt to the new environment I made use of two activities which stood me in good stead with my barrack room comrades: one was my skill as an artist and the other was my sporting prowess. Regarding the former, I was ordered by my superiors to decorate the mess hall with allegorical and emblematic motifs designed to stimulate not only the troops' appetites but also their fighting spirit. Captain Àlvarez, a hard and unbending show off, was to supervise the work. The central motif was a depiction of King Fernando III *El Santo*, holding aloft in his left hand a flag bearing the legendary insignia of our regiment. Trouble arose when I painted the flag in a glorious bright red. Captain Àlvarez, for whom there was no other color than blue, rushed off to inform the Colonel. Our commander came over to look at the mural and informed the big-headed bully in no uncertain terms that red was also the color of blood, and furthermore the players of our national football team wore red shirts.

From that day on the captain tried incessantly to persuade me to volunteer for combat duties in Sidi Infi (in Spanish Morocco), where gallant troops were needed to defend the fatherland. There was something of the stereotyped Wehrmacht officer about him—impeccably turned out, with a fine military bearing, he had the habit of slashing a hunting crop across his highly polished jackboots. I still have a number of press cuttings about the events in Africa where about a hundred soldiers lost their lives. They even staged an American-style show at Christmas to boost the morale of our heroic troops, with the participation of such artists as Carmen Sevilla [later star of *La Cruz del Diablo*], the comedian Gila [still working today] and many others.

As for my sporting activities, I was by now a leading athlete taking part in international competitions and so I was given the job of organizing a display of various feats of strength in order to inspire my comrades. I had to prepare it all very thoroughly since this exhibition was to be performed in front of my superior officers, their families and friends. Naturally I did my training in Madrid so I didn't spend a lot of time in camp. The great day arrived and I went through my routine, lifting weights, breaking chains with my chest (there was a bit of cheating here) and ripping up telephone direc-

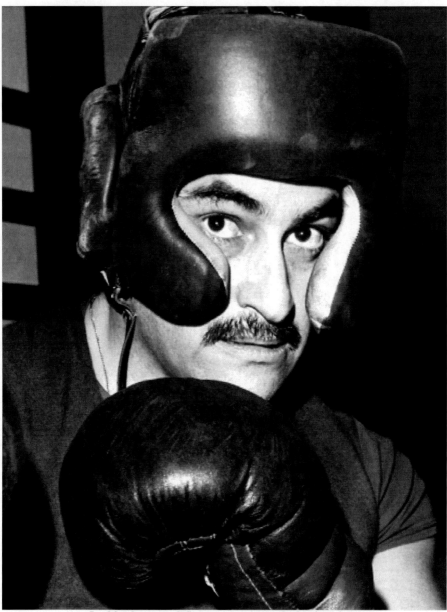

In this photograph I prepare to enter the boxing ring.

tories. Then a prize was offered to any soldier who was capable of reproducing any of my amazing feats. Luckily I had the advantage over them; apart from brute force, I had technique on my side.

I had a bit of trouble with a certain Sergeant Cobelas. He was a hairy, ugly fellow, built like a brick shit house, and he fancied himself as something of a "muscleman." He was always trying to get me into a bout of arm wrestling. I was wary of taking on this man from Galicia, winner of a well-deserved Black Cross for his participation in the African campaign; I foresaw that it could cause me certain problems. I know what I'm like and I don't like losing. Anyway, one day I couldn't get out of it because Cobelas ordered me to accept his challenge.

The sergeant wasn't aware that the sheer power developed by a weight lifter enabled me to lift six or seven thousand kilos. Up until that time I had only been beaten by the wrestler Hércules Cortés in a televised contest for a stake of 100,000 pesetas. Hércules weighed in at 140 kilos, the muscles of his arms measured over 50 centimeters and he could lift weights like a crane. In any event I had given him a good run for his money.

As was to be expected, Cobelas made a fool of himself and I beat him time and again, showing him no mercy. As was equally to be expected, from then on he did all he could to make my life a misery.

Years later I was destined to come across Cobelas again. It was during filming of *La furia de Johnny Kid* (1967) and he was working on the film as an extra. I spotted him standing, looking at my Mexican's costume. Since I was on the production staff he came to greet me in a most obsequious manner.

Later on during my spell in the army I was put on office duties, which was even more of a cushy job. I also started dating the Colonel's daughter who was a most attractive girl.

One day Franco visited the camp and I was able to take a close look at him. He was a very short and weedy looking man who addressed the high ranking officers in a squeaky little voice. But, as the Moors said, he had *baraka* [charisma].

To conclude my recollections of military life I have to describe a scene which could have been taken from one of the paintings of my admired Solana.

It was a depressingly gray Saturday. Four soldiers, two of whom were totally illiterate, took me to a cluster of semi-demolished old houses which stood in the middle of a marshy plain. The twisted branches of some half-rotten trees were outlined against the leaden sky. Two mongrels were fighting viciously and one of the soldiers put an end to the fight with a hail of stones. We came to the house which looked to be in the least ruinous condition. I followed the others and came upon a scene that I'll never forget. Inside the blackened room, whose cracked walls were daubed with obscene graffiti, time seemed to have stood still. Two young but wizened girls were lying half -naked on a couple of straw filled mattresses while a wrinkled old woman pocketed the measly fees handed over by the young soldiers who, in spite of the bromide put in their food, needed to satisfy their animal instincts. The only furniture in the room was some rickety wooden chairs and some large boxes upon which stood a number of bottles, probably containing rough wine or firewater. One of the whores was smoking and posing seductively for her select clientele. An open fire was burning in the center of the hovel, bathing the disgusting scene in a reddish glow. One of the privates dropped his trousers and his cheap pants and, wheezing like a man in his death throes, leapt astride one of these queens of pleasure. The man's hairy arse started going like the clappers and I decided that I'd seen enough. Feeling sick in my stomach, I left them to it. It was no wonder that lice, blennorrhœa and syphilis were rife among the troops. But I had a date with the Colonel's daughter. I found her smartly dressed, prettier than ever and wonderfully perfumed. It was quite a contrast with what I had just seen and I enjoyed my time with her that day all the more for it.

Spanish Championships, Lightweight Division, 1952

Pumping Iron

I was keen on sport from an early age. I soon started to stand out in athletics, gymnastics and soccer. I had a good turn of speed and was an excellent shot putter and javelin thrower. I used to go the plush Parra gymnasium which in those days followed a Swedish-style gymnastic training program which is no longer in vogue. At the gym I met (Manuel) Fraga Iribarne [Minister of Transport, Tourism and Communications and later Spain's ambassador in London under Franco's regime and currently President of the autonomous regional government of Galicia] and the actor and first rate theatre director Luis Escobar. Of course, neither of them got further than doing a few light floor exercises.

One summer's day while traveling on the Tube I bumped into Colonel Pastrana's grandson. I couldn't believe my eyes when I saw the size of the lad's muscular arms. I accompanied him to the gym where he did his weight training, putting the day's art classes completely out of my mind. We arrived at the Moscardó, quite an advanced gym for its time, where several champions were in training and, again, I couldn't believe what I was seeing. The sportsmen, each as strong as an ox, were lifting bars loaded with weights which seemed to me quite impossible to move. As I recall, they were being coached by an ex-champion from the Argentine called Domingo Saloco.

However it would be some time before I made up my mind to abandon gymnastics and take up bodybuilding. My idol, and that of all the lads in those days, was Steve Reeves, the cinema's Hercules. I enrolled at the Juventud gymnasium and started working out with the classic dumb bells. The atmosphere was a bit rough and ready down at the Juventud, which belonged to playwright Alfonso Paso's brother. It was run by ex-boxing champion Juanito Martín. The gym was used by many wrestlers, and also by Eduardini's midgets and a whole circus troupe. Toulouse Lautrec would certainly have felt at home there. The house specialty was obviously boxing. My source of inspiration was the famous book by Marcel Rouet. One day Juanito Martín persuaded me to give up the dumb bells and to dedicate myself body and soul to boxing. Soon I was fighting in amateur fixtures and, although I took my share of punishment, my right hand invariably sent my opponents sprawling to the canvas. It was obvious that I was a slugger rather than one for refined technique.

Around this time I was in the habit of going as a spectator to watch wrestling and boxing matches. Among other great fighters I saw my friend Hércules Cortés wrestling a washed out Primo Carnera [one time boxing champion whose life inspired the film *Más dura será la caída* (*The Harder They Fall*)].

Then came my big day—I was to fight in a final against a strapping great legionnaire who really put the wind up me. This brute gave me a thrashing. I was getting beaten to a pulp and really believed the legionnaire was out to kill me. Then the miracle occurred. With the instinct of self-preservation I resorted to my killer right hook and knocked the fellow out cold. However, it took me three weeks to recover from the beating and my parents put their foot down: My days as a competitor in the noble art of boxing were over.

After breaking my right ankle in a soccer match I went back to the gym and started weightlifting to strengthen my leg muscles which had become weakened by months in a cast. So began my weightlifting career.

During the '50s I trained in earnest and in 1958 I became the lightweight (67.5kg) champion of Spain. In my many years of competition I broke numerous records and, apart from National Championships, I repeatedly won competitions in Castilla and Aragón. In Zaragoza I was fortunate enough to make friends with Ignacio Almau, one of the greatest Spanish weightlifters of all time. We're still friends today.

Weightlifters were quite popular in those days and I would rate the most charismatic of them as being Luis Ortiz de la Torre, El Zorro, Espartaco Antón Moscoso, El Gladiador del Bocho and myself. I was signed by the Real Madrid team and we won the Generalisimo's Cup five times running. I represented my country several times in world and European championships. I had worse luck with the Olympics. I was preselected for the Games in Rome, Tokyo and Mexico. I couldn't make Rome due to injury. The reason I didn't participate in Tokyo deserves a detailed commentary.

There was a contest to find the athlete who would represent Spain in the Olympics to be held in October 1964. I lifted a total of 357.5kg in the 75 category, far surpassing the total required to qualify. I was overjoyed—my dream had come true. Uncle Emilio was among the spectators, along with the Trotskyist Mexican I referred to in the foregoing pages. It was an afternoon for joy and celebration.

Having achieved the necessary classification to take part in the Olympics, I awaited the orders of the Federation regarding my training program. The Federation's technical director was a man named Luis Bosqued, an unlikable character who limited his gym training to building up his arms—which were huge and pale with bulging veins—while his legs were skinnier than those of Don Quixote. Anyhow, Bosqued recommended that I take it easy, resting for a month to take my mind off the excitement of the Olympics. After this vacation period we would draw up a suitable training plan. So that's what I did, and off I went to Torremolinos with a French girl I was dating at the time.

Three days after returning to Madrid, brimming over with enthusiasm, I got a call from the Federation. When I arrived at the Moscardó gymnasium I discovered that instead of just one trial session, they'd organized a full scale competition. Apart from the rest of the athletes enrolled in all the various categories, they'd brought in a weightlifter from Valencia, a certain Aleix, who, combining strength and great technique, had been pressed into service at the last minute in order to beat me while I was on low form. Like all high level competitions it was absolute agony. The contest went on and on until we were fit to drop and Bosqued & Co.'s little scheme backfired. Aleix was unable to beat me. However, as I was far from being at peak fitness; I couldn't equal my previous best and only managed to lift 347.5kg. They rubbed their hands with glee because I'd lost my place in the Olympic team.

The injustice was so barefaced that the press unanimously sided with me. The affair reached the Spanish Olympic Committee and the National Sports Delegation which, meeting in urgent session, requested that the Federation respect my rights and

With the Madrid Weightlifting Team

required them to sign the necessary contract to allow me to represent Spain in Tokyo. Bosqued and his cohorts resisted this pressure and of course refused to sign.

The president of the Federation was one Pedro Várez. This individual was a banker who'd never seen a set of weights in his life and who was completely unknown in the world of sport. I later had another confrontation with this worthless character when he excluded me from a competition against Portugal, despite my being the Spanish National champion and record holder.

As things stood, it was evident that the chain would break at the weakest link—namely me. As usual the usurpers, the ones whose only skill is wheeling dealing behind the scenes, had taken control. In the case of halterophilia, the athletes, the ones who run the risk of serious injury while sweating under the pressure of responsibility and the weight of kilos, had little joy under the mandate of Pedro Várez and his acolytes. I carried on competing, but gone was the enthusiasm of the early days. I retired from weightlifting in 1971 holding the title of supreme champion of Castille and having broken the record for powerlifting with a mark of 130.5kg.

My 14 years in the world of weightlifting obviously brought me bitter disappointments but also great satisfaction —the titles, the records— but above all intense sensations. It was a huge thrill to overcome your fear and successfully culminate a gravity defying lift. The pioneers of this extremely tough sport were buried under the apathy and indolence of a few. I openly encourage the new president, who comes from the world of bodybuilding, to make good the injustices which the previous Federation committed with their best sportsmen. May the names of Luis Bosqued, Pedro Várez and others of their ilk be banished to the obscurity which they themselves created.

1961 World Championships in Vienna

Before leaving the subject of sport for the time being, I wish to recall the name of a legendary gymnast. I refer to Joaquín Blume. This unique athlete from Barcelona was the European champion and was considered the world over to be the leading figure in the world of gymnastics, superior to even the Russians and the Japanese. On the night of April 29, 1959, we met in the Moscardó gym after each finishing our respective training sessions. The following day he was flying to the Canary Islands to take part in a gymnastics display. Tragically, his plane went down in the mountains around Cuenca and all the passengers and crew were burned to death. It was the end of a Spanish sporting legend.

Thanks to my sporting activities I struck up a friendship with Miguel de la Quadra Salcedo, a brilliant discus and javelin thrower. He used to fling the javelin so far, utilizing the Errauzquin spin, that if he hadn't prematurely revealed his technique he'd have caused quite a stir at the Olympic Games. However, the Olympic Committee quickly made a rule forbidding the use of this spin in javelin throwing. But Miguel's aim had been simply to gain publicity, an aim he had certainly achieved. From then on he started to build up his legendary reputation as an intrepid adventurer. Someone once told me that de la Quadra had even been cast in a film as Juan Centella, the popular comic book crime fighter cum explorer, but the movie never got off the ground.

Those years were also notable for our summers spent in San Sebastian. On the beach at Ondarreta I met Marina, a woman who had a certain importance in my life. She was a dark-skinned beauty who exuded eroticism and mystery. The daughter of a Pakistani nobleman and a Basque woman, her oriental blood gave her a certain haughtiness and a notable intellect. It wasn't easy to seduce her but eventually I managed to get through to the apparently inaccessible Marina and we lived a torrid and passionate romance. To narrate it in detail would fill a whole book.

Despite being so young she was a talented writer, already having had some short stories published and she also wrote columns for various periodicals. I was inspired by her example and decided to try my hand at writing. I wrote a Wild West novel titled *Yo sé que ganarás* (*I Know You'll Win*) and I took it straight round to a publishing house called Editorial Rollán. I then wrote some others—*Dale la mano al diablo* (*Shake*

Paul Naschy

Hands With the Devil), *La muerte te acompaña* (*Death Rides With You*) and *La última pistola* (*The Last Gun*). All of them were published under the pseudonym of Jack Mills. However, the best novel I wrote was rejected by the censors for having too much sex and violence.

The second time I saw Franco I was with Marina. We were leaning out of a window when we saw the dictator being driven along the boulevard, accompanied by President Eisenhower. The Generalisimo was standing up in the back of his automobile, waving to the crowds. The thought flashed into my mind that had I been a sniper, it would have been a simple matter to shoot him dead. Maybe it was a vision of things to come, as we shall see later on.

Marina's family owned the Columbia record label and held the rights to the prestigious record companies Decca, London and Alhambra. Marina's uncle, who was the company director and knew that I was an excellent illustrator, asked me to sketch the covers for a number of records the company was going to release. That's how I was commissioned to illustrate the covers for the first records released in Spain by Elvis Presley and Bill Haley. I also did the cover of Frankie Lane's unforgettable song from *High Noon*. But the most important jobs were the luxurious Decca record covers, for which I did pen and ink drawings of Mozart, Bach, Haydn, Beethoven and Handel.

My love affair with Marina followed its course, although our relationship was becoming increasingly stormy and bizarre. At times I was plunged from the heights of ecstasy to the depths of depression in an instant. One day Marina informed me that she was leaving for Pakistan to spend some time with her father, and she said that on her return we would have to plan our wedding in earnest. I was very upset by her departure. Initially her love letters and promises of undying love reached me in a constant stream but one day she simply stopped writing. She didn't reply to my repeated, desperate letters. I put up with the anguish for some time but finally I plucked up courage and went to see her mother. Mary was aloof and concise: Marina had married a prince— her prince charming—in Lahore. I stumbled out of there like a groggy boxer and just wandered around aimlessly. I ended up in a cinema showing *The Alamo*.

Many years later my parents bumped into Marina's uncle at a party. He told them that she was separated from her husband, had returned to Spain and that she was still in love with me. By this time I was happily married and I had two sons. The lovely, enigmatic Marina had long passed into history.

It took me a long time to get over our break up, but I carried on with my life: my studies, sport, painting and drawing. In the summer it was fun to go out and try to pick up foreign women. The swimming pool at El Lago was a good place for this. All the musclemen in town used to gather there —weightlifters, wrestlers and bodybuilders, although a lot of gays and whores were also drawn to the celebrated leisure complex.

A short time later I met Conchita and we started going steady as it was called in those days. She was a medical student and her sister Teresa was studying architecture. They lived with their grandmother in Madrid. Their father was a doctor who was also the mayor of a place called Talavera de la Reina.

At about this time I met the great choreographer and dancer Luisillo who commissioned me to prepare some sketches of the sets and costumes for the musical adaptation of *Don Quixote*. I put my heart into it and worked non-stop for months. Unfortunately a Luis Bosqued-type had me excluded from the project. It was one of the greatest

Spanish poster for *King of Kings*

frustrations of my life. On the evening that Luisillo informed me that I wouldn't be working as set decorator on his production, I was alone in Madrid, in my parents' house in Calle Islas Filipinas. A tremendous storm blew up and in the midst of furious thunder claps and blinding flashes of lightning the film *Nosferatu* started on TV. I was literally scared rigid in my chair. The brilliant Murnau evoked memories of when, as a small boy, I had seen *Frankenstein Meets the Wolf Man.*

It was at this time that the desire to make movies really started to take a hold on me. I didn't miss a single movie at the cinema, especially if it was one with Marlon Brando or Montgomery Clift. As I was a regular patron at the movie houses specializing in re-releases and double bills, I often found myself watching on the same program Hollywood blockbusters like *Pirates of the Caribbean* and modest Spanish productions, such as Antonio Molina's pictures. Actually, I had already worked as an extra on the American superproduction *King of Kings* (1960) and in Luis Lucia's *El principe encadenado* (1960).

On *King of Kings* I worked a whole summer, playing the parts of an Egyptian slave, a Roman soldier and even as one of Herod's guards. I became quite friendly with the actor Jeffrey Hunter, a charming fellow to whom I acted as tour guide on several nights, showing him the monumental parts of Madrid and its old taverns. I remember that on one occasion I recounted for him the comeuppance of a famous Madrid bandit, Luis Candelas, who had been garroted to death under the arch of Cuchilleros. My account was quite gory, and Solanesque and I think it impressed him. I also had the chance, through Jeffrey, to meet Nicholas Ray, a likable and rather peculiar character. Both men were heavy drinkers. I would also work with Ray as an extra on *55 Days at Peking.*

As for *El principe encadenado*, I was taken on due to my muscular build and because my head was shaved. During the day I worked on the American production, and at night, dressed in the costume of a Mongol warrior, I filmed my scenes in Luis Lucia's picture on location at Casa del Campo. I recall that María Mahor was exceptionally pretty and I met the excellent actor and splendid romantic leading man Antonio Vilar. Later I worked with both of them and Antonio became a good friend of mine. The director, Luis Lucia, was always shouting and bawling and at one point he started to slag me off. Since I didn't really care too much, I took myself off to the costume tent to change into my ordinary clothes. But it seemed I had *raccord*, although I didn't have a clue as to what the term meant, and I was asked to stay on with a considerable pay raise. Lucia never shouted at me again.

Around the time of my relationship with Conchita, before I took up filmmaking on a serious basis, my parents were becoming increasingly fed up with my dabblings into art, literature and cinema. All they wanted was for me to get on and finish my studies. My father, as a replacement for my old Seat 600, had given me a brand new coupé. Although apparently things were going well, one day we had a terrific row and I left home. Now out on the streets, with only the clothes on my back, I hadn't the faintest idea how I was ever going to break into the world of filmmaking.

Luckily a good friend of my parents, a French clothes designer called Nicolás Vatelle, offered me sanctuary in the home he kept in Madrid. His studio was in Tangiers and he dressed celebrities like Elizabeth Taylor, Jeanne Moreau, Capucine and even Brigitte Bardot. Nicolás was away much of the time, so I had his flat to myself.

Conchita was a source of constant support and she found me a job as a draughtsman in an industrial freezer manufacturing company, of which her uncle was the owner. I gave up the job after a few months, fed up of this uncle who was a real slave driver.

After that I did it all. I was a professional wrestler, an interior decorator, a jobbing portrait painter, I even worked for a while repairing lamp shades. Conchita remained with me, doing the cooking and housework.

At last my parents and I made up. My father even put me in touch with his friends, filmmakers Pedro Lazaga and Manuel Mur Oti. But unfortunately the black shadow of death was about to reappear.

On their father's birthday, Conchita and her sister Teresa had driven to Talavera de la Reina to have lunch with him. I don't know why but some premonition filled me with unease that day. After lunch they came out into a menacingly black afternoon and before long the heavens opened up and down came a veritable deluge. On that fateful afternoon I was so listless that I decided to go and see a movie. The film was *Nevada Smith*. When I came out of the cinema it was still pouring like it had never rained before. At four in the morning the sinister reverberations of the telephone ringing shattered the silence. I heard the voice of one of my fiancée's aunts telling me the terrible news: Conchita had been killed when the car which her sister was driving went out of control and collided head on with another vehicle. Conchita had been the only one to die. I will never be able to describe what went through my mind at that moment.

Posing with some of my sports trophies

My father drove me to her house. I entered her bedroom and there on the bed were the skirt and jumper she had been wearing before the trip to Talavera. I picked up the jumper. It seemed to be still warm and so impregnated with her own characteristic aroma that it made me shudder. I couldn't bring myself to believe what had happened.

Before daybreak Conchita's body was brought to her home in Madrid. It was so mutilated that it had to be transported in a zinc coffin. Later on I learned of the terrible, macabre adventure which Conchita's father had been obliged to undertake to recover the body of his daughter. After the accident, the injured were evacuated under the relentless downpour and my fiancée's body was left lying under a blanket by the roadside. Apparently the J.P. of the neighboring village had refused to come to the scene to authorize the removal of the corpse until the rain stopped. A passing tractor driver had felt compelled by compassion to take the body to the nearby cemetery. Conchita's father was eventually informed and arrived to take charge of the body. It was pitch dark and after a long search he found it, lying in the mud. A terrible story.

Going back in my time machine to before my tragic affair with Conchita, I have to mention my happy years of study at the Faculty of Science of the University of Zaragoza. I had to successfully complete the first three years to be able to enroll in the School of Architecture. Maybe it was because it was the easiest course—or maybe because I knew the attractive daughter of a bank manager there—that I ended up in Zaragoza.

Another photo from the 1961 World Championships

They were happy years. I carried on with my weightlifting and apart from becoming champion of Aragón, I was taken on to coach the local team. I remember the bitter cold winters and the chilling howl of the wind known as El Moncayo. I lived in a guest house with four students of medicine, two Peruvians and two Basques. These latter were in favor of independence for their region and one of them was always going on about Sabino Arana.

I used to go drinking with other undergraduates and we were on good terms with a number of prostitutes. One of them, a young and pretty girl, did a roaring trade with the American servicemen from the military base and she was extremely generous with the occasional student who took her fancy. Her name was Viky and I was one of her favorites. She even came to watch me lifting in competitions.

One day I went to the faculty of medicine with the Peruvians to fetch a diagram of the muscles of the human body. We came to a low metal door; one of the South Americans rapped on it with his knuckles and, following the sounds of heavy bolts being drawn, the door opened. In the doorway appeared a beautiful blonde wearing a white coat and leather apron. Upon the tables in that crypt-like place were body parts and corpses which students had just finished dissecting. The blonde took great bites out of an omelet filled baguette while she nonchalantly sliced up a human liver. The place smelled terribly of formaldehyde and preserving fluid. I followed the two Peruvians who were lifting the lids of some long rectangular cases in which grayish, soon to be dissected, cadavers floated. They stopped before a huge refrigerated cabinet and as they opened it three bodies came into view, hanging upside down with drainage tubes protruding from them. One of the students reached out and swung round the corpse of a woman: it was Viky. She had been killed in a traffic accident following a binge with some American soldiers, and since nobody had reclaimed her body, she had been brought here as a dissection specimen.

Having passed the three exams in Exact Sciences, I left Zaragoza. My next destination was Catalonia where things couldn't have turned out better for me.

In Barcelona I did a course in artistic drawing which at that time was a requisite to be able to gain a place at the city's School of Architecture. I was given accommodation in the home of the Carol family, members of Catalonian high society who ran a textile business and who were also the owners of a well known basketball team called Joventut.

I was amazed by the creativity and artistic fantasy displayed by Gaudí, unequaled anywhere in the world. I discovered the wonders of the Sagrada Familia [Barcelona's unfinished cathedral], the Bell Esguard houses and the constructions of Milá, Calvet and Güell Park. It was a real adventure for me to study the fascinating legacy left by the Catalonian architect.

I learned to love opera thanks to the Carol family. They had their own box at the Liceo and on Wednesdays we would go to see a performance of the works of Verdi, Leoncavallo, Puccini, Rossini and other great composers. I was able to hear the leading singers of the day and was fortunate enough to meet divas Giuseppe di Stefano and Renata Tebaldi in their dressing rooms.

Partly through the course in artistic drawing and partly through my fondness for books on the subject of art, I became familiar with the works of artists like Kandinsky, Gris, Carrá, Chagall and Giorgio de Chirico, among others. The principal of the School of Architecture, Señor Rosbila, asked me to do some pen and ink drawings—scenes of low-life in the red light district—to hang in his home. I finished the course and was second in my promotion.

The time I spent in Barcelona left me with fond memories. I learned a lot in that city of culture.

1963 was a very special year because I started to get an inkling of where my future career lay—in films. It was also the year in which the assassination of President Kennedy shook the world. Other famous people passed away that year, such as the painter George Braque, writers Jean Cocteau (director of *Beauty and the Beast*) and Aldous

Huxley and the singer Edith Piaf. I was terribly upset at the death of the venerable Pope John XXIII. Also, in the city of Buenos Aires, José Gutiérrez Solana's close friend Ramón Gómez de la Serna passed away.

Around this time I was vacationing in Guadalmina, Málaga. There I met the tubby genius Edgar Neville, director of *La torre de los siete jorobados* (*The Tower of the Seven Hunchbacks*), who dazzled me with tales of Hollywood. The wonderful actress Conchita Montes had a crush on him. I also had the chance to get acquainted with Princess Soraya, then at the peak of her beauty. In Torremolinos we became great friends with the eccentric Jaime de Mora y Aragón, who made us a present of an enormous Great Dane which we christened Jimmy.

Conchita was dead. It was 1964. I felt really lonely and while still tormented by her memory, that summer I met a French girl, Fanny Canteloube. I had to keep a hold on life and although Conchita would always live on in my memory, Fanny was alive there and then.

In life, as in the theatre, there are some characters whose only mission is to say their lines and be gone. Fanny was one of them.

In the month of November 1966 Uncle Emilio was, as usual, at one of his *tertulias*, surrounded by friends. Suddenly he felt a sharp pain in his chest, but it passed and he made his way home. The minute he got there he dropped down stone dead in front of my Aunt Sagrario, victim of a heart attack.

When I arrived at the house my uncle was lying in the lounge, covered in a shroud and flanked by four huge great candles. Some neighbors were praying with the rosary. I was put in mind of Solana's paintings: it only needed the sweet cakes and the bottles of anisette liquor. I felt that something deep inside me had gone for good and I cried bitterly. The great artist would never again accompany me to meet "important fellows," as he called them. Today there is a Virgin of Lourdes which he sculpted in marble with his own hands atop my father's grave.

I took a long time to get over my uncle's death for I knew that along with him my years of initiation had come to an end. However my father, that strong and level-headed man from the Basque country, would become my confident and companion for many years to come.

A Passion For Movies

I started working in movies thanks to my father. I was assistant to such disparate directors as Pedro Lazaga, Mariano Ozores, Gianni Puccini and Manuel Mur Oti, *The Genius*. My original intention was to work as an art director, but fate held something different in store for me. I worked my way up, doing several jobs including assistant to the director. I won my union ticket which at that time was issued by the National Show Business Union. Naturally I was still watching a lot of movies and my personal harvest now included the Hammer films directed by Terence Fisher and starring the charismatic Peter Cushing and Christopher Lee.

I had managed to see numerous masterpieces of German Expressionism and I was becoming familiar with some of the legendary Universal pictures with Boris Karloff, Lon Chaney, Sr. and Jr., Claude Rains, Bela Lugosi, Peter Lorre, Basil Rathbone and Vincent Price. They were my idols. My beloved Westerns were losing ground to the fascinating world of horror fantasy. After my apprenticeship with Ozores, Lazaga, Puccini and Mur Oti, it was clear to me that I was hooked on celluloid.

Mariano Ozores was a jovial fellow who filmed fast and made up in ingenuity what he lacked in talent. I worked as gopher for him. I even managed to arrange location filming free of charge at the National Institute of Physical Education since I

One of my first film roles in *Operación Plus Ultra*

With Gianni Puccini I made *La furía de Johnny Kid.*

was a good pal of the principal, José María Cagigal, and he loaned us the building before it had been inaugurated. I don't think Ozores was very impressed by this because he never called me again. The truth is, I didn't learn a great deal with him and his films have never held the slightest appeal for me.

Pedro Lazaga was quite different; he was talented and he knew how to show his appreciation for the efforts people made on his behalf. Some of his great titles are *Cuerda de presos, Posición avanzada* and *La fiel infantería*. It was Lazaga who gave me my first bit parts (in *Las viudas* and *Operación Plus Ultra*), against my will, funnily enough. Working with him was a real pleasure.

Manuel Mur Oti was a dear man as well as an excellent scriptwriter and a worthy director. Moreover, I never heard anyone speak as well as he did. It was delightful to listen to him and his favorite topic apart from cinema was women. I didn't make any films with him but at his side I learned a lot about editing, dubbing and planning. That's how I learned all about post production. I feel a great admiration and fondness for the genius.

I became great friends with Gianni Puccini. With this Italian I made *La furía de Johnny Kid* and he soon realized how well versed I was in the paraphernalia of the Western. So I became a consultant to the art director, to the head of wardrobe and to the armorer, much to the chagrin of executive producer Enrique Cabezas who had helped get me involved in the movie in the first place. Gianni had a blind faith in my judgment, even going so far as to ask for my advice about the script and certain scenes. On one occasion I had to play a gunman in place of one of the Italian actors. In a scene in the saloon I had to engage in an arm wrestling match with another character. The props department came up with the idea of placing wooden planks with real, sharp-pointed nails under the forearms of each actor. So when I forced down the arm of the Italian actor the nails went into his flesh, sinking into several veins and splattering blood over the continuity girl, who almost fainted. As a result we had to wait three or four days to carry on shooting, this time, obviously, using fake nails.

Puccini was very pleased with the job I'd done and offered to take me with him to Italy to work with him there, in spite of the problems posed by the Italian trade unions. I was all set to travel to Rome to start work on a new movie with Marcello Mastroianni and Monica Vitti. I had the plane ticket and everything arranged, but half an hour before I was due to leave for the airport the phone rang. I heard the sobbing voice of Gianni's wife who told me her husband had been struck dead by a heart attack. I cursed my luck. Once again Death had swung his lethal scythe to cut down my latest dream.

Some time passed and I met a really picturesque character, Juan López García (Juan Logar). He was short and tubby and he was putting together a picture entitled *Agonizando en el crimen* (1967) of which he was to be scriptwriter, star and musical composer. The film was to be directed by the workmanlike Enrique López Eguiluz. Once again I was taken on as general dogsbody, although this time I also had an important role as an Inspector of the Sûreté.

The film was shot in Paris and we froze our butts off as well as having to put up with all sorts of tribulations. We filmed day after day, 24 hours non-stop. One day, out of sheer exhaustion, I fell asleep at the wheel and nearly killed myself. But the trouble didn't end there. Logar and Eguiluz had a row because the director had increased my role too much. I witnessed the conversation and, sick to the back teeth of it all, I went to my hotel and resolved to have nothing more to do with the picture. Presently Juan Logar came and persuaded me to carry on. I've always wondered how actors of the caliber of Irene Gutiérrez Caba and Tomás Blanco got involved with such an insignificant project.

We carried on filming in other locations but troubles remained. There was one particularly complicated scene in which the psychopath kills off my character, smashing his head in with a large stone. We used a real lump of rock and I came within a hair's breadth of being brained for real.

During one of the breaks in shooting, sitting in my car to get away from the extreme cold, I spoke to Enrique López Eguiluz about writing a script dealing with lycanthropy and vampirism. He was also fond of horror movies—his film school finals project had been Poe's "Cask Of Amontillado." Enrique was sincere in his conviction that it would be useless to try something along those lines with such an unimaginative film industry that existed in Spain. And anyway, what about the special Wolfman makeup?

Dawn came and the tough shoot came to an end. We packed up and left and, as the red blaze of the sun crept up over the jagged peaks of the Cabrera mountain range, I felt convinced that my enthusiasm would overcome everything and my dream would one day become a reality.

At that time my agent was the late Fernando Butragueño. I was always urging him to find me work as an art director but I don't think he took much notice of me. One fine day he called me up with the offer of an acting job in an American TV series. In the early hours of February 25th 1966 he picked me up in his car and we drove out to a large expanse of moorland outside Madrid. This was where the American production company had set up all their usual amenities: kitchens, luxurious trailers, trucks, generators, tents and marquees.

We walked over toward a round shouldered man who was sitting near the makeup van. He was heavily wrapped against the intense cold and a kind of thick hood covered his head. It was none other than the legendary actor Boris Karloff, a true living legend and one of my longtime idols. I felt a shiver run down my spine when he looked straight at me with his piercing, hypnotic green eyes. He spoke with a deep voice and proved to be a most kind and considerate man. Just then he was called to shoot a scene and with a considerable effort he got to his feet, apparently due to a pair of leg irons which he had to wear to enable him to walk. While I watched him at work I came to realize just how important facial expression could be for a film actor.

I worked for a few days with Boris and other cast members Robert Culp and Bill Cosby. The series was called *I Spy* and I appeared in the episode entitled "Mainly on the Plains" (1966). The censors didn't allow it to be shown in Spain because it painted an unflattering picture of the Civil Guard.

One day I saw Boris cry. The old man was complaining of the bitter cold, he was tired and the production company's car was late coming to collect him. I was surprised: I must have been one of the last people to see the terrifying Frankenstein monster cry. Three years later in a Munich hotel I heard on the TV the news that Boris had passed away. Something withered inside me when I learned of the death of this venerable monster.

The Mark of the Wolfman

After having the odd bit part in a modest *peplum* and a few co-productions, in 1967 I took the big decision to write the script of *Mark of the Wolfman* [aka *Frankenstein's Bloody Terror*, 1968]. Using an old fountain pen I worked for a week in my parents' home in Calle Islas Filipinas. It's the only story I've ever written to a musical accompaniment, with Albinoni's *Adagio* predominating. My girlfriend at the time, Elena, helped me to type up the manuscript and between the two of us we bound the pages.

I then started off on my pilgrimage with the book tucked under my arm. The world-wise producers' rejections ranged from the lighthearted to the vehement. It started going around that a hare-brained muscleman was on the loose with the idea of making a vampire movie, with a werewolf in it to boot, when everybody knew that only the Americans or the British could make that kind of picture. The only kind of Spanish films that were successful in those days were crude domestic comedies, ones with shapely girls in mini skirts and, above all, "queers," and if there was a character with a speech impediment in it too, so much the better. Spaghetti westerns, made in Almería in co-production with Italy, were also a safe bet.

I recall that my last, desperate visit was to Amando de Osorio. He welcomed me politely and explained that he was just about to start filming a movie about the Royal Canadian Mounted Police. After a couple of whiskies he told me, in fatherly fashion, that this horror business was very appealing but just not viable—that's what Hammer were there for—and a genre picture made in Spain just wouldn't work. He had his own model and SFX workshop, and his dream was to make a movie about a giant crocodile or sea serpent. He was good at that sort of thing. I was wearing a very tight red T-shirt which showed off my muscles and at one point Osorio looked at me critically and proclaimed that I was far too muscular to be an actor. Years later, Profilmes put my name forward for the star-

With Aurora Alba in *Mark of the Wolfman*

ring role in one of his films and he refused. He must have still held the same opinion of me. He obviously would never have given a chance to Jean Claude Van Damme, Sylvester Stallone or Arnold Schwarzenegger.

When I least expected it Enrique López Eguiluz called. Two production companies, Maxper PC of Spain and Hi-Fi Stereo 70 of Germany, were willing to undertake the Wolfman project. The film was to be shot in 3D and 70mm. I was over the moon. At last my script was going to be filmed.

But then the first problem arose: the werewolf couldn't be Spanish (as I had written it he was a native of Asturias), and we had to cut down on the religious and erotic content as well as the graphic violence. I complied with the dictates of the censors and the Polish nobleman Waldemar Daninsky was born.

The second problem was to find an actor for the leading role. It had to be someone who could convincingly play both man and werewolf. First we got in touch with Lon Chaney, Jr., but the reply was most disheartening. He was ill with throat cancer, overweight and decrepit, in a pitiful state. There was no way he could take on the role. The project nearly fell through since we were unable to come up with a suitable leading man. When everybody's morale was touching rock bottom, one of the German producers pointed his finger at me; I could play the part. Despite my fears there seemed to be no alternative. They called on the formidable makeup artist José Luis Ruiz, brother of the great Julipi, and working from designs I had made, we went to the Ballesteros studios to do the necessary tests.

We decided that we would use, for the first time in the history of movie werewolves, a set of upper fangs; those first fangs were made of pieces of potato! Then Ruiz improvised the heavy makeup, applying it hair by hair and subjecting me to five interminable hours of torture. Everyone liked the trial makeup and overnight I had become the star of the show. My dream of becoming an art director was once again put on hold.

So began the filming of *La marca del hombre lobo* (*The Mark of the Wolfman*, 1968), which ushered in the golden age of Spanish horror fantasy films. My fellow cast members were José Nieto, Carlos Casaravilla, Julián Urgarte, Aurora de Alba, Dianik Zurakowska and Rossani Yanni. The cinematographer was Emilio Foriscot. I got on well with everyone except Zurakowska, who was something of a snob. We shot most of the film on location in the Cerralbo Museum and at the Castle of San Martín de Valdeiglesias, which was located in a place called El Cercón and had once belonged to don Àlvaro de Luna. [Don Àlvaro de Luna was a member of King Juan II's court in the 15th century who exercised a Svengali-like hold over the weak willed monarch, an influence which jealous noblemen attributed to sorcery, subsequently putting him on trial for black magic. Of course he was found guilty and sentenced to death. He was beheaded in Valladolid and buried in unhallowed ground.]

I remember a violent scene in which the Wolfman is on the rampage. Craving fresh human blood he smashes his way through the door of a gamekeeper's house. Instead of making a false door frame out of balsa wood, the SFX people, with a laudable sense of economy, merely made a few saw cuts in the real, massively compact door. On hearing the magic word "action!" I went hurtling at the door like a meteor and nearly smashed myself to a pulp. I broke through the door but the impact left me black and blue all over. On another occasion while filming in the underground tunnels

La marca del hombre lobo [*The Mark of the Wolfman*] ushered in the golden age of Spanish horror fantasy films.

of the Conde Duque barracks in Madrid, I nearly suffocated amid all the smoke that we were using for atmospheric fog.

A funny thing happened during the making of the film. It was in the early hours and I was waiting in the doorway of the production company's building for a car to drive me to the set. The street lamps were still alight and there was a fine drizzle. I heard footsteps approaching and assumed that it was somebody from the company.

Dianik Zurakowska in *The Mark of the Wolfman*.

Decked out in full Wolfman make up I stepped out into the street and bumped into an unwary construction worker on his way to work. The man's eyes nearly popped out of his head, he let out a shrill scream of fear that went echoing down the street and took off at such a rate of speed that his heels beat a tattoo on his backside. Without a doubt he was convinced that he'd come face to face with a monster in Madrid.

The Mark of the Wolfman opened in Madrid's Cine Boulevard; a macabre coincidence which reminded me of the years when I'd known the murderer Jarabo. As was to be expected, the Spanish critics didn't look kindly on the film. It was only natural: What did those hacks know about horror fantasy, vampirism or lycanthropy? One scathing reviewer, who wrote under the *nom-de-plume* of Bitibinovsky in *La Codorniz*— "the more audacious magazine for the more intelligent reader"—slagged it off in no uncertain terms, although he also predicted that it would go down in history. And it undoubtedly did. It sold the world over, being shown in 3D in the USA, Argentina and Germany. Today it is revered as a genuine cult movie. As was also to be expected, the reviews garnered outside Spain were excellent: In this life everything is so subjective... The main thing is that the Waldemar Daninsky mythology had been born. Along with him was born Paul Naschy, as I shall now explain.

Filming had finished some months previously and once post-production had been completed, it was time to market the film. The German producers phoned me at home from their office in Munich to tell me that the overseas distributors wouldn't accept the name Jacinto Molina to head the cast list. Spanish names didn't work in foreign markets in those days so I had to come up with an acceptable pseudonym. The release date was already set and they had to prepare the front of house stills, posters and credits on the master copy. They gave me 30 minutes to think it over.

Posing with champion Hungarian weightlifter Imre Nagy

On my desk was a newspaper and I spotted the name Paulo VI; I'd be called Paul. As for the surname, I recalled the world champion weightlifter who I'd made friends with at the 1961 Vienna championships, the Hungarian Imre Nagy. I Germanized the spelling and came up with Naschy. With Teutonic precision the phone rang after exactly 30 minutes: I told them the name and they liked it. And so Paul Naschy began his lengthy career.

A few years ago in France, a black and white version of the film was released. It's an absolute delight and lends the picture a very similar feel to the legendary Universal pictures.

During my time teaching film composition at the Official School of Film Making I appeared in a movie called *Plan Jack 03* directed by Cecilia Bartolomé as a final exam project. I was accompanied in the cast by Charo López. It was then that the idea of creating the Sitges Film Festival arose.

I was in the office of Antonio Cervera, the School's secretary, when Antonio Rafales, owner of a photographic shop in Sitges, phoned. He and a group of colleagues wanted Cervera's advice and help to set up a festival of comedy films. It occurred to me that instead of comedy, they might hold a terrific festival of horror and fantasy movies. Rafales thought it was a great idea and he accepted the proposal. I even programmed the movies for the first festival myself.

The festival soon gained great prestige and started to attract the best that the industry had to offer. It became a real treat for the fans and Antonio Rafales did an extraordinarily good job. Thank you Antonio.

A scene from *Los monstruos del terror* (*Assignment Terror*)

In 1980 I was on the International Panel of Judges for the last time. A bunch of clueless, self-seeking opportunists took Rafales' festival from him and obtained the support of the Generalitat (The Catalonian Autonomous Government). And they're still there. In 1996 they invited me back to the festival where I was subjected to all manner of rudeness and mockery. But they had the smiles wiped off their faces when Quentin Tarantino, another of the guests, publicly expressed his admiration for my work.

After filming *Las noches del hombre lobo* (*Nights of the Werewolf,* 1968) and *La Esclava del Paraíso* (1968)—with Raf Vallone and Bond girl Luziana Paluzzi—it was time to do *Los monstruos del terror* (aka *Assignment Terror* or *Dracula vs. Frankenstein*, 1970). This film has quite a story behind it.

I got a call from the producer—an excellent fellow called Ramón Planas—at the request of Jaime Prades, the last survivor of the formidable Samuel Bronston empire (he had produced, among others, *Pampa Salvaje*, directed by Fregonese and starring Robert Taylor). The production company wanted me to write a script for a big-budget horror movie. I penned an outlandish story which involved Dracula, Frankenstein's Monster, the Wolfman, the Mummy and even the Golem as well as aliens and flying saucers. Incomprehensibly Prades decided to engage director Julio Coll (*Un vaso de whisky*). At a meeting in the company's office, the aforementioned Coll just kept on making one stupid comment after another and he was quickly taken off the assignment. Some time later with the film *La araucana* he established an all time record audience for a film premiere—zero! I heard no more about him until, a few years ago, Antonio Gregory, a journalist from Burgos, told me that he'd interviewed Coll in a tiny little room crammed with books, old documents and papers about Franco. He was planning to make a movie about the Generalisimo and had spent years researching the subject. An odd fellow.

Los monstruos del terror was originally to be helmed by a great director from Hollywood, Hugo Fregonese. I had to go to his house in Rome to get him to agree to the project. We argued over the final draft of the script for several days but in the end a deal was struck.

Very few people know that Robert Taylor, the great Robert Taylor, phoned me at home, much to my surprise. Somehow he'd read the script and was very keen to play the part of Odo Varnoff. He was in Spain to make a commercial for a brand of TV sets and he invited me to dinner at the Hilton Hotel. He had a very pleasant manner and although he'd aged somewhat, he still kept his exceptional good looks. I was full of enthusiasm and the next day I rushed to tell Prades the great news: Robert Taylor wanted to be in the picture. Prades, to my amazement, frowned and told me that Warners had insisted on the part being given to Michael Rennie. When Rennie turned up he was suffering from severe asthma and could only shoot very brief scenes at a time. The female lead was Karin Dor (*Topaz*) and the other main part was taken by Craig Hill.

Filming took several months and was fraught with financial difficulties. After a few weeks Fregonese walked off the job and was replaced by Tulio Demicheli, a good friend and wonderful director, who had to deal with all sorts of problems. Eventually, I gather, Isasi Isasmendi lent his support to the project and the film was able to be completed. There are some spectacular moments in the movie, such as the explosions near the end and a really superb materialization of Count Dracula which probably counts as one of the best ever filmed.

The film has a double climax—the Wolfman (Waldemar Daninsky) engages in almost surreal combats with the Mummy and the Frankenstein Monster in two scenes which clearly pay homage to the classic *Frankenstein Meets the Wolf Man.*

During the long and troublesome shoot I became acquainted with a stunning German actress named Barbara Muller. She led me to witness something so ghastly that I've never told anyone about it until now, something which has long haunted me and given me many sleepless nights. I hope that writing about it in these memoirs will serve as a kind of exorcism.

The Night of Satan

Barbara Muller had incredible greenish-blue eyes, a sensual red-lipped mouth and a perfect body; she was almost too beautiful to be true. The cinema screen just couldn't do her justice.

I met Barbara on a darkened Munich street, filming a scene in which Waldemar Daninsky attacks her and rips her throat out. It was snowing and an unpleasant cold wind was blowing the snowflakes around. Fregonese was taking his bad temper out on everyone, above all on Ferrer, the useless Spanish makeup man. At one point while they were rearranging the lights I followed the actress to a bar, still in my Wolfman makeup. We got into a lively conversation, as if we'd known each other all our lives. I was surprised to learn that Barbara was a fanatic of the occult and of black and red magic. She knew a lot about demonology, vampirism, the practice of magic and ghostly apparitions.

The day's filming over, she offered to drive me to the hotel. I remember that Narro, an ex-soccer player for the Real Madrid team and production assistant on the film, winked at me and gave me a look of lecherous complicity. We went to the actress' apartment on the outskirts of Munich. It was snowing harder. Barbara turned out the lights and lit some candles. The yellowish light from the little tongues of flame produced an atmosphere at once intimate and disturbing. We had a few drinks and then she offered me hashish and marijuana. I'd never tried it before but temptation over-came me in that place where unreality seemed to take hold as if anticipating some kind of ritual. I felt like one of those 19th century writers who sought inspiration by smok-ing pipes of kif. We talked for a long time. This beautiful woman spoke to me of esoteric rites, and of characters like Gilles de Rais—The Marshall from Hell—or Erzebeth Bathory de Nadasdy, the bloodthirsty Hungarian countess.

She confessed that she belonged to a sect of Devil worshippers who met in a secret place to make diabolical invocations. We both knew the stories about Madame Lugardi, the Magyar aristocrat Mariya Zojjus, the undead Boris Jalavich, the dreaded Lajos Vileyii or Marta Khoresima—a whole legion of diabolical beings that she spoke of incessantly. Perhaps the shades of *El Mariscal del Infierno, Latidos de pánico, El espanto surge de la tumba* or *La noche de Walpurgis* started to take form in my subcon-scious on that weird night.

Filming continued and, as soon as I was free, I would go out with Barbara. I was never in the hotel but I confided in Narro who always knew where to get a hold of me. Barbara took me to the cellar where Adolf Hitler, the most terrifying devil in history, used to meet with his sinister comrades. There we talked about *Phantasmagoria*, the Teutonic anthology which had inspired the Villa Diodati group of Byron, Polidori, Shelley, Claire Clairmont Hobhouse, Davies and Pellegrino. Later she presented me with an old book, the diary of Hobhouse, which starts off sounding like an epitaph: "Of those friends who often used to dine together in the Villa Diodati in Geneva, namely

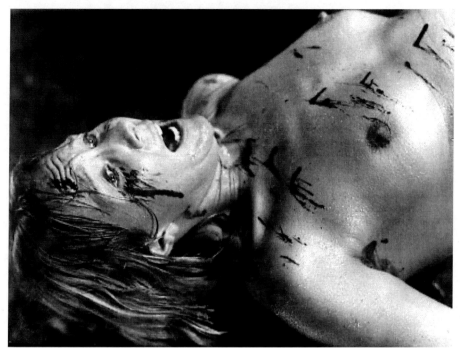

Perhaps *Latidos de pánico* started to take form in my subconscious on that weird night.

Polidori, Shelley, Byron, Scrope, Davies and I, the first committed suicide, the second drowned, the third was killed by the physicians, the fourth is in exile and I...." Such was the insalubrious atmosphere which surrounded the attractive German woman.

Barbara gradually introduced me to the people in her circle. They were a varied bunch who all had something in common: an interest in the occult and devil worship. There were doctors, teachers, models, students, actresses and even civil servants. During filming my mind was in a such a whirl that even work seemed something distant.

The bad weather put a stop to location shooting for several days. Obviously this did nothing to improve Fregonese's temper. Then Barbara made me an offer that I had been looking forward to: to accompany her to one of the secret meetings. Torn between fascination and fear, I accepted. Almost 30 years have passed. I hope that telling all this doesn't matter now. I hope it doesn't.

Night was falling as we left the apartment. She handed me a kind of habit which I was to put on later. She had one too. We went through the Isar Gate, over the Maximilian Josef bridge, past the Nymphenberg Castle and across Teresenwiese. That's as far as I remember. Later on I retraced the route but I never found the big old house we went to. It was terribly cold and the roads and byways were still frozen over.

Finally we came to a large, typically Bavarian house. We were joined by 17 other people and each of them handed over a considerable sum of money for the society. I could hardly contain my anxiety at what might happen. However everything appeared perfectly normal: The people gathered together, 10 women and seven men were chatting as if it was a mundane meeting and a waiter of indefinite age was serving hors d'hoeuvres and drinks.

We were in a magnificent lounge adorned with valuable furniture and splendid paintings. For a moment I thought I must have been mistaken: Nobody had horns, cloven hooves or tails and there wasn't the slightest smell of brimstone. After about an hour Barbara came up to me and said it was time to change into those strange robes. When I put my habit on over my clothes she pointed out that we weren't allowed to wear anything underneath.

Shortly afterwards we descended a flight of narrow stairs to an enormous cellar. It was decorated in a very peculiar way and hung with heavy black drapes covered in five pointed stars and cabalistic symbols which I didn't understand. On the main wall a large inverted cross made of black wood hung, presiding over the sinister chamber. Several censers gave off a smoke smelling of incense and opium. Large flaming torches threw a reddish glow over the scene of the supreme rites.

The participants filed into the cellar. From somewhere came the strains of *Dies Irae*. Full of unease, I felt Barbara by my side. Her face was half-hidden by the hood of her habit. The music swelled and from behind the drapes, as if materialized from the darkness, emerged the Great Leonardo, the Goat Devil of witches' covens. I wondered whether it was one of the worshippers wearing the Devil's head of Eliphas Levi.

Maese Leonardo went and sat upon his Gothic throne to preside over the black mass. The introit commenced at once, one of the young women acting as minister, holding in one hand a chalice—half of a skull set upon a ram's horn—and in the other a sinister massbook from which she read Satanic prayers. I wondered whether the book was bound in the skin of an unbaptised infant as the rite stipulated.

Next a small black goat was placed on the altar below the inverted cross. While two of the worshippers held it fast, one of the priestesses took up a dagger which glinted under the light of the candles. I started to feel sick. The woman slit the animal's throat and a jet of blood came spurting out. I was choking on the fumes from the censers and saw all this as through a mist. The priestess ripped the goat's heart out and offered it to the two worshippers who started to devour it. The *Dies Irae* kept booming out and smoke swirled around the Dantesque scene.

Then the body of the sacrificed animal was thrown to the floor and a female acolyte removed her robe and stood totally naked. Her lovely body was glistening with sweat. It was time for the ritual and her body was anointed with an aphrodisiac lotion. She went down on all fours on the altar and the priestess scattered some grains of wheat with a dedication to "the dweller in darkness and the ripener of crops." At that moment the devil figure stood up and approached the girl from behind to consummate the diabolical act. The worshippers removed their vestments; in my delirium I saw their writhing bodies and heard their cries of ecstasy or, perhaps, of death. I had sunk into a deep red nightmare Hell.

Barbara took me out of there. We didn't speak to each other on the way back. What for? She dropped me at the hotel and I watched her disappear across the frozen asphalt like a specter. I didn't see her again after the night of Satan.

At noon the next day Ramón Planas called me at the hotel because there had been a change of plans and I was needed that night. A few days later we had finished filming in Munich and flew to Rome to do the remaining location work. After turning the events of that terrible night over in my mind and prompted by my Catholic upbringing, I went to see a priest. The act of confession brought me solace.

Paul Naschy

My Companion for Life

By this time I had met the woman who was to be my companion through the good times and the bad times. Elvira Primavera was a pretty girl from Burgos, the daughter of an Italian diplomat. Our relationship began in Burgos and continued in Rome. I recall that on the first night we went out to stroll around the old Castillian town a full moon was shining brightly and I told her about my filmmaking ambitions, about my interests and about the many things that meant anything in my life. Inevitably the subject of lycanthropy cropped up. The moon hung huge in a star spangled sky. Some of the places where we wandered I had walked with Fräulein María Ronge when I was knee-high to a grasshopper. Many years later our own two children would walk in those same places.

I talked about the post-war years, about my childhood and I remember we passed by an old bookshop where I used to get picture cards of the popular cartoon character *Garbancito de la Mancha*, as well as comic books and the well known tales of Calleja. It was wonderful.

We had met years previously, when she was a tourist guide in a stately Madrid home. She was the niece of close friends of my parents and one day she had lunch with us in a restaurant in the old quarter of Madrid. I gave her a lift in my tiny car to the Palacio Real; she really looked good in her smart blue uniform. We both had partners already and neither of us ever dreamed that we'd end up marrying each other. As we said our farewells I gave her a red apple which I had picked in Lozoya. Yes, a red apple like the one the witch gave Snow White, but without the poison.

We met again in Burgos by chance, as I had only stopped over in the town to visit my parents who were spending a few days there. We went sightseeing together. Later we would meet again in Rome, first when I was filming there and again when I went to train with the Italian national weightlifting team.

On one of these visits to Rome I had the harebrained idea of taking her to see *Brides of Dracula* with Peter Cushing . The cinema was on the other side of town. We had a job to get there because we ran into a demonstration. There were hundreds of people yelling and shouting, holding clenched fists aloft and waving red flags with the hammer and sickle. Even Mussolini and his Blackshirts would have been impressed. We eventually made it to the cinema, which happened to be next to a cemetery. Elvira was very young and I don't think she enjoyed it very much. When we were newly married she sat through *La Máscara del demonio* [*Black Sunday*]starring Barbara Steele and that one certainly did frighten her.

We were married on October 4, 1969, in Burgos Cathedral surrounded by the Fly-catcher, the tomb of El Cid, the tragic Christ painted by Solana and the stony tombs of bishops, deans and other worthies. The altar looked splendid, adorned with flowers and shining bright like a glowing ember. Such was the totally Gothic atmosphere which impregnated one of the most important moments of my whole life.

Our wedding day October 4, 1969

Elvira brought me love, peace, stability and, above all, understanding. I had found the perfect partner.

In this country which has many virtues but also numerous vices, the usual petty-minded crowd always let me know their own mean-spirited opinion of me. They said I made movies because I was a spoiled brat and my family financed all my films. They didn't know that when I got married I had only 30,000 pesetas in the bank, or that I never took a penny from my family and friends. My wife and I had to make our own living as best we could. I never had the good fortune of certain other smooth operators who manage to pick up generous subsidies from all sides. The truth is that Naschy, like the dog in Goya's painting, always swam against the tide.

The spirit of Groucho Marx's famous phrase lives on in these memoirs: "Starting from nothing I have scaled the heights of absolute poverty." I have little to thank anybody for, and those who have helped me I can count on the fingers of one hand—and have fingers to spare.

After *Los monstruos del terror* I made other films but I want to say something about one particularly bizarre affair. I refer to *La furia del hombre lobo* (*Fury of the Wolfman*, 1970), directed—for want of a better word—by José María Zabalza.

This picture was started by Enrique López Eguiluz who had done a very creditable job on *La marca del hombre lobo*. However, Maxper PC for some reason replaced him with the aforementioned champion boozer.

José María Zabalza was a very odd character. Although he seemed to be an intelligent man, he started drinking first thing in the morning. I must say he had an amazing sense of balance. I once saw him fall flat on his back with a brimming beer tankard in his hand and he didn't spill a drop.

Filming *La furia del hombre lobo* was a real torment.

Filming the picture was a real torment. Zabalza did as he pleased with my script and directed in his usual state of inebriation. One time I even came across a 14-year-old kid making alterations to the text of the screenplay. According to Zabalza, this was his nephew, a very talented lad who was writing down some extra scenes that the director had dreamed up. So I threw in the towel. Predictably it turned out that the film was too short. Without the slightest qualm the director spliced in clips from *La marca del hombre lobo*. The Wolfman appeared in the same scene alternately wearing a white shirt and a black one. What's more, for so-called reasons of economy, a double was hired to film long shots of my character. The fellow swaggered around more like a Madrid city pimp than a ravening beast.

Things came to a head when it was decided to show the film to a potential distributor. The man drove to the screening accompanied by his wife and their daughter. On arrival the beam from the car's headlights illuminated an individual urinating at the curb. Who should it be but our great director. Negotiations were broken off then and there. The amazing thing is that *La furia del hombre lobo* was sold abroad and has a legion of admirers. Andy Warhol would probably have loved it.

Later Zabalza tried to prove that he could shoot a movie in just one day! He didn't manage it. The poor actor involved was Simón Andreu.

Between one piss up and the next, José María Zabalza made Westerns in which the saloons advertised malted milk and gangster movies with (comedians) José Truchado as a Mafioso and Jesús Puente playing Al Capone.

When Zabalza died the Spanish film industry lost its own genuine Ed Wood. Maybe one day he'll be lucky and find his Tim Burton.

Memoirs of a Wolfman   **103**

El gran amor del Conde Drácula (*Count Dracula's Great Love*, 1972)

Paul Naschy

The Legend of Walpurgis

1970 heralded the beginning of something of great importance for horror fantasy in general and for Paul Naschy in particular: *La noche de Walpurgis* (aka *Shadow of the Werewolf* and *The Werewolf Versus the Vampire Woman*). The film was to be a co-production between the German company Hi-Fi Estero 70 and Hispamex Films. I had written the screenplay and it was to be filmed in English. Waldemar Daninsky was back. Alberto Platard wanted a fast and reliable director and I put forward the name of León Klimovsky. Thus began a long and fruitful friendship.

Before filming began somebody from Hispamex phoned to warn me that the producer wanted to replace me with some other blue-eyed boy wonder (I had a strong suspicion that this was Máximo Valverde) or that, at the very least, the new fellow would play the human Waldemar while I would be left with the part of the lupine Waldemar. Logically, this state of affairs didn't appeal one little bit to the Germans and they soon put a halt to the scheme.

A whole book could be written on *La noche de Walpurgis* but I'll just mention a couple of anecdotes. The first occurred on the night we were to film the opening scene, in which the two pathologists remove the silver bullets from Waldemar's body and the

La noche de Walpurgis (aka *Shadow of the Werewolf* and *The Werewolf Versus the Vampire Woman*)

With León Klimovsky, Pascual Cebollada and Alberto Platard on the set of *La noche de Walpurgis*

werewolf comes back to life. We arrived at the cemetery and León Klimovsky came furtively over to speak to me, drawing me aside from the crew. He asked me to follow him, and the graveyard attendant took us round the back of a sinister looking building which turned out to be a morgue.

He unlocked the old door with a huge key and we entered a small autopsy room. There was a marble slab, with little channels for draining away blood and body fluids, and upon this there lay the corpse of a young man who had been killed in a motorcycle accident. He was covered by a grubby, grayish sheet from which protruded his blood-less hands and wax-like feet. Leo expressed himself quite clearly: "Do you feel able to lie down there after the corpse has been removed? It's up to you whether we shoot or not." It didn't take me long to consider and I agreed. Then another man came in and with the help of the attendant carried the body away. There were bloodstains on the slab which the man proceeded to scrub down energetically.

Shortly afterwards the crew was ready to start filming. The pathologists were played by the veteran Hungarian actor Barta Barry and the great Julio Peña. I lay down stark naked on the cold marble slab and got chilled to the bone. For some reason I thought of my uncles Jacinto and Emilio and of the fabulous José Gutiérrez Solana. What would he have thought of it all had he been able to see it? I bet he'd have found inspiration for one of his paintings.

The second anecdote is in lighter vein. We were filming in the cemetery and while a shot was being lined up I went for a stroll wearing my Wolfman make up. Absent-mindedly I stepped out from behind a headstone where an old lady was laying some

1970 heralded the beginning of something of great importance for Spanish horror fantasy in general and for Paul Naschy in particular: *La noche de Walpurgis.*

flowers. She let out a scream of terror and almost had a heart attack on the spot. She even tried to sue the producers.

Klimovsky and several of his closest collaborators, me included, went to a screening of the master print at the Fotofilm laboratory. Once the projection was over my reaction to the film was none too positive and the director chided me for my lack of enthusiasm. Despite my reservations, *La noche de Walpurgis* was a worldwide box-office sensation and went on to become a movie legend and a genuine social phenomenon. Even the hospital for tuberculosis sufferers in the Madrid sierra where part of the film was shot became known from then on as the Walpurgis sanitarium. This modest production marked the high point of Spanish horror fantasy and revitalized the genre throughout the world.

The actress Patty Shepard (Wandesa Dárvula de Nadasdy), who played the evil, bloodthirsty, undead, lesbian countess, regretted having accepted the role. But today she is remembered only for having portrayed Erzebeth Bathory (the names Wandesa Dárvula are a homage to the terrible Hungarian aristocrat's bloodthirsty servant women).

Patty Shepard (Wandesa Dárvula de Nadasdy), who played the evil, bloodthirsty, undead, lesbian countess, regretted having accepted the role in *La noche de Walpurgis*.

The truth is that Patty played the part to a "T." Had there been a proper film industry in this country, Ms. Shepard would have become a new Barbara Steele.

A short time ago I saw the film again with a group of friends. At the end I asked them if it had been worth it. They replied that it undoubtedly held a kind of magic.

Klimovsky really knew how to move his camera and in the slow motion scenes evoked an eerie, unearthly world of darkness which has since been imitated time and time again. Whether the usual crowd of airheads want to believe it or not, *La noche de Walpurgis* had a profound effect on two generations.

Little by little I was creating a style of my own, what the fans call "The Mark of Naschy." My sources of inspiration were old movie serials, German expressionism, the Universal films, certain doses of Hammer's Victorian style and a little of the Italian school. These were complemented by the influence of age old cultures, ancestral folklore—notably that of the Balkans, the Romantic movement, which had embraced the English ghost story and the German *Phantasmagoria*. The epic poems and medieval folk tales also had an influence.

As for the visual aspect and use of color, my influences were Solana and Goya, as well as Vermeer de Delft, although sometimes I was unable to achieve the desired results. Evident examples from my filmography are *El caminante, El huerto del Francés, El retorno del hombre lobo* and *Latidos de pánico*. I consider myself to be the instigator of a shockingly realistic visual style within Spanish cinema —I'm not referring to gore, although I also inaugurated that genre in Spain—combined with an extreme Gothicism.

My Judeo-Christian upbringing also had a bearing on my work, as professor Adolfo Camilo pointed out in his doctoral thesis, which explains why I came up with the Mayenza cross and chalice, transforming the classic silver bullets into a liberating religious symbol harking back to the Holy Grail.

My personality was forged by the war, by my exposure to religion, by a partially frustrated sexuality, by my family and social background, by the people I knew, by love and by the ever present shadow of death. All this is reflected in my films as well as the somewhat sinister and cruel universe of childhood during the Second World War. My toy soldiers fought and died to satisfy my overpowering desire for destruction. Circus clowns didn't make me laugh, they frightened me, because behind those painted faces—behind the masks, the Bogey Man or Bluebeard were waiting to get me. I smashed up my toy cars in chases which the police always lost. And I always liked Richard Widmark better than Gary Cooper, who is, undoubtedly, in heaven [this refers to the title of Pilar Miró's 1980 film *Gary Cooper, que estás en los cielos...* (*Gary Cooper, who art in Heaven....*)].

Marginal characters have always held an appeal for me, the same kind of appeal you find with broken toys. I remember meeting the great boxer Urtaín when he had been reduced to working as a bouncer at a nightclub in Burgos where everyone laughed at him. I've seen a film producer who had administered budgets of several million pesetas begging for alms in a Tube station. I was witness to the sad demise of Antonio Vilar, abandoned by all, of Lola Gaos and Gracita Morales. I can readily identify with them; I've felt like a broken toy myself.

Characters like Wolfgang Gotho (*El jorobado de la morgue*), Waldemar Daninsky, Count Dracula and Alaric de Marnac are creatures with no future who share both my own bitterness and the cinematic ostracism to which they are subjected by the poisoned pens of frustrated and envious individuals. However all these alter egos, whether of my own creation or borrowed, will outlive us all, friend and foe alike, because they have been immortalized on celluloid.

Jack, el destripador de Londres (*Jack the Ripper*, **1971**) **brought me my first award from the Sitges Festival.**

I wrote one of my next films, *Jack, el destripador de Londres* (*Jack the Ripper*, 1971), a co-production with Italy, for my good friend José Luis Madrid, who produced and directed it. It brought me my first award from the Sitges Festival. The flamboyant DP, Enrique Salete, was never seen without a cigar between his lips. Since I was playing a physically impaired ex-trapeze artist he told me earnestly that he'd light my scenes with "cripple light!"

The film was shot almost entirely on location in London and on British Railways, a fact which didn't prevent one smart-arse reviewer from writing that the word RENFE (Red National de Ferrocarriles Españoles—Spanish Railways) was clearly visible on the wagons. However the film received mainly favorable reviews.

Doctor Jekyll y el hombre lobo (*Dr. Jekyll and the Wolfman*, 1971) also had its peculiarities. The script was commissioned by the producer José Frade, who was confined to bed with hepatitis. I held Frade in great esteem and considered him to be the most capable young producer in Spanish cinema. I spent several days at his home reading him the text and he gave me his suggestions. We eventually agreed on a draft which we both liked. However, after he'd recovered from his illness he sustained an ankle injury during a soccer match. Time went by and Frade gave no sign of life. I called his office several times but he was always busy. I got fed up with trying. Shortly afterwards Arturo González called to ask me for a horror screenplay. I offered him this one, which he liked and decided to put into production. A few days later Arturo González told me that Jose Frade had got wind of the situation and had phoned to advise him not to make the film. But the project went ahead all the same.

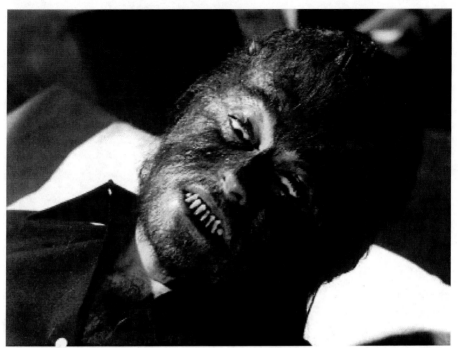

Preparing *Doctor Jekyll y el hombre lobo* (*Dr. Jekyll and the Wolfman*, 1971) for filming also had its share of peculiarities.

Now we come to *El gran amor del Conde Drácula* (*Count Dracula's Great Love*, 1972). This film was produced by the great writer and journalist Manuel Leguinche. For this Gothic tale I transformed the terrifying Transylvanian Count into a Romantic vampire who destroys himself for the love of a beautiful mortal woman. The female

lead was played by French actress Haydée Politoff who had made her name as the star of *La Coleccionista*. To tell the truth, we didn't get on too well and filming love scenes with her was none too easy. The film was well directed by Javier Aguirre. Several important scenes were filmed on the grounds and in the stately home of the Duke and Duchess of Osuna. The catacombs where the vampire had his lair were in reality part of the labyrinthic bunker which served as General Miaja's refuge during the Civil War.

There were numerous mishaps during filming; the actresses were injured in a traffic accident; a set collapsed and almost crushed three of the crew; Ingrid Garbo was almost asphyxiated by a leak of toxic gas. Come the presentation of the film at the Paris Festival, the hostess

With Ingrid Garbo, Haydee Politoff and Rosanna Yanni in *El gran amor del Conde Drácula.*

who introduced me was injured falling down the stairs leading to the stage and, what's more, my speech had disappeared and I had to make it up as I went along. It seems that Vlad the Impaler wasn't on our side. Luckily though the critics and box-office takes were with us. In France the film was compared to Stendhal and today it's a favorite with the fans. I look back on the film with melancholy.

In *El jorobado de la morgue* (*Hunchback of the Morgue*, 1972) several things worth mentioning happened. This film was also directed by Javier Aguirre and once again the producer was Manuel Leguinche. It was the story of a poor hunchback, Wolfgang Gotho (named after Mozart), who loved a girl beyond death. His mission in this world—it couldn't have been any other—was to be custodian of a macabre mortuary where he cut up corpses for subsequent dissection by medical students.

The film was mainly shot inside some labyrinthic cellars that once belonged to Felipe II, while the most unpleasant part was filmed in the morgue of Madrid's Hospital Provincial. There was even an homage to Lovecraft with the inclusion of an Ancient One in the film.

I recall a scene which made a tremendous impact on the audience. I refer to the scene where the hunchback defends himself with a flaming torch from the attack of a pack of starving rats. It was as terrifying as it was real. The Ibys Institute caught a load of rats in the sewers and left them without food for some time. Once loosed on the set

With Alberto Dalbes in *El jorobado de la morgue* (*Hunchback of the Morgue*, 1972).

the filthy little beasts proved able to leap up to a meter high, sinking their needle sharp teeth into anything at hand. I felt their bites on several parts of my anatomy and wondered what would have happened to me if I hadn't been wearing protection. It wasn't a nice scene to shoot.

Just like that mortuary I recalled from my student days in Zaragoza, the hospital morgue stank of formaldehyde and embalming fluid and there was a constant stream of cadavers. The corpses were put into coffins to be taken out to the hearses. When the attendants couldn't get a body into the oblong box, one of them would get on top and cram it in by force. On one occasion a dead man's head was left poking out of the casket, and when one of the attendants pushed down on the rotten corpse, it sprang up and spewed a green viscous liquid over him.

Another day we had to shoot the scene where Gotho cuts the head off a corpse. The body we were given was due to be dissected shortly and the man in charge intimated that we could do as we liked with it. I knocked back two whiskies and picked up the knife. However, once I'd started the business I couldn't get past the first cut so a death mask was taken and a sensational wax head was made which is what actually appeared in the film.

The man in charge of the morgue had been repeatedly accused of committing acts of necrophilia with the female corpses, and he'd had his hand burned with sulfuric acid. He insisted on showing me his new *guests* every morning. He used to say: "The dead are wonderful, they never complain." This odd character would be the inspiration, years later, for the macabre butler played by the late, fondly remembered Howard Vernon in *El aullido del diablo* (*Howl of the Devil*).

Memoirs of a Wolfman

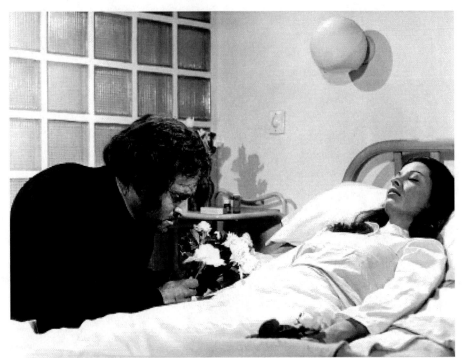

El jorobado de la morgue **won me several international awards including the special Georges Méliès award for best actor at the International Festival of Paris.**

El jorobado de la morgue won me several international awards including the special Georges Méliès award for best actor at the International Festival of Paris where I was fortunate enough to meet Peter Cushing and Terence Fisher. The legendary Hammer director congratulated me for my portrayal of the hunchback and talked about working with me in a new version of *Dr. Jekyll and Mr. Hyde.* He could visualize me in the part. Unfortunately he died shortly afterwards and the project fell through.

Cushing was a true gentleman, polite and extremely kind. He used a white glove when smoking and among all those present he was the first to come over to congratulate me. It was a great night, a really terrific night. Here I also struck up a long standing relationship of respect and friendship with the critic, writer and president of the International Fantastic Film Society, Gilbert Verschooten. The name of Paul Naschy was beginning to mean something on the international scene.

In conclusion I must just say that Javier Aguirre was in top form for this picture and did a splendid job in creating a true classic, blending horror, metaphysics and Gothic into a uniquely successful whole, not forgetting some savage gore touches. Thank you Javier.

Following *El jorobado* I made several other films which gave me certain satisfaction. I would pick out *Disco rojo* (1972), a film which daringly addressed the alarming problem of drug trafficking which was starting to affect the Iberian Peninsula. I wrote the script for my unforgettable friend Antonio Vilar and as usual it was harshly criticized. I was pleased with my character, the villainous Segio Meleter, an elegant but

When I wrote the screenplay of *La rebelión de las muertas*, I must either have been under the effects of hashish or, like Bram Stoker, I'd had one hell of a nightmare.

unscrupulous individual. *Disco rojo* won two important prizes awarded by the National Show Business Union.

When I wrote the screenplay of *La rebelión de las muertas* (aka *Vengeance of the Zombies* and *Night of the Walking Dead*), I must either have been under the effects of hashish or, like Bram Stoker, I'd had one hell of a nightmare. Maybe it wasn't hashish but cheap wine. The critic and booze connoisseur Marcos Ordoñez would opt for that.

La rebelión de las muertas (1972) was a delirious tale involving oriental gurus, voodoo, black magic, the devil and zombies.

La rebelión de las muertas (1972) was a delirious tale involving oriental gurus, voodoo, black magic, the devil and zombies. José Antonio Peréz Giner and Ricardo Muñoz Suay read the script and liked it. The film was directed by León Klimovsky.

Since I find it very hard to evaluate the picture myself, I'll reproduce here university professor, writer and anthropologist Adolfo Camilo's opinion of it:

> A highly entertaining piece of cinefantastique in the spirit of (George A.) Romero, spoilt by the worst movie score in history—the music was by Carlos Calderón—it should be viewed like a comic book and savored like a sepia print. It contains some really wild moments.

I knew that after my experience with the Devil worshippers in Munich anything could happen... and happen it certainly did. One fine day, following the release of *La rebelión de las muertas* in Germany, a man turned up at my home. He was about two meters tall, wearing an ivory colored tunic and his long hair and beard lent him a kind of Jesus Christ look. Around his neck hung a chain at the end of which dangled a metal eye-shaped medallion. The fellow was really quite impressive.

He and his cronies had seen the film. He claimed that I had sent them a message from the screen and he had come to fetch me to be the spiritual leader of their esoteric sect. Frankly, such a suggestion scared me shitless. I went through a thousand and one arguments to persuade him that I was just a mere actor, that I didn't have any powers whatsoever. It occurred to me that it must be some kind of practical joke or maybe a con trick or even some scheme of Barbara Muller's. I eventually realized that I was wrong. It was all in deadly earnest, which frightened me even more. You just don't play around with the occult. He remained with me for hours, until dusk. The dying sunlight lit up his face with disturbing scarlet tones.

He rambled on about auras, astral projections, other dimensions, ancient rites and, above all, of the need of my presence for his people. Luckily my wife, Elvira, arrived back home. On taking his leave the weirdo told me that sooner or later I'd drop everything and go and join them. I remember his name was Klaus.

Somebody else who entered my life at the time of this film was a famous parapsychologist named Carol Ramys. Carol used to write about these matters in magazines and books. She was elderly but she must have been quite a looker in her youth. Together with Ramys and an Austrian actress whose name escapes me, I got involved in psychophonia, experiments in spiritualism and telekinesis. We even went to visit the place where the mysterious Faces of Bélmez had appeared. I have to admit that some of these things gave me food for thought. Ramys showed me several photos—wonderfully retouched I imagine—showing strange human forms intruding into everyday scenes. She told me they were photos of ghosts and that one of the apparitions was Cleopatra herself. One fine day Carol Ramys and her obsessions disappeared from my life and I never saw her again—I don't even know if she's still alive.

People who died that year included George Sanders, Maurice Chevalier, Ezra Pound, Américo Castro, Antonio Vico and Jorge Mistral.

Around that time my cousin, the famous furrier José Luis, gave a sumptuous dinner at the Hotel Ritz where the latest prototype Ferrari was being presented. The most famous models of the day were there to show off his spectacular fur and leather creations, these latter all in red especially for the occasion. It was a great society event and among the guests were Vittorio de Sica, Bette Davis and celebrities from the world of politics, the arts and show business and all the in-crowd. José Luis was said to have spent 14,000,000 pesetas on the event. I went along with my parents and had a chance to speak to De Sica whom I found to be jovial and polite. He told me he was a great admirer of the comic actors Mario Moreno *Cantinflas* and Totó who had died in 1967. I also managed to talk to Bette Davis, the grand dame of world cinema who seemed to be constantly giving a performance. She was quite friendly towards me and told me something that surprised me. Bette had been going to play a role in *Frankenstein* together with Leslie Howard and Bela Lugosi. When the project was handed over to James Whale none of them stayed on board.

My cousin was very fond of organizing spectacular dinners and fashion shows. When the fur and leather trade went into decline he lost the factory. The famous store in the Calle Génova no longer exists. José Luis died when he was only 62.

El espanto surge de la tumba (*Horror Rises from the Tomb*, 1973)

Paul Naschy

The Profilmes Years

Several more films went by, such as *Los crimenes de Petiot* (1972) and *La orgía de los muertos* (aka *The Orgy of the Dead, Return of the Zombies* and *Beyond the Living Dead*, 1972)—the only film of any interest ever directed by José Luis Merino—until we come to a really emblematic title. I refer to *El espanto surge de la tumba* (*Horror Rises from the Tomb*, 1973).

Pérez Giner called me up in a terrible hurry—he urgently needed a horror screenplay, since the creation of a production company depended on it. I didn't have one but I told him I could write one pretty fast. I had to do it in a day and a half. With the help of amphetamine tablets I managed it in what is obviously a record time.

The film was directed by Carlos Aured, Klimovsky's assistant, because the latter was unavailable. Shooting started in the middle of winter 1972 in the valley of Lozoya and a large part of it was filmed on location on the grounds and in my parents' country house. It was a dark, claustrophobic story with a terrifying climax. Alaric de Marnac (Gilles de Rais) and his companion, the evil Mabille, a pair of sorcerers, cannibals and vampires, came back from beyond the grave thirsting for blood and vengeance. This nightmare combined black magic, hidden treasure, the living dead and all manner of shock tactics. The beleaguered characters, mercilessly menaced by the unleashed forces of darkness, were unable to escape from the fateful mountains, trapped as surely as the characters confined inside the house in Buñuel's *El angel exterminador*. The music by the great maestro Carmelo Bernaola—composer of the scores for *El jorobado de la morgue* and *El gran amor del Conde Drácula*—underlined the horror perfectly. Mention must also be made of the marvelous work of makeup genius Julián Ruiz Julipi.

El espanto surge de la tumba was a dark, claustrophobic story with a terrifying climax.

Let me recount an anecdote from the movie. The area where we filmed the beheading of Alaric and the hanging of Mabille was known as Roble Gordo (Great Oak). The reason is simple: The outstanding feature of the district was a huge,

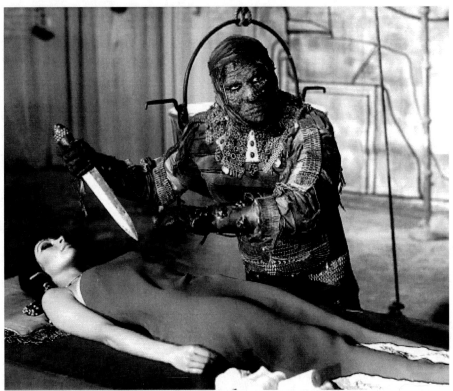

La venganza de la momia (***The Mummy's Revenge***, 1973).

ancient oak tree, steeped in history and legend. The famed Count Fernán Gómez's hordes camped by the tree in preparation for one of their battles. Naturally this oak was listed as part of Spain's national heritage.

Well, we finished filming a medieval scene which had featured a lot of horses and soldiers carrying standards and flaming torches. Early the following morning Julipi rushed in to wake me. All that was left of the famous tree was a pile of smoldering ashes. Apparently a torch had been left alight and the strong wind took care of the rest. As a result the forestry engineer who had granted permission for us to film there got the sack and the mayor of Alameda got into deep water with the Environment Department.

I made three more films with Carlos Aured, all of them frankly worthy pictures: *El retorno de Walpurgis* (aka *Curse of the Devil* and *Return of the Werewolf*, 1972), the thriller *Los ojos azules de la muñeca rota* (*House of Psychotic Women*, 1973) and *La venganza de la momia* (*The Mummy's Revenge*, 1973). Afterward something happened which halted any possible future collaborations.

At the time I was under exclusive contract as both actor and scriptwriter to Profilmes, the production company which had been set up by Pérez Giner and Muñoz Suay at the time of *El espanto surge de la tumba*. Pérez Giner called me to say that I'd be working with Aured on a new movie. I was to get in touch with him to discuss the script and make any necessary improvements and to familiarize myself with the character I would be playing. I happily phoned the director but he replied coldly and categorically: There was no part in his project for me. I was absolutely stunned and quickly phoned up the producer. He couldn't believe it either but there was nothing he could do about it: Carlos Aured had already signed the contracts and had the upper hand.

My next job was a part in *Tarzán en las minas del rey Salomón* (*Tarzan in King Solomon's Mines*, 1973), with the breathtaking Nadiuska. She was an extremely pretty woman, with the eyes of a panther and a terrific body... and very little acting talent. I also appeared in a *giallo* style thriller called *Una libélula para cada muerto* (1973), with Erika Blanc. It was shot mainly on location in Milan by León Klimovsky and I think it turned out to be a fairly decent detective story. I enjoyed playing the exuberant Italian police inspector Paolo Scaparella.

So we come to *Todos los gritos del silencio*. This wasn't a particularly relevant film in itself but there are a few unusual events surrounding the filming that warrant a few lines.

A journalist from *El Alcázar* newspaper named Juan José Porto, whom I loved like a brother—God help me—brought me a one page synopsis of a story with the original title of *El búho negro* (*The Black Owl*). I set to work to write the script—Porto didn't add so much as a comma—and when I had finished it I took it along to César Gallego, the partner of Maximiliano Pérez at Maxper PC. They had produced *La marca del hombre lobo* and José María Zabalza's strange movie. César was a likable fellow, a chubby, bald-headed man and something of a gourmet. He showed an interest in the script which by then was titled *Todos los gritos del silencio* (1974). The director would be Ramón Barco, a peculiar character who was taken on board the project at the insistence of Porto. According to my *friend*, Barco had directed a classy arthouse picture called *Mecanismo interior* starring María Mahor and which had been selected for the San Sebastián Film Festival.

Filming commenced with the main roles played (apart from myself) by the excellent José María Prada, María Mahor, Blanca Estrada, Máximo Valverde, Mirta Miller and the famous Argentinean boxing champion Goyo Peralta. Ramón Barco wasn't a bad fellow but, apart from being a bit pretentious, as a director he left a lot to be desired. I had endless problems with him. Meanwhile Porto in those days went chasing after any actress who came anywhere near him.

The picture was being shot in Madrid and Paris, where the key scenes were due to be filmed. Then big trouble hit the production; Barco was arrested. It was rumored that he had been picked up on charges of child molesting, but frankly I never found out the truth of the matter. A little while ago I read a short item in the paper which saddened me: Barco's body, in an advanced state of decomposition, had been found on New York's subway.

Poor César Gallego was on the verge of ruin: suddenly without a director and everything ready and waiting to roll in Paris. He got in touch with several other directors and naturally they asked to see the scenes that had already been filmed and to study the script. The crisis deepened and the producer was moving closer to bankruptcy with every day that filming was held up. Then he begged me to direct the picture. I worked flat out and within the limitations imposed by the footage already shot by Barco but I saved the day and César Gallego could breathe again.

Exorcismo (1974) was a Profilmes-Pumares co-production directed by Juan Bosch. I wrote the script three years before the release of *The Exorcist.*

Paul Naschy

The Marshall from Hell

Many people may find some of the things I've written a little hard to believe. But what I'm about to relate in this chapter goes beyond the bounds of the most overheated imagination.

El Mariscal del Infierno (*The Marshall from Hell*, 1974) was the first sword and sorcery movie ever made in Spain and, unless memory fails me, also the last.

The title character was a glory-steeped Marshall of medieval France who, after a number of military campaigns, retired to his isolated castle to immerse himself in a world of horror, black magic, devil worship and horrific cruelty. He abducted village girls and tortured them just to satisfy his depraved appetites. He hired sinister sorcerers and alchemists to aid in his maddened quest to obtain the Philosopher's Stone, an obsession which led him to keep his people under the yoke of the most savage tyranny. In other versions this character, clearly inspired by the real-life Gilles de Rais, went by the name of Alaric de Marnac. De Rais went insane trying to turn metal into gold and has always been one of my personal favorite characters.

The film was packed with spectacular swordfights and jousting tournaments which made it into something of a tribute to those legendary Hollywood movies starring Douglas Fairbanks, Errol Flynn and Basil Rathbone.

And now we come to the unbelievable part. After filming in places like Talamanca del Jarama and Toledo we moved on to the castle of San Martín de Valdeiglesias which as I have previously mentioned had belonged to Don Alvaro de Luna.

Don Alvaro de Luna was a Castillian courtier and a member of the Order of Saint James[The Patron Saint of Spain]. He served King Juan II well and was fond of banqueting, jousting and hunting. His wealth was beyond reckoning. The king bestowed upon him all manner of civil and ecclesiastical powers which he abused on numerous occasions. It was on his advice that Juan II resumed the bitter war against the Moorish king of Granada, which was beneficial to the nobleman's interests. On his advice Don Juan married the princess Isabel. This beautiful

El Mariscal del Infierno (*The Marshall from Hell*, 1974) **was the first sword and sorcery movie ever made in Spain.**

El Mariscal del Infierno

young woman, paradoxically, brought about the downfall of Don Alvaro whose arrogance and abuse of power had led the people to hate him. From Burgos he was taken to Portillo where he was tried and sentenced. On June 22, 1453, he was led to the gallows in Valladolid. His bloodied severed head was displayed on the point of a pike as a warning to others.

In this unique character's castle we had a strange experience. The place had been bought from the Colón (Columbus) family, direct descendants of the famous discoverer, by an eccentric individual of American origin. One day when the crew were taking their lunch break the owner of the castle came up to us. The actors were all dressed in medieval clothes and, upon seeing me, this tall, thin, gray-haired man of about 50 years of age exclaimed: "Thou art not the Marshall from Hell!" Although I was taken aback by his manner of speech I decided to humor him.

But a little later I had a feeling that something odd was going to happen. Modesto Pérez Redondo, the film's line producer, invited him to eat with us but he declined. Before leaving he once again addressed himself to me and with an odd look on his face he cried: "You were who you were. I shall explain."

At dusk León Klimovsky called a halt to the day's filming. The director, his wife Erika, the electricians and several other technicians left. Some of us stayed behind. There was Rosa García the wardrobe mistress—today a film producer herself—the Argentinean actresses Norma Sebré and Graciela Nilson, the DP Francisco Sánchez and a few others.

The title character *El Mariscal del Infierno* was a glory-steeped Marshall of medieval France who retired to his isolated castle to immerse himself in a world of horror, black magic, devil worship and horrific cruelty.

I was still made up and dressed in medieval costume when the castle's enigmatic owner appeared and invited us down to the ancient wine cellars to try the excellent wine from his own vineyards. So we descended into the damp underground passages and came to the stone crypt-like cellar. Soon everyone was drinking and merrily toasting each other's health. Then the owner came up to me and led me to the courtyard. Suddenly he told me: "Thou art not Gilles de Rais. Thou art not the Marshall from Hell. Thou art the reincarnation of Don Alvaro de Luna!" Just then, I don't know how, a white horse galloped through the courtyard, mane flying in the wind and at one of the phantasmagorically illuminated barred windows I thought I caught sight of a woman's silhouette. We returned to the cellar and shortly afterwards this weird character led us to the castle's great hall.

The room was full of burnished suits of armor, panoplies, heavy medieval furniture and dark old paintings, among which was a portrait of Carlos II *The Bewitched*. The film people, who by this time were pretty well drunk, stood up on a kind of minstrels' gallery which overlooked the hall. I didn't know what the man intended but I did notice a heavy iron gate set into one of the massive walls. From outside came the rumblings of a thunderstorm. The man shot the thick bolts of the front door and the two of us were locked in the hall. He opened a cabinet and took out a jug and two goblets, which he claimed were made of solid gold. We drank a toast to Carlos II *The Bewitched* whose spirit was said to haunt the castle.

El Mariscal del Infierno

I couldn't believe it. Up above, the film crew were having a great time watching this surprising spectacle which, to be sure, had only just begun. The owner grabbed two swords from one of the panoplies and threw one to me. "Thou art Don Alvaro de Luna! Show thy skill and thy valor!" And without pausing to draw breath he went at me with sword flailing. I realized it was for real and defended myself as best I could. The fencing lessons I had taken in preparation for the movie certainly stood me in good stead.

The fight went on for several interminable minutes and just when I was starting to fear the worst, my opponent ceased his onslaught. I was bathed in sweat from fear and exertion. "Thou hast not done badly. And now I wish to introduce thee to a loyal friend." Above us my colleagues were shouting, "Viva el mariscal del infierno! Viva Gilles de Rais!"

The fellow then pulled a lever and the gate opened. I just couldn't believe what I was seeing: Out of the tunnel strutted an enormous great lion. The peaceful feline let its master stroke it. Accompanied by the huge beast we walked around the hall. We even drank another toast to Don Carlos *The Bewitched*. Suddenly the lion started to turn nasty: Its mighty roar reverberated around the stone walls and it sent my goblet flying with a swipe of its claw. Its master uttered a few sharp commands and managed to get it back in the tunnel. By this time I had totally lost my nerve.

I don't know how, but eventually the madness ended and I found myself back in the car and heading for Madrid. Then a tremendous storm broke. Tongues of lightning chased across the sky and thunder boomed while the rain poured down. The driver lost control of the vehicle and we skidded off the road and ended up in a bog. All at once Graciela Nilson lost her head and leapt out of the car and went running off. I went racing after her and managed to catch her, although she struggled like a wild thing. Eventually we got back to Madrid.

It had been a great night, worthy of the Marshall from Hell or perhaps of Don Alvaro de Luna.

At last we came to the filming of the finale, in which the good guy fights the bad guy. The famous Argentinean actor Guillermo Bredeston had to engage me in a long and spectacular swordfight among the ruins of a monastery. Guillermo misjudged one of his moves and his sword broke the thumb of my right hand. Luckily—yes, luckily—it was the very last shot to be filmed.

Such was the strange story surrounding *El mariscal del infierno*.

After the film was finished, the castle remained locked up. The owner was hardly ever seen in the village and all sorts of odd rumors began going around. Some years later I read in the papers that the eccentric character had taken a gun and blown his brains out.

By the end of 1974 my career had taken a great leap forward. I had won awards: from Paris, Sitges, Antwerp—my name meant something on the international scene and articles and features dedicated to my films appeared in specialized magazines like *Fangoria, L'Ecran Fantastique, Eurocinema, Famosos monsters del cine, Creepy, Fantom, Terror Fantastic, Vudú* and many others. My name now appeared in most foreign movie encyclopedias, especially those in English, French and German. But possibly the most important accolade was having my own display in the legendary Forrest J Ackerman Museum. Props from my movies went on show alongside Bela Lugosi's ring and cape, various items and masks belonging to Lon Chaney, Sr. and Jr., some of Vincent Price's costumes and mementos of the great Karloff. I had my own showcase displaying one of the bloodied shirts from *La noche de Walpurgis*, the now famous cross of Mayenza, masks, stills, several handwritten scripts, production sketches, lobby cards. To have a place in the Ackerman Museum means you're really somebody in the world of genre cinema.

While all this was going on in the world at large, in Spain everything was so much more difficult, although I did have a number of prestigious admirers such as Luis Gasca, Luis Vigil, the *Terror Fantastic* team and several other critics and writers. But also, there were those who in their arrogance chose to totally ignore the existence of a type of cinema which the people loved.

I had received several offers to work abroad, from Germany, from the United States, even from England, which was always a hard nut for Europeans to crack. My family, the love of my own country, the mistaken belief that my work would finally be recognized in Spain, together with fear of the unknown and a touch of complacency led me to stay put. Without doubt it was a tremendous mistake and I probably let the chance of a lifetime slip out of reach forever. Still, you never know. An unexpected Paul Naschy revival may be starting at this very moment.

In 1974 I suffered one of the most traumatic and depressing experiences of my career. I had always loved writer Gustavo Adolfo Bécquer's *Leyendas* and I came up with the idea of making a totally indigenous horror fantasy movie by adapting some of Bécquer's works for the big screen. The tales I chose were *El miserere, El monte de las ánimas* and *La cruz del diablo*. I set to work and wrote a script which took me a long time and a lot of effort. At last I was satisfied and offered it to John Gilling, a workmanlike director who could lay claim to the considerable prestige of having worked for Hammer Films. Gilling, who was then living in Spain, was delighted with it and I started to get in touch with actors of the stature of Peter Cushing, Christopher Lee, Herbert Lom and James Franciscus as well as a number of first-rate Spanish actors.

Everything was coming up roses, and it seemed that this was going to be a major motion picture. But, alas, I went to my close *friend*, my *brother* Juan José Porto and offered to let him have a hand in the project. He accepted the offer enthusiastically and soon he was telling me about Quique Herreros, Jr., a man with great prestige in the film business. Without a doubt he was the man who could bring it all together for us by having his company Bulnes Films produce the movie and then making a deal with one of the top distributors. I knew that Quique was the son of the great artist, painter and talent scout Enrique Herreros.

I was in Barcelona and the project was underway when Quique turned up and asked me to sign a contract for the screenplay with Bulnes, as if the company had already bought it and owned the rights. This was indispensable in order to get things moving since we didn't have any funding. I was suspicious, but then the fellow, in an extravagant display of theatricality, went down on his knees—much to the amazement of the customers of the café where our meeting was taking place—and with outstretched arms swore his total allegiance to me. And I, like a prize idiot, went ahead and signed.

I finished my work in Barcelona and went off to the Sitges festival feeling quite confident. One fine day Juan José Porto turned up in the beautiful Catalonian city and told me that John Gilling had broken his ankle and that shooting would be held up. He also mentioned that the producers had made a few small changes in the cast, but that everything was going ahead.

Some time later I returned to Madrid. By pure chance I happened to buy the magazine *Triunfo* and imagine my surprise on seeing three color pages about the making of *La cruz del diablo* (*The Devil's Cross*, 1974). My name was nowhere to be seen in the credits and Gilling was now claiming that he didn't consider me as a star of the genre.

I managed to get a hold of Porto, a smarmy devil who could have sold ice to Eskimos, and he managed to convince me that he too had been an innocent victim of the underhand machinations of the treacherous Quique. I felt humiliated, cheated and miserably deceived. I had been stripped of my role, my script and, worst of all, my self esteem.

I hired a lawyer and got Herreros to pay me 100,000 pesetas and to include my name in the credits—below Porto's, of course. I'll always regret getting a billing on this picture because after seeing the film I came out of the cinema feeling ashamed: They had ruined the script and Gilling's direction was deplorable. *La cruz del diablo* will always hang like a weight around my neck, even though I had nothing to do with the end result.

Many more films came along. To name a few, there was *Los pasajeros* (1975), a surreal tale filmed by a strange director, José Antonio Barrero, in which the wonderful Aurora Bautista appeared in the nude for the first time. It caused quite a stir. I also appeared in *Exorcismo* (1974), a Profilmes-Pumares co-production directed by Juan

Bosch. I wrote the script three years before the release of *The Exorcist*, as a visit to the archives of the Sociedad de Autores (Writers' Guild) will prove. In *Muerte de un quinqui* (1975) I worked with the fabulous Carmen Sevilla, the beautiful Julía Saly, Enrique Gónzalez Macho and the late prince Henry Gregor. Then I had a small part in *Ambición fallida* (1975) with Gert Fröbe and John Philip Law, directed by none other than Christian Jaque.

I appeared in a forgettable picture called *Pecado mortal* (1976) directed by Miguel Angel Díez and in which the inevitable Juan José Porto was involved. In *El último deseo* (1977) I had to put up with the intolerable bouts of egocentric posturing from Alberto de Mendoza

As Louis XIV in *Los pasajeros* (1975)

and glamour girl Nadiuska. I won several awards for *La maldición de la bestia* (*Night of the Howling Beast*, 1975), including best actor in a Spanish language picture at the Festival of New York.

Now I must once more go back in time. The artist Juan Carlos Eguillor had incorporated my Waldemar Daninsky character in his comic strip in the newspaper *El correo español/El pueblo vasco,* where Waldemar co-starred with the artist's own famous character Mari Aguirre. I was honored. Meanwhile in Spain many things had changed following ETA's car bomb assassination of Admiral Carrero Blanco and the death of Francisco Franco. My exclusive contract with Profilmes had expired and the company went off on a new tack, hiring Jorge Semprún [a future Spanish Minister of Culture] as a scriptwriter and making big-budget pictures with Yves Montand and Glauber Rocha. Profilmes could have been the Spanish Hammer but they didn't last many years longer. It was a shame.

As I was writing these lines I heard the news of the death of Ricardo Muñoz Suay, a well known intellectual and a friend of mine. Ricardo founded Profilmes together with José Antonio Pérez Giner. We worked together on a few scripts, although I hadn't seen him for several years. His name will forever be associated with the Spanish *cinefantastique* genre. With his passing our cinema has lost one of its most important figures.

Inquisición (1976)

Paul Naschy

A Nightmarish Time

In 1977 I made my debut as a fully-fledged director by tackling a tricky subject: nothing less than the Holy Inquisition of the Roman Catholic Church. In order to carry out my research I requested an interview with Julio Caro Baroja, thanks to whose help I was able to compile a lot of crucial data I needed to help me write the screenplay. I discovered that the Inquisition in France, Germany and Switzerland was far bloodier and much crueler than the Spanish Inquisition, for all Torquemada's reputation. Undoubtedly the dark legend had survived and flourished for centuries. The European trials for witchcraft, the topic I was concerned with, were far more numerous and spectacular than in Spain.

The plot was largely based on true events which took place in the French region of Carcassone, where a judge fell in love with a woman accused of being a witch and they both ended up being burned at the stake. The film, *Inquisición* (1976), was made as a co-production with Italy. It was an ambitious project but personally I was quite satisfied with the end result. One anecdote comes to mind; while filming in the church at Colmenar Viejo, we discovered a mummified corpse from the 15th century when an old wall fell.

During filming an unpleasant incident occurred. A well-known film producer of those days, well-known as a drunkard, put in an appearance at Colmenar accompanied by his bodyguards. He'd come to fetch Juan Luis Galiardo, who had been hired by our producer, to start work on another picture. It seems this other producer had been forced to change his schedules and he wasn't at all pleased about it. Four guys in dark suits, reminiscent of Lucky Luciano, got threateningly out of their cars in an attempt to take

Inquisición **was an ambitious project but personally I was quite satisfied with the end result.**

away the actor by force. Naturally I couldn't allow such an intrusion. I whipped off my jacket and confronted them, armed with a heavy metal bar. Later I would have another confrontation with this producer at the Sitges festival. It was an unpleasant scene but I certainly ended any argument. The last I heard of him was that he was wanted by the police.

My film roles continued. I was reunited with María José Cantudo in *Secuestro* (1976). I had first worked with her in *El*

I was reunited with María José Cantudo in *Secuestro* (1976).

espanto surge de la tumba, her film debut. At times I had a job to put up with her prima donna behavior. I was surprised that a filmmaker of the caliber of producer Rafael Gil would call me up every night to inquire about his star and to remind me to take the utmost care of her. The film was based on the Patricia Hearst case and dealt with the Stockholm Syndrome.

Next I undertook two projects which were to bring me serious trouble. I refer to *Comando Txikia* (aka *Muerte de un presidente,* 1977) and *El Francotirador.* The first of these, a film lacking artistic merit, narrated in a realistic fashion the assassination of Carrero Blanco carried out by the ETA terrorist group. To be sure, nobody but me could have come up with idea of making a movie about such a touchy subject in the midst of Spain's tense political transition.

The atmosphere which surrounded the shoot was one of tremendous nervousness and we tried to film in secret, although we were beset by all kinds of problems. While we were filming some scenes outside the Admiral's house the police came along and in no uncertain terms forced us to leave.

An anecdote in a lighter vein happened when we were filming in the village of Leiza, in Navarra. They were holding the world log cutting championship. I had to act as just another aizkolari (the Basque name given to these ax wielding competitors) while we filmed the scene with hidden cameras. In those days I was pretty muscular and I certainly looked the part. My Basque blood came to the fore and I chopped away at the thick log like a true aizkolari. When the scene was in the can, it had to be explained that I was really an actor, and fortunately, those spectators who had placed wagers on me, took it all in good part. This was really the most pleasant thing which happened to us amid all the tensions of filming in the Basque country.

When we got back to Madrid our tribulations continued. Once when we were filming in a church where Carrero used to worship, a newspaper reporter had the bright

Comando Txikia (aka *Muerte de un presidente,* **1977**)

idea of hiding himself inside the confessional in order secretly to take photos of the production. Juan Luis Galiardo really blew his top over this incident.

However this troubled production was nothing compared to the one that followed it. *El francotirador* (1977) sparked off one of the most bitter and miserable episodes in my movie career. The film narrates the story of Lucas, a Basque watchmaker who loses his daughter in a terrorist bomb attack. Lucas, who is a widower, decides to assassinate the head of state whom he considers responsible for his tragic loss. Armed with a 9mm pistol, he heads for Madrid to draw up a plan for the assassination of Francisco Franco during a Labor Day rally held in the Santiago Bernabéu football stadium.

With Blanca Estrada in *El francotirador*—**I think** *El francotirador* **was a good movie, full of suspense, well paced and wonderfully acted**.

Exercising the utmost caution he takes a room in a boarding house run by a sympathetic middle-aged lady. The other guests are a motley bunch, including an elderly Fascist, a young trendy and an over the hill Bohemian. The well-endowed young maid is most accommodating to any of the guests who take her fancy.

ETA knows all about the amateur executioner's plans and decides to utilize him, preparing a car bomb as a back up in case he fails. Lucas falls in love with a ravishing prostitute, bringing an unexpected glimmer of hope for the future to the lives of both these marginal characters. But first he has to achieve his aim: to kill Franco.

When the day comes the terrorist takes up a strategic position in the stadium, inside a storeroom from which he has a clear view of Franco and the princes of Spain. He fires and misses, alerting the security forces to his presence. He manages to give them the slip and escape from the crowded stadium but then he discovers to his horror that a bus, full of children, has parked next to the car packed with explosives. He rushes to deactivate the bomb only to find himself surrounded by police and he dies under a hail of bullets. The reports of pistols and submachine guns are drowned out by the detonations of fireworks. To the strains of the national anthem the dictator leaves the stadium. The beautiful prostitute awaits the return of her lover in vain. The film finishes with a close up of a bullet on her bedside table.

I think *El francotirador* was a good movie, full of suspense, well paced, wonderfully acted and with a surprisingly skillful use of documentary footage intercut with the fictional action.

It was the only real quality film that director Carlos Puerto made in his brief career. Outstanding among the large cast were José Nieto, Carlos Casaravilla, Elisa Montes, Pep Munné, Carmen de Lirio Blanca Estrada and Antonio Vilar. I believe I gave a highly creditable performance as the wretched Lucas, the watchmaker turned terrorist.

While we were filming there were violent riots going on in the streets which the notorious grays [the Spanish National Police of Franco's regime were known as "the grays" from the color of their characteristic uniform] put

Eventually *El francotirador* went into general release and there was trouble in many places.

down ruthlessly. We were going through the most tense, conflictive time of the Transition. It was then that the nightmare began. The telephone, at times an infernal contraption, kept ringing at all hours, conveying a message of death. I heard horrible, threatening voices: "Commie bastard! Motherfucker! We're gonna kill you, your wife and your kids. Your whole family's gonna die. We're gonna blow you away."

The worst thing about it was that they knew my every movement, and I felt myself under constant surveillance. They even knew what school my sons went to and what my wife and parents were doing. I went to the police and spoke to Commissioners Vila and Conesa who told me it could all be a bluff—or it could be for real! I knew then the limitless horror which can be inflicted by man's capacity for inhuman cruelty.

The police investigated but without making much headway since it was a complex case. The worst part of it is that I believed every word; I was convinced they were going to murder us all. One day they even forced me to sing "Cara al Sol" ("Faces to the Sun," the anthem of the Franco regime).

Eventually the film went in general release and there was trouble in many places. People started fighting in the cinemas and more than once the police had to intervene. I was becoming more and more afraid and I decided to send my family to Algiers where my Italian diplomat father-in-law was posted. I couldn't go away myself due to work commitments; moreover, if anyone had to die, it should be me. The threats grew worse and I began to receive anonymous letters.

After about a year the calls suddenly stopped. The police never got conclusive evidence but they let me in on a number of details and I put two and two together. I finally realized the identity of the swine who had been behind the macabre scheme. Unfortunately I couldn't prove it. I must admit that the hell I went through marked me for the rest of my life and I will never forgive them.

With Agatha Lys in *El transexual* (1977)

Then came a rather ill-fated movie, but one which I personally deem to be of considerable interest.

One night I was having a beer at the bar of a rather special establishment when a stunning blonde came up to me—a bit over made-up as I recall—and started to chat to me in a very familiar way. I invited her to have a drink with me and we carried on with our friendly chat.

Lisa was surprisingly well read and spoke with a deep, husky voice. The cigarette smoke in the place was so thick you could have cut it with a knife and the DJ was playing music so loud that we had to shout to make ourselves heard. All of a sudden she surprised me by asking whether I'd read anything by Restiff de la Bretone. I happened to be familiar with the works of this 18th century French libertine and author of pornographic writings. The girl looked me in the eyes and asked me: "So come clean, what's a man like you looking for in a place like this?"

I should point out that I was in the famous Gay Club in Madrid. I explained to Lisa that I was a scriptwriter and I wanted to write the story of Lorena Capelli, a transsexual who had recently died in strange circumstances and who had been a regular patron of the Gay Club. In 1977 sex change operations were forbidden and only a few special doctors would carry out the dangerous vaginoplastia operations. At that moment the entertainer Paco España was on stage doing an impersonation of folk singer Lola Flores. Somebody called Lisa over and a few moments later I had to go to the gents. I was still standing at the urinal when Lisa came in, lifted her skirt and started to urinate. Lisa was a she-male. Later she introduced me to Yeda Brown, a good friend of hers who had undergone the sex change operation.

That night I learned a lot of things, out of which a film was born—*El transexual* (1977). They were all warmhearted people and gave me every cooperation, even taking acting parts in the film. The director was the jinxed José Jara and the late-lamented screenplay writer and good friend of mine Antonio Fors worked with me on the script.

My role was that of a pushy journalist investigating Capelli's death. I was joined in the cast by Vicente Parra, Agatha Lys and José Nieto, among others. I also acted as co-producer.

I got to know the homosexual scene quite well and made a lot of good friends, many of whom were great artists. One magical night the excellent Catalonian female impersonator Pierrot gave me a heartfelt tribute at the Gay Club. Pierrot was

In *El transexual* I play a pushy journalist investigating a death.

editor of the magazine *Vudú* and was an exceptionally good illustrator. I have great affection and admiration for him. He would work with me some years later, taking a part in *El último kamikaze*.

I was a step ahead of other prestigious filmmakers who didn't deal with this subject until many years later.

It was at this time that my wife and I, in the company of León Klimovsky, his charming wife Erika and Prince Enrique Starhemberg—known in the movie business as Henry Gregor—went on a tour of Eastern European countries, ending up in Austria.

I'd like to say something about Hungary, a country close to my heart and which holds a great significance for me personally. I have been there both when it was under the iron rule of Communism and again after it gained its freedom. My wife had lived in Budapest when her father was posted to the Italian embassy in the Magyar capital.

When we crossed by train into Hungary some Hungarian border guards came to our compartment. Their over-bearing uniforms and weapons lent them a sinister appearance, reminiscent of the Nazis. They demanded to see our passports in a gruff, hectoring tone. They scrutinized us with disquieting looks and discovered that Erika was Hungarian but naturalized Spanish. The men's granite-like faces took on an even harder expression and one of them spoke the word "traitor." On a word of command from the officer, the guards started to rummage through our hand baggage and then they set about taking the seats apart.

My wife and I, in the company of León Klimovsky, his charming wife Erika and Prince Enrique Starhemberg (Henry Gregor), visit the Lenin Estate in Hungary.

I addressed them politely in German. One of the soldiers unexpectedly thrust the cold barrel of his sub machine gun into my ribs. I felt a shiver run down my spine and the tension became unbearable. The officer relented, gave a curt command to his men and they put the seats back and returned our passports. Their jackbooted footsteps echoed along the corridor as they left. Enrique Starhemberg was as white as a sheet.

This unpleasant incident did nothing to dampen our spirits and we arrived in Budapest in good cheer. We were staying at a luxury hotel called the Duna. There was a sordid contrast between the palpable poverty in the streets and the abundance and extravagance of the Duna Hotel. Foreign tourists were a protected species because we paid in dollars.

My wife knew the city well since she had lived there for quite a time. We went to visit the street called Alcotmani Utsa to see, standing opposite the old Parliament building, the quaint Austro-Hungarian mansion house which had been her home. There were still bullet holes in the walls, grim reminders of the past conflict. Elvira became quite emotional and told us how the aristocrat who had given up his house to her father—the Communist government had ordered him to put it at the Italian diplomat's disposal—lived miserably in one unheated, practically unfurnished little room on the lower floor of what had once been his beautiful home. When the Hungarian peoples' cries of freedom had been crushed by Soviet tanks, Nonna Kepess, the aristocrat, had committed suicide.

We visited the city and I remember Lenin Square with its statue of the Revolutionary leader standing opposite the spectacular red marble building which housed the Communist party headquarters. While we were there a number of black limousines with tinted windows pulled up outside and disgorged several high ranking officials, dressed in ostentatious overcoats and astrakhan hats. The cheaply attired passersby watched them stony faced.

Two famous film directors invited us to their finely furnished home where we partook of the traditional Hungarian goulash. Incidentally, set in an old stone wall close to their residence, I discovered a number of tombs of medieval warriors who had fought against the Turkish invaders. I was surprised to see several Spanish names among them.

In Austria Enrique Starhemberg gave a terrific party for us in his fabulous castle. I was reminded of the more lavish scenes from the Sissí films. The European aristocracy turned out in full. The following day he screened *La muerte de un quinqui* for his guests, a film which he had produced.

Later on I know that the Prince set up a chain of cinemas together with Enrique González Macho and both León Klimovsky and I were excluded from his circle. For years he used to send me a calendar which he published, illustrated with his own photographs, until I recently received the news of his death and an invitation from his family to attend his funeral in Vienna.

Henry Gregor was a mediocre actor, but he might have become a noteworthy producer. He certainly had plenty of money.

Paul Naschy

My Most Personal Phase

Now I come to what I believe to be the most interesting and, above all, the most personal phase of my movie career. I had made my directing debut with *Inquisición* and now I started preparing another project which would turn out to be one of my most emblematic and highest quality films. I refer to *El huerto del Francés* (1977).

It all began when I started wondering about the origin of the common Spanish expression "cuidado, que van a llevarte al huerto" [an approximate and partial English equivalent which retains the simile could be rendered by "they're leading you up the garden path"]. I was so intrigued by this that I started to do some research. It's clear that the phrase is a warning which bodes no good. Eventually I made a trip to the news cuttings library and after several days I came across the source of the story.

"The Frenchman's Garden" was a sort of tavern in Peñaflor, a village located between Córdoba and Seville. It was here that a cold, ruthless murderer had done away with several victims, together with his partner Juan Muñoz Lopera. The sinister serial killer was called Juan Andrés Aldije, nicknamed "The Frenchman" because he was said to have come from that country, although this point was never really clear. Juan Andrés married the richest woman in the village, Elvira Orozco, and settled in Peñaflor. After buying the tavern his string of horrific crimes commenced.

The murder victims were usually people who had come to gamble at the tavern. The poor devils ended up buried under the beds of flourishing tomato plants. However Aldije made one serious mistake: He spurned a young lover, whom he forced to have an abortion and subsequently tried to prostitute. The girl betrayed the horrors of the Frenchman's Garden to the Civil Guard and Juan Andrés Aldije and his partner, the unlucky Muñoz Lopera, were executed by garroting in October 1906. When I shot this scene, with Luis Ciges playing the executioner, I couldn't help but remember Jarabo.

I wrote the script and Antonio Fors collaborated with me on the final draft. The excellent ballad was written by Rosa León and the music was composed by the late Angel Arteaga, a great and unjustly forgotten composer.

I had a great cast with such quality actors as Pepe Calvo, José Nieto, Carlos Casaravilla and Nélida Quiroga. The leading ladies were the fashionable starlets Agatha Lys and María José Cantudo. They were constantly at odds with each other, quarrels and fits of jealousy were the order of the day and they really made shooting difficult, especially Ms. Cantudo. During one of their rows she threw a plate at Ms. Lys which missed her and injured the makeup artist Angel Luis de Diego. Another day she went and ripped the other woman's costume to shreds. I remember how the poor wardrobe mistress came weeping to me with the news. The thing came to a head when they had to act out a real fight scene. I warned them that if there were any incidents which put filming at risk they'd have the fight with me. I remember that María José Cantudo's husband, Manolo Otero, who was watching the scene whispered in my ear, "Just let

María José Cantudo gave a great performance in *El huerto del Francés* despite the

them smack each other about a bit. You'll get a bloody great scene." The animosity between the two made a good ongoing story for the gossip magazines.

I worked hard and ended up with a good film. Both Lys and Cantudo gave great performances. I saw Agatha again recently in a theatre production and she was excellent. I've never met María José Cantudo since. I only know that she's currently reaping great success with the play *Mariquilla Terremoto*. In spite of our problems I sincerely wish them both all the best.

The most interesting part of shooting *El huerto del Francés* was the time we spent in Andalusia.

When we got to Peñaflor we found that the production team hadn't gone over the ground too well and a number of difficulties cropped up. Naturally, my wish was to film in the same places where the real events had taken place. First we had to locate the Frenchman's Garden if it still existed, to lend the film as authentic a flavor as possible. The trouble was that time seemed to have stood still in the village, and whenever I asked the locals about the sinister place, nobody knew anything. There had never been any such place in Peñaflor. I realized that the subject was totally taboo. Unbelievably,

When I shot this scene in *El huerto del Francés* with Luis Ciges playing the executioner, I couldn't help but remember Jarabo.

and despite the fact that we had all the necessary permits, the town hall official who I had to deal with didn't know anything either. I felt as if I'd been transported back to the deepest, darkest Spain depicted in José Gutiérrez' paintings.

The solution to this problem came from an unexpected quarter: the village priest, a young, intelligent man who gave me his unconditional support. In the vestry of the parish church he took out some bundles of old documents and showed me the birth certificates of Muñoz Lopera and Elvira Orozco. He also came up with Juan Andrés Aldije's marriage certificate and the pathologists' reports on the people who had been brutally murdered.

These documents carried detailed sketches of the injuries which had caused the deaths of the Frenchman's clients. There were drawings of skulls smashed in with axes or iron bars. It was a veritable gallery of horrors. Afterwards the priest took me to the old cemetery where he showed me the grave of one of the victims: "Félix Bonilla, cattle dealer, met his death in The Frenchman's Garden on November 8th 1901 at two o'clock in the morning."

Later the helpful priest took me to the actual Garden itself. In fact, only the walls were still standing, and even those weren't intact. I was able to speak to the current owner, a stockbreeder whose grandfather had bought the sinister place for a song. When turning the soil the man's forebear had unearthed a rusty crowbar, an old, corroded *L'afouché* revolver, a large knife blade and some pieces of human bone. All these finds were handed over to the authorities. Strangely, none of this was reported in the newspapers.

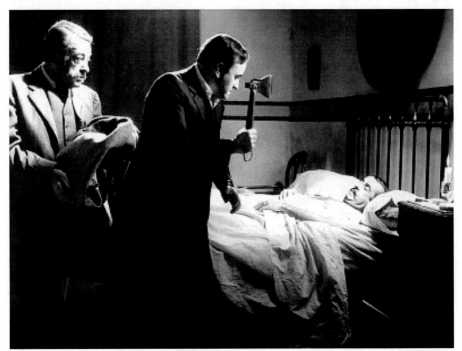

I am proud to be able to include *El huerto del Francés* in my filmography and I consider the trouble I had filming it to be time well spent.

Thanks to the priest I was able to film the facade of Juan Andrés Aldije's real residence, as well as the authentic garden walls, the church where the terrible murderer and the lovely Elvira (played by Julia Saly) were married and, with a bit of set dressing, a tavern which had belonged to Muñoz Lopera.

One evening the clergyman took me to a really old tavern with a zinc bar counter, tiled walls and illuminated by a single opaque light bulb from which hung a strip of flypaper. Villagers were playing cards and dominoes at the tables. We were served wine by a surly, balding man of about 40. He gave me a black look but said nothing. It was almost dark by the time we left the bar and the priest told me: "The man who served you is Juan Muñoz Lopera's great grandson."

I am proud to be able to include *El huerto del Francés* in my filmography and I consider the trouble I had filming it to be time well spent.

On the night of the premiere I received many congratulations as is usual on these occasions. However there was one compliment which I was really pleased to receive. José María Forqué told me in all sincerity: "You've made a magnificent picture. The dark side of deepest Spain at the turn of the century has seldom been so well recreated as in *El huerto del Francés*."

I was still competing in powerlifting championships and it was in Burgos that I sustained a very serious injury. I tore my triceps while attempting to lift a weight of 155kg. The injury was so severe that the doctors told me I'd never be able to take part in the sport again and that my left arm would be impaired even for everyday activity. Luckily, as we shall see, they were wrong.

The wrap party for *Madrid al desnudo* (1978) which was an ironic and scathing comedy with an all-star cast: Fernando Ferán Gómez, Agustín González, Rosanna Yanni, Silvia Aguilar, Pastor Serrador and myself.

In fact it was in a gymnasium where I first met Eduardo Franco, a bodybuilder, journalist and writer.

Eduardo spoke to me of Eduarda Targioni, a novelist friend of his of Italian origin who wanted to make a film of her novel *Madrid al desnudo*. We got in touch and Ms. Targioni suggested that I write a screenplay of her novel and that I should direct it myself. I liked the story and I agreed. What I obviously didn't know was that this film would bring me almost as much trouble as *El francotirador*. Juan José Daza recommended me to line producer Enrique Jiménez, a good-looking, amiable fellow who knew how to get his own way.

Madrid al desnudo (1978) was an ironic and scathing comedy with an all-star cast: Fernando Ferán Gómez, Agustín González, Rosanna Yanni, Silvia Aguilar, Pastor Serrador and myself.

We filmed the picture in Madrid and Marbella. After a week and a half spent working on the film I started to notice certain odd reactions coming from the media. I mentioned this to my DP, Alejandro Ulloa, who replied in his usual wry manner: "You dickhead. Don't you know what film you're making?" I said yes, I'm making a film based on a novel. "Yes, a novel that makes a laughing stock of the most powerful members of Madrid high society," he said.

The film's release caused a commotion; once again I received threatening, anonymous phone calls. Besides which, a certain very powerful figure of those times tried his utmost to put an end to my career. He banned my name from appearing in the media and he endeavored to have the major production companies slam their doors in my face. He almost managed it.

With Irene Gutiérrez Caba in *El caminante* (1979)

Following *Madrid al desnudo*, I suggested to Eduarda Targioni that we shoot a script which I'd written three years previously, *El caminante*. I was really keen to make this film.

El caminante (1979) narrates the adventures, the misadventures, the glory and the disaster which befall the Devil himself during his voluntary pilgrimage on Earth. In order to commit his felonies the Devil must accept incarnation in a mortal body so that he may be vulnerable to pain, illness and even death. I had a magnificent cast: Irene Gutiérrez Caba, Sara Lezana, more beautiful than ever and at her zenith as an actress; Blanca Estrada, the prettiest eyes in Spanish cinema; Paloma Hurtado; José Ruiz; the attractive Taida Urruzola; Adriana Vega; David Rocha and Rafael Hernández, among others.

The director of photography, who achieved splendid results, was the ubiquitous maestro Alejandro Ulloa. As was our custom, we took a trip to the Prado museum and ascertained that the light and color effects we wanted were to be found in the paintings of Jan van Eyck, Peter Brueghel (the elder) and Vermeer de Delft. Each one of them would contribute to a specific atmosphere. These same artists were also the inspiration for the out-and-out Gothicism of *El retorno del hombre lobo*.

I wrote *El caminante* in a very special frame of mind. Life had dealt me several harsh blows and I had gained a pretty negative impression of people. For me personally, friendships had been a lamentable disappointment. I knew all about betrayal and lack of loyalty and apart from my family—my parents, my wife and my two sons—I didn't believe there were many things worthwhile in this filthy rotten world. Later on

For me the high point of *El caminante* is when the Devil, crucified opposite a stone Christ, admonishes: "Lord, how could you give your life for these swine?"

three people appeared in my life whom I consider true friends. However, the cry of anguish from the bottom of my soul which found expression through this movie is still valid today.

The seven deadly sins are present in *El caminante*. For me the high point of the whole movie is when the Devil, crucified opposite a stone Christ, admonishes: "Lord, how could you give your life for these swine?" I believe it's clear enough who the swine are. *El caminante* is a medieval comedy—set around Burgos during the reign of the Catholic Monarchs—which includes picaresque and romantic episodes as well as incorporating legends about the Devil. Friars and nuns, pilgrims and bandits, nobles and commoners form a frieze presided over by the figure of the Devil. He's an evil devil but at the same time mocking and jocular, like any devil worth his salt.

Perhaps this isn't the most perfect film of my career but it's definitely the most personal and heartfelt.

It won the Eurocón 78 award for best fantasy film of the year and it also won prizes at the International Fantasy Film Festival in Paris and at Imagfic in Madrid.

Although the film only took four weeks to shoot, the sets, costumes and period detail were excellent.

Since I have a wealth of comments about the film I could quote, I've opted for what Professor Adolfo Camilo wrote in his doctoral thesis on Spanish Horror Fantasy:

> Satan walks the Earth—we witness his rise, his tri-
> umph and his downfall, by men defeated, in the
> most impressive and quintessentially Spanish fan-
> tasy film ever made, photographed in the colors of
> ancient Grimmoire parchment.

For the specialist Gilbert Verschooten, *El caminante* is a minor masterpiece. Coming from him, I find this appreciation most gratifying.

As an anecdote, I remember one bitterly cold night when we were filming in a melon field, I looked for a little respite inside an old shack. As I entered I came across the head of production and our lady producer locked in amorous rapture in the cozy glow of a blazing log fire. I stepped outside and a freezing wind buffeted my face. I looked to the sky, saw the crescent moon and told myself with absolute conviction that my career with Horus Films had come to an end. Undoubtedly that moon was an omen, but to tell the truth, I was already sick and tired of the woman's *affairs de coeur*.

In any event I'll always be grateful to Ms. Targioni for giving me the chance to make my beloved *El caminante*. I never saw her again. Years later I heard that Enrique Jiménez had directed a hard-core pornographic film called *La seta española* (*The Spanish Mushroom*). That's showbiz.

I was working on *El retorno del hombre lobo* as producer, scriptwriter, lead actor and director when, through my good friend the journalist Hugo Astiarain, I received the offer of a small part in *Mystery on Monster Island* which was being produced and directed by Juan Piquer Simón. I also knew that Peter Cushing and Terence Stamp were going to be in the film. I agreed to do it, even though it meant rearranging my own shooting schedule.

I had met Juan Piquer at an edition of Imagfic and he had struck me as a very nice man, really pleasant to deal with. To be frank I wasn't too familiar with his work and what little I had seen of it didn't appeal to me very much, but I was willing to work with him.

However, when I'd done my stint on the movie I wasn't overly enthusiastic and most of the reviews concurred. There was one in *Fangoria* magazine which went something like this:

> The film sounds promising. The names of Peter
> Cushing, Paul Naschy and Terence Stamp all ap-
> pear in the opening credits. Well, save your money:
> they're hardly in it and the rest of the film is a total
> waste of time.

To top it all, I was nearly blinded during filming. The special effects technician, who had lost a number of fingers in an earlier accident, overdid it with the explosive charges and I was almost blown sky high. If I had been, my disappearance would have been so realistic that it would have been worth buying a ticket. I promise to say more about Juan Piquer later on.

The Wolfman's Finest Hour

As previously mentioned, in 1980 I was busy filming *El retorno del hombre lobo*, one of the most significant titles of my whole career in the horror fantasy genre. Waldemar Daninsky was back to confront his worst enemy, the perverse, vampiric Bloody Countess Erzebeth Bathory de Nadasdy, this time portrayed by Julia Saly. Other cast members included Narciso Ibañez Menta, Silvia Aguilar, Azucena Hernández, Beatriz Elorrieta, Pepe Ruiz, Tito Fernández, Rafael Hernández and Ricardo Palacios. Regarding the latter, whenever possible I would invent a role for him since I liked to have him in my movies. Of course, when Ricardo came to direct his own pictures he didn't feel the need to reciprocate. Only natural, isn't it?

The superb makeup was the work of Angel Luis de Diego with photography by Alejandro Ulloa. I really enjoyed making this picture, giving full rein to my love of heavy Gothic imagery, blended with both real historical detail and unbridled flight of fancy. I was also able to give vent to my most intimate fantasies.

When I was writing the script I had in mind those privileged individuals who abuse their power to crush the weak and defenseless. Just like Bathory who exercised

El retorno del hombre lobo **is one of the most significant titles of my whole career in the horror fantasy genre.**

In *El retorno del hombre lobo* Waldemar Daninsky was back to confront his worst enemy, Bloody Countess Erzebeth Bathory de Nadasdy, portrayed by Julia Saly.

the power of life and death over her wretched subjects, seeking eternal youth through the power of blood. Waldemar the Wolfman had to blindly do her bidding, a slave utilized by Bathory to impose her infernal tyranny.

In actual fact the character symbolized others like Wolfgang Gotho, the pathetic hunchback, or my own personal take on the evil Count Dracula, both of whom had become frail, oppressed and marginal figures.

El retorno del hombre lobo contains all the coordinates of my own life, fitting together like the pieces of a jigsaw puzzle: the claustrophobic castle, the Gothic tombs, the ill-fated love affair, the menace of the undead, the ostracism of someone who is despised for being different and the all pervading shadow of death. All of these elements go to make up my personality and my work. Movies, even horror fantasy movies, can carry real depth of meaning because through fantasy we can convey a far deeper message than would appear possible at first sight.

After finishing this picture, something happened which I must relate. I heard from Klaus Rabe, the German mystic who had visited me in my home one day long before. One morning the phone rang in my study. I remember that it was raining hard and the raindrops were beating on the window pane. I was writing the script of *Los cántabros*. From the other end of the line came a hoarse, croaking voice. He told me his name and I couldn't help but shudder. The mysterious Klaus told me things I still haven't forgotten. He was in the last stages of throat cancer and had only a few months to live. He told me that my life was going to change, that I would find work in a faraway land, that I would meet with certain success during a number of years but things would then go wrong. I would be increasingly misunderstood in Spain and enter my own Walpurgis, a dark tunnel with no clear way out. I would no longer be self-sufficient and would need a great deal of help to survive. The forces of evil would be unleashed against me on the night of Saint Walburga. He admonished me for not having listened to him and refusing to be the Führer of his sect. Although I didn't understand anything at the time, hearing all this was somewhat unsettling.

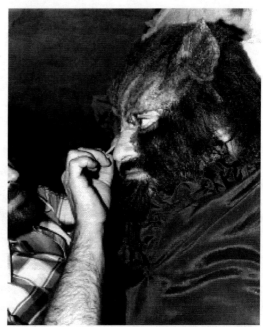

The superb makeup in *El retorno del hombre lobo* was the work of Angel Luis de Diego.

Not long afterwards Barbara was in Madrid and she brought me Kraus' metal, eye-shaped medallion. It was the legacy which he'd left me when he died. I refused the amulet and declined to go with her to Germany. I now realized that there had always been a link between Barbara Muller and Klaus Rabe. I've never seen her since.

Los cántabros (1981) came about in a strange way. The film was started by Amando de Osorio, with a certain Dan Barry playing the barbarian chieftain Corocotta. It must have been going wrong because the film's chief of production, Agusto Boué, offered me the task of directing it. But I wouldn't settle for resuming work on a picture which had been started by another. A totally new script needed to be written for an almost completely new cast. I would have to have control over the whole project. And so it was. I did thorough research to give the film maximum authenticity. I recall that Carlos Saura made me a present of a book about the conquest of Cantabria which proved to be very useful.

I had a fine cast to work with, including Alfredo Mayo, Andrés Resino, Antonio Iranzo, Julia Saly, Ricardo Palacios, Luis Ciges, Verónica Miriel, Manuel Pereira, Paloma Hurtado, Adriano Domínguez, Vidal Molina, Pepe Ruiz and David Rocha. They were all a pleasure to work with. I also have fond memories of the late, lamented Sebastián Almeida, my assistant director.

The great problem which we had to address was the lack of both photogenic qualities and acting talent displayed by Dan Barry, a third-rate bodybuilder who had worked as a stuntman and fancied himself a big star. He gave me a lot of trouble. What's more I had to work with very limited resources; if I asked for 75 horses, I got 30.

We shot the picture in January, and apart from the extras going on strike, we also suffered the loss of several horses that died from the cold. On top of that we didn't

In *Los cántabros* (1981), it gave me great pleasure to don the helmet of the Roman general.

have enough Roman helmets and armor and I had to shoot a cavalry charge of Marco Vipsanio Agripa's troops by filming the same group of riders coming from behind a large mound over and over again. It turned out quite spectacular to see horses and warriors multiplied a hundredfold. As can be seen, in my movies I've had to use my wits to make up for lack of resources to an astonishing degree.

In the film the powerful Caesar Augustus, played by Andrés Resino, has to confront his general Marco Vipsiano Agripa (my own character). The final scenes were shot on Jachú beach in Santander, the actual scene of the historical events, where the rival leaders engaged in a spectacular swordfight.

I think I made a highly creditable *peplum*, and what's more a homegrown one, and it gave me great pleasure to don the plumed helmet of the Roman general. I'd like to see this movie again on the big screen. Maybe someday, at some retrospective.

And then, much to my surprise, the dying mystic Klaus Rabe's predictions started coming true.

The Samurais

It was through the Japanese embassy that the country's leading production company Horikikaku Seisaku got in touch with me. The impenetrable doors of the mysterious Orient were opening for me. I hope I'm able to explain properly the most interesting period of my already lengthy career.

It was towards the end of 1980, if I remember correctly. I was set to encounter an enigmatic and fascinating world.

At that time there were no airlines flying directly to Tokyo so there was no alternative but to make a stopover in Moscow. What today seems a perfectly straightforward business was quite an odyssey in those days, when there was another great red Czar in command—I mean Brezhnev—aided by his sinister Nomeklatur. We flew with the Soviet airline Aeroflot, and we were given accommodation for the night in a hotel belonging to the company.

Before boarding the bus we had to wait around like a flock of sheep inside a great circular, windowless room, suffering from the extreme cold: The temperature was about 20 degrees below zero.

Afterward we were shepherded to the main airport building that housed a large hall where there were a few shops, a shoddy exhibition of rickety furniture and some shelves with cheap paperback books of party propaganda. The only thing of any interest on sale in the shops were the famous Russian dolls. The walls of the airport were covered in photographs of famous Soviet athletes, one being substantially larger than all the others—that of the colossal Alekseiev, the best weightlifter of all time, a giant Ukrainian who would have put Hercules to shame. Not even Leónidas Brezhnev occupied such a privileged place as the legendary strongman. Obese women with swollen, blue veined legs were monotonously swabbing the airport floor with their mops. I needed to go to the bathroom and it felt like I was back in post-war Spain: The toilet paper had to be taken off of a spike and the lavatory bowls looked like they were of 1930s vintage. Then came passport control. Stern looking, stony-faced soldiers wearing uniforms somewhat reminiscent of the Nazis made a show of repeatedly examining your passport and staring at you as if they were about to dissect you. Eventually the passport was exchanged for a piece of red plastic with a number on it.

The journey from the airport to Moscow was made aboard a decrepit coach which drove us along a frozen highway. We were packed in like sardines in a tin. Night was falling and the poverty stricken wooden houses which skirted the Russian capital were illuminated by candlelight.

On arrival at the hotel a fat woman checked out my credentials. We were assigned rooms, which we shared. I lay on the bed with my coat on and even so I almost froze to death. Presently we heard the sound of jackboots and my door was locked. It was unlocked at eight o'clock the next morning. In the snowbound streets I saw enormous crows everywhere, ochre-painted Fiat cars and soldiers, a lot of soldiers.

With Takeda and Sasai at the press conference for *El Museo del Prado*

When we landed at Narita airport I felt like I'd arrived in another galaxy. It was a huge culture shock, everything was so different, so modern. I was given a grand welcome by the Japanese executives who whisked me away to the great metropolis in a spectacular black limousine. After dropping my things at the luxurious Miyako Hotel, I dined with the high ranking executives in a pricey French restaurant. Early the following morning I would have my first meeting with the company's President, Sasai San.

During the meeting in Sasai's huge office came an unexpected surprise: They offered me the job of making a major documentary about the Prado Museum, no less than nine hours long. They'd seen my films and considered that I was the right man for the job.

I returned to Spain conscious of the incredible prospects opening up before me. What's more, a special set of circumstances also worked in my favor. I was great friends with Julia Saly, *La Pocha*, whom I had met during the filming of *La muerte de un quinqui* and she happened to be a friend and partner of Masurao Takeda, a Japanese living in Spain, where he'd come as coach to the Spanish national judo team. The moment was right for us to join together to constitute a production company which would operate fundamentally with Japanese capital. Agusto Boué came in with us as general production manager.

The Prado Museum was a tremendously successful documentary series in Japan, to the point of winning an award as the best cultural film of 1982. We filmed at night, when we had the entire museum to ourselves. I thoroughly enjoyed the experience. At times I had the orgasmic sensation that all this beauty had been created for me alone. The director of photography was, as usual, Alejandro Ulloa. The series was divided into two long chapters: *Great Spanish Painters* and *Great Universal Painters*. The Japanese producers let me have the rights for Spain and I offered the series to TVE. They didn't even bother to watch it. Sometimes these things happen in this country.

After filming this documentary, Takeda and I returned to Japan where many projects awaited us.

Masurao Takeda was a noble person, faithful to the last and totally unable to tell a lie; he gave me everything and asked for nothing in return. He was, in short, a friend, my best and only friend, someone who will live on within me until the day I die.

In Japan all doors were opened to judo legend Takeda. I remember that my first official act there was to present an exhibition of European painting. I met many celebrities from the world of culture, business and politics: Takeo Fukuda, ex-Prime Minister of Japan and a key figure in the contemporary history of the country; the famous actor Toshiro Mifune; the legendary director Akira Kurosawa; Yamaha, president of The Deadly Hundred, a group rooted in the most ancient Samurai traditions; Sigheru Amachi, celebrated theatre, cinema and television actor; the president of Toho... and also leading writers and painters, some of whom I would collaborate with at a later date. It was a great day for me.

Takeda showed me the typical ancestral ceremonies, such as the tea ceremony with Geisha girls, and I had the chance to talk to the legendary actors and actresses of the fabulous Kabuki theatre. By the way, the geishas are not high class prostitutes as is commonly believed in the West. They are educated in special, very strict schools in which they learn music, song and dance and the exquisite ceremonials which they have to master in order to be able to properly serve the wealthy customers of the luxury restaurants where they work. True to the cliché, they look like China dolls with their pretty faces covered in white rice powder makeup. I must admit that I dreaded these ceremonies because so many hours in a crouching position played hell with my knees. At first everything seemed very reverential and orthodox; later on the sake took a hold and the diners would start to relax and lose their rigid composure. Strangely, I was afraid of taking my shoes off, being absurdly worried that I might have a hole in my sock.

One day Takeda took me to the beautiful lake Hakone, at the foot of Fujiyama. Wonderful galleons were anchored on the lake, looking like something out of a Hollywood movie. It was like going back centuries in time. Mount Fujiyama was gen-

A galleon on Lake Hakone at the foot of Mt. Fujiyama

erally obscured by dense clouds. According to tradition, it brings good luck to see it free from cloud from Lake Hakone. I saw it like that several times, clear cut and a marvelous shade of blue. Leaning on the rail of one of the galleons, Masura Takeda gazed into the water below and told me that the bodies of many a businessman who had made the wrong decision were to be found at the bottom of the lake. I was shaken by these words. The Samurai spirit apparently still lived on.

Takeda usually took me to Tokyo's most refined European restaurants, since I thought raw fish was revolting. Eventually I tried it at a wedding and soon developed a taste for it.

Logically, in such an exotic country, one so different from our own, there were plenty of anecdotes. Here's one example. One night we went to a very peculiar establishment. It was a huge World War II submarine which had been turned into a luxury restaurant. We were surrounded by katanas, officers' uniforms and caps displayed on metal hangers and yellowing photographs of the, probably, heroic crews. We met a group of veterans, one of whom was an ex-kamikaze pilot. I even dressed up in an old imperial tunic and cap while we drank toasts with sake and sang old army songs.

We visited a lot of temples, both Buddhist and Sintoist, where we burned little papers in honor of ancestors. I also remember the *I Ching* sticks which told my future. In one of these temples there was a museum which contained a collection of Spanish arms and armor, once belonging to European warriors and adventurers whose errors had led to Japan, the Cipango of antiquity, shutting herself off from the rest of the world for centuries.

On another occasion we made contact with the dreaded Japanese Mafia. They all wore black and their chief, Masanori Yoshimo, prided himself on having all his fingers intact, something which his subordinates couldn't claim—all of them had some digit missing. Takeda justified this meeting by telling me that there was some unfinished business pending between the Yakuza and a friend of his, the daughter of one of Sanyo's major shareholders.

The Hory-Kikaku-Seisaku company commissioned me to produce a TV movie which they planned to shoot in Spain to mark their 25th anniversary. The film, called *Amor blanco* (1980), starred the two leading Japanese actors of the day—he was the greatest romantic leading man and she was the most popular, adulated singer and actress in the land of the flowering almonds. The director, Kotami, was a tricky customer although I knew how to deal with him. One day he wanted the trains to be a different color, the next he wanted to change the upholstery in the jumbo jets. My small team and I kept him under control and gave him a dressing down whenever necessary, although we let him have the best whenever possible.

The director wanted to include Spanish actress Charo López in the cast. Her agent, seeing a great opportunity, charged an astronomical fee. However, at first this amount was agreed to. But when he wanted wardrobe and makeup sessions to be paid at the same rate as a day's filming, as general production manager I put my foot down and refused. I've often thought that Charo probably didn't know anything about all this.

There was a highly risky sequence in *Amor blanco* which required painstaking preparation. This was a reproduction of the spectacular bull running event which takes place during the San Fermín festivities in Pamplona. Kotami wanted to film the real thing but I pointed out that this was not viable since it was impossible to mix actors with the real action, and much less given that at one point a balcony had to collapse plunging stuntmen into the path of the charging bulls while the male lead rescued the girl, just as she was about to be impaled on a bull's horns.

So I had a set built in Torrelaguna to represent the Pamplona location and I bought five bulls, including a real monster of a beast. The inhabitants of Torrelaguna were given berets, neckerchiefs and red cummerbunds and dressed to look the part. We even changed the cars' number plates. When it came to shooting the scene there were all sorts of mishaps and upsets. One of the bulls tossed a poor stuntman up in the air. He came down on his backside, crashing through a wooden barrier with an almighty wallop.

Torrelaguna was brought to a standstill for several hours until the scene was in the can. But our troubles didn't end there, because the monster bull refused to be brought under control. We had hired a wrangler to take care of any bulls that got out of hand. When it came to the crunch, the wretched man went down on his knees and begged me for his children's sake not to make him confront the massive beast. I understood why the fellow was in such a funk and in the end the Civil Guard shot the dangerous creature dead.

That night, in a restaurant in Rascafría where we had ordered supper for the crew, Takeda insisted that the Japanese contingent, who had been shaken by the incident, should eat only fish as their stomachs weren't up to dealing with meat after their upsetting experience. But when it actually came to it they happily gorged themselves on juicy beef steaks.

Another day we caused mammoth congestion in Madrid's main thoroughfare, the Gran Vía. We were there to shoot a difficult scene, and cameras, lights, specially prepared cars were all set, but things were being complicated by the stormy weather. The first assistant director, a Japanese know-it-all, ordered filming to continue. Of course, it was a total disaster and he was downgraded to pushing the trolley with the cans of film around the studio. The price of failure is high in Japan.

Once the difficult shoot was completed I was congratulated by Hory-Kikaku-Seisaku who then commissioned me to produce an eight hour documentary, including docudrama footage, to be called *Historia de España a través del Palacio Real de Madrid* (1981). I had a great time making it. The cast included Andrés Resino, Julia Saly, David Rocha, Charlie Bravo, my eldest son Bruno and myself. I combined objects from the museum with historical docudramas. The script went

I had a great time making *Historia de España a través del Palacio Real de Madrid* (1981).

In *Historia de España a través del Palacio Real de Madrid,* I combined objects from the museum with historical docudramas.

from the bit of Witiza's horse to the enthronement of Juan Carlos I, by way of characters like Hernán Cortés, El Cid and Napoleon, among others.

Once filming was over the objects we had used were returned to their display cases. But one of Hernán Cortés' swords, one which I think he had used in the famous battle of Otumba, failed to appear. After searching high and low we found it wrapped in a piece of cloth inside one of the props trucks. I like to think it was just a little mix up.

After this documentary we made one about the monastery of El Escorial, once again with docudrama footage included. The cast was the same. This time I played an aging Felipe II.

There was a peculiar anecdote to this production. There is a chamber near the royal crypt which is known as the Rotting Room. Royal corpses had been laid inside this macabre chamber for hundreds of years to undergo the decomposition process after which the bare skeletons were transferred to their sarcophagi. The Japanese knew about this place and they asked me to film it. This was easier said than done because filming was not allowed there. Our activities were watched at all times by a curator, which logically made it completely impossible.

It so happened that I needed to set up a dolly for a traveling shot of the tombs and I asked the curator to open the door of the Rotting Room so I could get a longer run. I had a job and a half to persuade the man and I had to promise not to cross the threshold. We had set up the lights when we had a stroke of luck: Somebody called the curator away on some business. I exchanged a glance with Alejandro Ulloa, who got my meaning and Eduardo Noé picked up his camera. We filmed the whole room as thoroughly as possible. There was a row of open niches with drainage channels and a larger channel running down the middle of the floor. There was a body in one of the niches, barely visible in the shadows but we filmed it all. We came out of there with

Here I portray Filipe II in *El Monasterio de el Escorial.*

our footage and shortly afterwards the curator returned. Everything had gone unbelievably well. I felt well pleased with myself.

I am proud to have contributed with these films to bringing greater knowledge of our history and our culture to the Orient. I used the plot device of a father and a grandfather (Andrés Resino and Eduardo Fajardo, respectively) telling stories to their son/grandson played by my eldest boy, Bruno, which allowed me to bring into play the dramatizations of historical events.

Next up was *La prehistoria en Cantabria* (1982) and *Las cuevas de Altamira* (1982). The former was a magnificent documentary about the men who did the famous cave paintings, their customs and beliefs. I was aided in writing the script by the help I received from the Altamira Heritage Trust and from several eminent paleontologists. I was able to do research and take notes at the diggings then being carried out at the famous caves.

It was quite an odyssey getting a permit to film inside the caves themselves. We were given a time limit and filming was complicated by the structure of the caves. We shot in 35mm and working with the amount of equipment we needed, we almost became contortionists. However my DP, José Enriquéz Izquierdo, did a great job.

It was also quite tricky to reconstruct on film the sensational discovery of the caves made in 1876 by the archeologist Marcelino de Sautuola. I came up with another dramatization in which I myself played the part of the Cantabrian scientist, basing my characterization on photographs and old prints. The marvelous cave paintings we shot

With Julia Saly in *La Prehistoria en Cantabria*

in traditional documentary fashion: the horses, the hog, the graceful deer and the spectacular bison.

In another tunnel which leads off the main cavern are to be found lesser known designs such as a boldly rendered human head with a prominent brow, decorative friezes and indecipherable symbols.

Don Marcelino had made several visits to the cave but the great discovery came about when his little daughter went with him and pointed out the "oxen" on the roof. The archaeologist fought to have his peers acknowledge the immense importance of the discovery but unfortunately he died before the authenticity of the incredible cave paintings, sometimes referred to as the Stone Age Sistine Chapel, was accepted.

I requested an interview with the banker Emilio Botín, grandson of the little girl who had discovered the oxen. A famous journalist and TV presenter for NHK also came out from Japan to conduct a further interview with the elderly banker for the documentary. In the sitting room of his luxurious home I re-encountered my admired Solana, since one of the greatest collections of Don José's works belonged to the Botín family. I also filmed the wonderful monument which stands in the grounds of the bankers residence and even the family pantheon.

This documentary proved highly successful on Japanese TV and was regularly repeated over the years.

Next I made a documentary entitled *El descubrimiento de la máscara del Juyo* (1982). This remarkable discovery didn't have much repercussion in Spain but in Japan it filled page upon page in the papers and was seen as a cultural event of the first magnitude. The mask was found in a cave, known as Juyo cave, some nine kilometers from Santander. It is actually the first religious image in the history of mankind. Strangely enough it comprises a double face; one visage is that of a bearded man and the other is of an animal, a feline according to the archaeologists, although to me it's always looked like a wolf. Those who wish to see it can view it on display at the Altamira Caves Museum. With this rough and ready head prehistoric men must have been trying to represent the duality of Good and Evil at the heart of man, preceding by thousands of years the mythical face of the ancient Greek god Janus.

Once more I employed the docudrama format. I wrote the script based on data supplied by a learned Spanish priest and a renowned American archaeologist, among other researchers.

Around this time the influential businessman and politician Yammaha, along with some others, started to lobby the Japanese government to bestow on me one of its greatest decorations in recognition of my great contribution to culture. Meanwhile, at the suggestion of Takeda, we requested an audience with the Spanish director general of Fine Arts, Javier Tusell. We wanted to propose several projects which would be beneficial for Spain: exhibitions, cultural exchanges and other interesting collaborations with Japan. We had been told that Tusell, son of a movie producer, was at the time the top dog for cultural matters within UCD (Unión del Centro Democrático, then ruling party in Spain). But what happened was most unpleasant. We were received by a short little man in shirt sleeves who seemed angry with us, with the world at large and even with himself. He implied that we had no idea about culture and were wasting his time, that he and the government he represented were the only ones who could deal with such matters.

All these documentaries were made in collaboration with diverse companies over a period of time up to 1983. I would make one further documentary, a very different one. The title *Infierno en Camboya* (*Hell in Cambodia*, 1983) sums up how I felt about it.

I have dreamt one war and lived another. In Cambodia I was a horrified witness of executions, hangings and beheadings, savage rape and subhuman tortures, a whole catalogue of atrocities. I was thinking of devoting a whole chapter to this accursed assignment which I was given by Tokyo's Channel 9 one day in 1983. But I don't think the time is right; it would take a whole book to speak about the horror, the mosquitoes, the malaria, the leeches, the murderous knife wielding kup-kups, the death and the savagery, a book which I don't feel like writing. What's more, the recent merciless killing of the innocent Miguel Angel Blanco Garrido (a Socialist M.P. killed by E.T.A. terrorists) has left me with no desire whatsoever to recall what I never should have lived through. The wolves are still among us and it's astonishing how easily we turn on each other with murderous intent, as reflected in *El caminante, El carnaval de las bestias* and *El último Kamikaze*. The black shadow of death, which I have seen at such close quarters, once again spread wide its scaly wings like those of some insatiable bloodlusting vampire.

As Waldemar Daninsky in *La bestia y la espada magica*

Paul Naschy

The Co-Productions

Apart from the documentaries, I made a number of films and TV series wholly or partly produced by the Japanese. The first Hispano-Japanese co-production in movie history was *El carnaval de las bestias* (1980), a weird, claustrophobic, erotic and cruelly perverse story. The cast included Lautaro Murúa, Silvia Aguilar, Eiko Nagashima, Koji Moritsugu, Azucena Hernández, Luis Ciges, José Ruiz, Ricardo Palacios, Tito García, Roxana Duprey and José Hernández.

The film tells a terrible story of sex, violence and cannibalism. It all starts when a European hit man is hired by a Japanese terrorist group. He double crosses the organization and kills several of its members, subsequently running off with a fortune in stolen diamonds. The hit man, played by me, was also the lover of the terrorist leader's sister. So began a wild chase which would end up with much bloodletting in Spain. Having been wounded, the protagonist seeks refuge in a solitary house inhabited by an apparently ordinary family comprising Don Simón, his beautiful daughters and their black servant. He is treated with the utmost kindness and begins to regain some degree of humanity. However he is actually in the midst of a family of cannibals and is the next item on the menu.

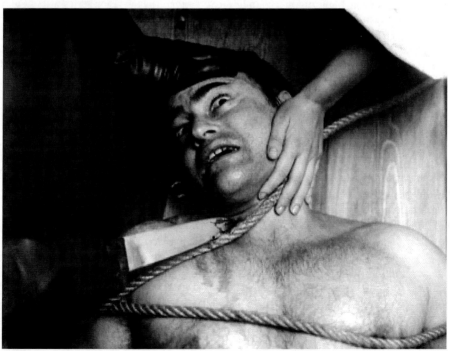

El carnaval de las bestias **(1980) is a weird, claustrophobic, erotic and cruelly perverse story.**

With Julia Saly and Sigheru Amachi in *La tercera mujer*, the television series where I play an Interpol agent.

In short, a pessimistic film dealing with the inevitable impossibility of redemption which brings the concepts of life and death as seen by two very different and ancient cultures into brutal head-on collision. Today *El carnaval de las bestias* is a cult movie.

I allowed myself the indulgence of having the story start on the breathtakingly beautiful Lake Hakone, aboard one of the galleons, and ending up in the valley of Lozoya in the heart of the Madrid Sierra.

I can't end my commentary on this movie without mentioning the totally professional way the Japanese actors went about their work. In order to make their job easier I told them they could deliver their dialogues in Japanese, because they found our language very difficult. However they were so conscientious that they said all their lines in Spanish, and what's more with almost perfect diction.

Personally speaking, I was well pleased with *El carnaval de las bestias* which, like *El Caminante*, sums up my position as regards human behavior.

Besides films, I had the chance to work on three Japanese TV series, namely *La tercera mujer* (1982), *El dragón negro* and *La espada del samurai*.

In the first of these I played an Interpol agent on the trail of a Japanese psychopath, portrayed by Sigheru Amachi. This 13-part series was based on fact: The shocking story of an employee who, out for revenge, poisoned the entire production of a well-known biscuit manufacturer. The action packed episodes were filmed on location in France, Germany, Italy, Yugoslavia, Japan and Spain. The finale was filmed on the Costa Brava and in Barcelona, with some very spectacular scenes shot in the Madrid

Paul Naschy

sierra, El Paular, the vicinity of La Cabrera and at my own country home. It was really hard work and given the Japanese concept of the working day, there was no mention of working fixed hours and we ended up absolutely exhausted.

I scored a point with the producers by virtue of gaining the collaboration of the Civil Guard, through the good offices of a close friend of mine who was a colonel in the corps. For the scenes in the Madrid Sierra they deployed an impressive force of vehicles, armed men and helicopters.

Filming went smoothly until the day we had to shoot a chase sequence involving two speedboats at sea. I had become good friends with the stuntmen, two of whom were brothers. As the cameras started to roll the unexpected happened. For some unknown reason one of the high speed craft lost control and crashed into the other one. The vessels burst into flames and one of the brothers was killed and another stuntman was seriously injured. The armorer and the other brother miraculously survived. But no time was lost in lamentations and a few hours later the scene was being repeated. Through an interpreter I spoke to the surviving brother, who was to repeat the action. He spoke in deadly earnest: "What more could my brother have asked? He has had a glorious end. Last night he made love to his fiancée and today he has met an honorable death. Is there any greater happiness?" You couldn't argue with the man. The Japanese are like that.

I must mention that Julia Saly played an important part in *La Tercera mujer*. She gave a fine portrayal of an audacious journalist.

El dragón negro (1981) brought me a change of register. I became a dangerous Armenian Mafia boss with plans to import drugs into Japan. In the end I was killed when the plane in which I was escaping crashed.

In *La espada del samurai* (1982), I played a half Japanese, half Dutch adventurer endeavoring to prevent the plunder and pillage carried out by his ruthless Dutch com-

In *La espada del samurai* (1982), I played a half Japanese, half Dutch adventurer.

rades. The makeup man, a remarkable specialist who had worked with Akira Kurosawa many times, did a most remarkable job in making my character convincing.

Two tragic events occurred around this time. The generous and influential politician Yahama, an out-and-out womanizer, gourmet and *bon viveur*, died of a stroke. We lost a valuable advocate and I had to forget about being decorated by the Japanese government.

On one of our trips to Spain, Julia Saly and Augusto Boué were waiting for us at Barcelona airport. Before we came out of the baggage reclaim hall, Julia held up to the glass a magazine which carried news of the death of Félix Rodríguez de la Fuente (de la Fuente was a famous naturalist, very popular in Spain for his wildlife documentaries on TV). Félix was a good friend of mine and of my family. We used to visit him at his house in Madrid and often bumped into him in his home village of Pozas de la Sal. Félix and I chatted a lot about wildlife and I recall one melancholy evening in his office when I asked him what he considered to be the most ferocious, bloodthirsty creature of all. He answered without hesitation: The great white shark was a perfect killing machine. Well, obviously second only to man, the world's greatest predator.

Before moving on to the next chapter, I'd like to set down a sentimental anecdote which shows the extent of the generosity I received from the Japanese. As I've already mentioned, the Spanish Weightlifting Federation in a display of contempt and petty mindedness which spoke volumes about its leaders had gone out of its way to discourage me and make me give up competing. Not to mention the gang of envious individuals who darkened my training sessions in the Guzmán el Bueno gymnasium for years. I only had one excellent colleague, the prematurely deceased champion Antonio Cerdán. By complete contrast the Japanese Weightlifting Federation staged a warm tribute for me, for which I shall always be grateful.

Having returned to Spain, Germinal Films, through José Antonio Pérez Giner, called to offer me a part in a comedy, *La batalla del porro* (1982), directed by Joan Minguell. I played the comically fierce captain Matarraña, alongside Victoria Abril.

I played the comically fierce captain Matarraña in *La batalla del porro* (1982).

Paul Naschy

Following this incursion into comedy it was the turn of *Latidos de pánico* (1982) and this film certainly is worth talking about.

Once again Alaric de Marnac (Gilles de Rais) was back from the grave craving blood and vengeance. The story is set in an old dark house somewhere in France and tells of the sinister schemings of an architect who is in love with his pretty and conniving maid. In order to eliminate the man's wife, a hypochondriac with a heart condition, the pair decide to utilize the terrible legend of the bloodthirsty medieval knight. A loyal servant, played by Lola Gaos, discovers the plot and is murdered without pity.

The architect and his lover subject the wife to the *Gaslight* treatment until they frighten her to death from a heart attack, utilizing all manner of diabolical tricks including the apparition of Alaric himself, clad in battle armor and wielding his deadly chain

Latidos de pánico (1982)

mace. Everything goes as planned until a string of magical phenomena concur and horror rises from the tomb again. Thus, death and horror are once more unleashed and the wretched lovers pay dearly for their wickedness.

The film was shot on location in an abandoned house once belonging to General Franco. The title of a painting by Valdés Leal sprang to mind: *Sic transit gloria mundi*. I came across a host of diplomas, family photographs, letters, busts, portraits and even crockery and cutlery, all strewn over the floor. These were the last traces of a man who had held the whole of Spain in his hands for 40 years. It was pathetic. In the garage, where we set up the location canteen, were parked the armored Mercedes which Hitler had presented to Franco—the same car in which the general had entered Madrid—and another vehicle, apparently a gift from Mussolini. It was quite amusing to see the delightful Lola Gaos, who was such a devout communist that she even wore red knickers, nonchalantly filming in the home of one who had undoubtedly been her worst enemy. But as she said herself, "It's one thing to be a communist and another to be a professional. If we have to make a movie, we make a movie, even if we have to go to hell to do it. And this isn't really hell." I had been warned by the malicious gossip mongers that Lola had a really foul temper, that she was a pain in the arse, that I'd be sorry and other drivel in the same vein. I found Lola Gaos to be an extraordinarily professional actress whom I'll always remember with affection.

The DP on this film was Julito Burgos—the favorite pupil of the maestro Pepito Aguallo—a good friend and a sensationally creative technician. The makeup by

Latidos de pánico **is a revisitation of the claustrophobic, phantasmagorical world of the most characteristic Naschy works.**

Fernando Florido, a true artist and another faithful friend, was up to the exceptionally high standards we had come to expect from him. Besides the aforementioned Lola Gaos, the cast included Julia Saly, Pat Ondiviela (Miss Spain), José Vivó and Manolo Zarzo.

Latidos de pánico is a revisitation of the claustrophobic, phantasmagorical world of the most characteristic Naschy works. It was very well received abroad and premiered at the Gran Vía Cinema in Madrid.

Now we come to a film which represents for some the high point of my filmography. I refer to *La bestía y la espada mágica* (aka *The Beast and the Magic Sword* and *The Werewolf and the Magic Sword*, 1983). The making of this film was an incident-packed adventure in itself and as such deserves a few lines.

The idea had come about while I was having lunch with Yamaha in a revolving French restaurant located atop an enormous cylindrical building. The panoramic views of Tokyo were magnificent. I don't know why but I mentioned the possibility of making a Japanese sword and sorcery picture but which included the character of Waldemar Daninsky. I feared the worst, feeling that the subject of lycanthropy was too European. To my great surprise, Yahama told me that this ancestral tradition also exists in Japan, where the Wolfman is known as the "okami."

That evening our influential friend gave a party at one of his homes to show off the reforms he had made to his private modern art gallery. Yamaha had an impressive collection of modern paintings, but his pride and joy were three large canvases by the great Japanese painter Fujita. Sigheru Amachi and Toshiro Mifune were both there

Some consider *La bestía y la espada mágica* (aka *The Beast and the Magic Sword* and *The Werewolf and the Magic Sword*, 1983) the high point of my filmography.

too. Takeda brought up the idea of making a film combining Japanese ghost stories with the traditional European werewolf.

Some time passed and towards the end of 1982 I came back to the idea. I wrote the screenplay based on the Japanese legend of the bandit known in Kyoto as The Beast. This outlaw had murdered a number of people in the forest—in the 16th century Japan still possessed considerable areas of woodland. The events occurred during the time when the legendary warlord Oda Nobunaga held sway, having emerged triumphant from the Shogun wars. The legend tells how The Beast was captured and made to take part in a singular combat against a Bengal tiger. The man from the woods won the fight.

Taking this idea as a starting point, I decided to tell the story of the Daninskys, whose line went back to the time of Otón the Great. They were cursed by a Magyar witch who used a wolf's skull to bite the swollen belly of Polish hero Irineus Daninsky's pregnant wife. In this way the pentagram stigma was passed down from generation to generation. Unlike the films about Lawrence Talbot (Lon Chaney, Jr.) which had a certain continuity, Waldemar Daninsky can move freely through space and time.

In the 16th century, at the height of the Inquisition, Waldemar, condemned because of the mark of the pentagram, seeks a remedy for his terrible affliction. He makes his way to Toledo where a learned Jew called Salom Jehudá (played by Conrado San Martín) endeavors to bring about his salvation, but the Hebrew is murdered by the fanatical inquisitors.

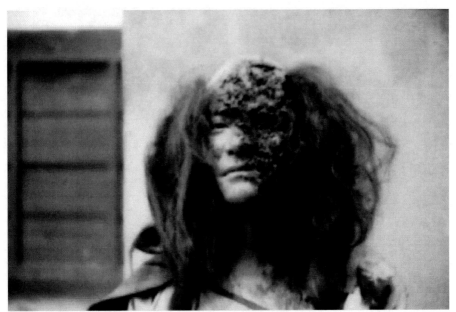

In *La bestía y la espada mágica* **Waldemar comes up against the terrifying world of Japanese black magic.**

Before he dies, Salom Jehudá directs Waldemar to Cipango (Japan) in search of the wise man Kian, the only person in the world capable of attempting to cure him.

In Kyoto Waldemar finds Kian but he also comes up against the terrifying world of Japanese black magic. Only the love of Akane and a magic silver katana can save him.

I researched the subject thoroughly in order to write the script. Thus I found out that in Japanese sorcery the high sorceress always wears red and her servants dress in white. She has the ability to mobilize an army of warriors whose souls are adrift in the netherworld and she can manipulate the elements of water, wind and fire. The witches who in life were the head of their clans inhabit phantom castles and, as in Western witchcraft, talismans are effective weapons against them. They are protected by a pretorian guard clad in red armor and armed with spears. I added detailed historical touches, recreating real names and situations. Names like Nobumago, Eiko Watanabe, Yukio Gotho, General Taikasoma and Kian are names of people who really existed.

The script was duly accepted but then we came up against the first problem. The Japanese production company possessed all the elements from the 17th century: wardrobe, sets, weapons... but not from the 16th century. I proposed we change the period to keep production costs down but I was in for a big surprise. They wanted to make the film as scripted. Everything would be specially made for the film because everything—from the samurais' hairstyles to the color of the clothes, even the sets and the buildings—had to be very specific. As for the werewolf makeup, we were asked for something reminiscent of the legendary kabuki theatre masks. Fernando Florido, my habitual makeup artist, based the characterization on an old engraving. As regards the magic sword, they actually went and made a katana of real silver. I still have it because it was presented to me as a souvenir.

I based the screenplay for *La bestía y la espada mágica* on the Japanese legend of the bandit known in Kyoto as The Beast.

Filming was to take place in Toshiro Mifune's superb studios on the outskirts of Tokyo. They were really well equipped: sound stages, makeup rooms, training schools for actors and technicians, lighting equipment and everything that one could want, even vitamin vending machines. Of course there were also restaurants, projection rooms, editing and dubbing suites. To cast the picture, those actors and actresses who had come through the video and photo selection stage were brought before me in an audition room where, through an interpreter, they told me of their professional merits. Set decorators, artistic directors and assistants all consulted me about everything and no decisions were taken without my approval. However, the chief of production adopted a hostile attitude at first, since he couldn't comprehend why a Westerner should be directing a movie about Japanese culture and customs when it wasn't a major co-production, however "fantastic" the film was to be. On the other hand, Julito Burgos with his characteristic bonhomie soon had the rest of the crew eating out of his hand.

At last work began on this incident filled shoot. Our first enemy was the intense cold. Besides that, due to the demands of the distributors, we had to work against the clock. There was no trouble with the Japanese but the Spanish assistant director and the continuity girl left a lot to be desired. To offset this Fernando Florido, his wife Loli and Julito Burgos were always at my side, even at the most trying moments, of which there were many.

The first of these occurred one night when Amachi, in a fit of artistic temperament, threw his katana to the ground and stormed off the set. He explained that he wasn't prepared to make a film for a director who filmed his back, not understanding why these reverse shots were needed. I was so maddened that I threatened to abandon the production. Fortunately the Japanese actor realized his mistake and came to apologize.

Memoirs of a Wolfman   **171**

The cast of *La bestía y la espada mágica* was graced with excellent Japanese actors and the finest of professionals.

Another time we were filming at night. The actress Yoko Fuji was required to lie half-naked on the soaking wet boards of a small boat. The temperature was only fit for polar bears. The lights were being set up when I gave the order for Yoko to be taken to her dressing room as she was likely to catch pneumonia. To my surprise the chief of production opposed this, alleging that she was a professional and it was her duty to remain in her place. The Japanese can be incredibly cruel at times. Of course I had a blazing row with the man, but meanwhile Yoko Fuji went back to her dressing room.

Then came the day of the fight between Wolfman and tiger. After numerous inquiries, circus lion tamers and animal trainers told me that the fight could be filmed with the realism I wanted using panthers, leopards or lions but with a tiger it would be impossible. I was about to give in when I heard that the tigress from the TV show *Sandokán* was in Holland and it might be possible to use her. Her trainer arrived with three big cats in a huge cage. It was strange to see that the fierce beasts were kept under control by an intelligent dog of uncertain breed whose intervention was on occasion decisive. Before shooting the tigress had to be fed 25 chickens. If she'd been hungry the critter would have eaten me and the trainer for breakfast.

Another particularly unforgettable sequence was the *hari kari* scene. It was important for me to get it exactly right, so I sought assessment on how this tragic ritual was carried out in the period in question. I found out several things, for instance that the samurai always had to fall forwards at the last moment. To avoid suffering he had to be beheaded by a kinswoman who would be at his side ready to perform the grisly task. When we filmed the scene most of the crew were in tears. This was the old Japan where death and honor were inextricably bound.

Paul Naschy

The cast of *La bestía y la espada mágica* was graced on the Spanish side with three wonderful veterans: Conrado San Martín, Gerard Tichy and José Vivó. I was less inspired in my choice of Violeta Cela and Beatriz Escudero, although in the end they didn't do too badly. The Japanese actors were excellent: Junko Asahina, Yoko Fuji, Yoshiro Kitamachi, Mitsuaki Hori and all the rest of them proved to be first class professionals. I did my utmost to plan the numerous action sequences as carefully as possible and to polish the direction. But above all I aimed to recreate the Japanese *tempo*, so difficult for a Westerner.

Eventually the master copy was ready for the first screening for the producers and the crew. Among the guests were Akira Kurosawa and Nagano. I was a bundle of nerves. When the film finished there was hearty applause. Kurosawa, the legend, came over to me, shook my hand and congratulated me. In his opinion I had achieved just the right period atmosphere and tempo for the film. Although the whole project had been incredibly tough, I felt totally recompensed by that evening's events.

After the screening, all the cast and crew members went off to a typical karaoke establishment where I was made to make a fool of myself singing, or rather murdering, corny old Spanish songs like "Niña Isabel ten cuidado" and "Princesita." Sake does have side effects. Sigheru Amachi, who had several discs to his credit, sang several lovely songs, including the one he had composed for the film.

The film was distributed in Spain by CIC and premiered at the Gran Vía Cinema. It was a grand affair with floodlights, journalists and all the usual paraphernalia that surrounds these events. Basically I was happy because of my father's pride in me; nobody could foresee that it would be the last premiere he'd ever attend. Neither could the smiling and satisfied Sigheru Amachi know that he wouldn't live to see the premiere of his film in Tokyo. Some months later he died from a stroke while recording a TV show.

Professor and film critic Adolfo Camilo Díaz wrote the following about *La bestía y la espada mágica*: "This is the Spanish cinema's best ever fantasy adventure film." I think it was Séneca who said: "Never speak well of yourself because nobody will believe you; and never speak badly of yourself because everybody will be quick to believe you." That's why I prefer to use the above quotation from Camilo. In any event, for me this film holds the enormous sentimental value of being the last of his son's films that Enrique Molina ever saw.

Scouting locations for *El último Kamikaze*

Paul Naschy

The Curse of the Pharaohs

A few months later I had the idea of filming a melodrama with a child protagonist. Actually, perhaps subconsciously, what I was really trying to do was to recreate my own childhood in the form of a sentimental journey back to the time when I used to dream of avenging cowboys, the Three Musketeers, the audacious Zorro or the fabulous Robin Hood. In order to find a child actor we thought of putting advertisements in the papers, but then Julito Burgos came along and suggested that we audition my younger son Sergio, then eight years old. This we did and we were all pleased with the result, so

Sergio became the star of *Mi amigo el vagabundo* (1984). He was accompanied in the cast by José Luis López Vázquez, José Bódalo, Florinda Chico, Gracita Morales, Julia Saly, Yolanda Farr, Alejandra Grepy, Manolo Zarzo and Pep Corominas. My role was a that of a tycoon with a heart of gold. As we all know "the rich also cry" [this refers to a Mexican soap opera which was incredibly popular in Spain, *Los ricos también lloran*].

This sentimental comedy did excellent business at the box office. I've lost count of the number of times it's been shown on TV. The plot was simple but I put a lot of myself into it. Yolanda Farr was an excellent Fraülein Ronge; Alberto Fernández played an unlikable friend of my father's, a loud-mouthed hunter and angler who used to tweak my ears when my parents weren't watching; Florinda gave a great performance as his wife, who was always going on about how good she was towards the needy; Gracita Morales was an old

My son Sergio became the star of *Mi amigo el vagabundo* (1984).

maid who thought she was a descendant of El Cid. The characters were not wholly fictional.

I got the basic plot idea from an Argentinean globetrotter who at the time was earning a living playing the accordion on the Madrid underground. This busker, whom I met while I was buying the newspaper, told me the story which I took as my starting point. The rest I took from my imagination and memories.

The story could have had a tragic ending. It was during the filming of the scene in which the boy has a dream involving my character in a shoot out with a bunch of gunslingers. I had given the order to "cut" and was being helped up off the ground when Pep Corominas' gun went off accidentally, hitting me in the eyes. I was on the verge of losing my sight but luckily the ophthalmologist got the gunpowder out of my eyes in time

The gunfight almost had tragic consequences in *Mi amigo el vagabundo.*

and after a few days we were able to continue filming.

There was an amusing incident. One of our actors, made-up and costumed for his role, was arrested by the police on the underground; they thought he was a real pickpocket. The producers had to go and rescue him.

The film was finished without further setbacks and it was distributed once again by CIC and premiered at the Gran Vía Cinema. Sergio still reminds me that we didn't take him to the premiere of his film.

Now we come to a film with very special connotations. I refer to *El último kamikaze* (1984). This film took me at last to Egypt. It's worth recalling and, for the first time, writing about what happened to us there.

The film was a fast-moving action adventure about the ruthless struggle between organized crime syndicates. These murderous organizations used contract killers to eliminate, whenever necessary, those individuals who posed a threat to the syndicates' dirty dealings. In *El último Kamikaze*, two of these sharks have been engaged in a long-running contest to show who is the best, combined with the desire for revenge on the part of Christian Danton (Manuel Tejada) over his deadly rival El Kamikaze, whom nobody has ever seen. Danton is refined and cruel, using the most sophisticated methods of execution—poisoned darts, walking sticks with retractable steel blades—while El Kamikaze employs more brutal weapons like machine guns, automatic pistols and explosives, earning himself a reputation for savagery. Each in his own way is a maestro of crime.

Paul Naschy

El último Kamikaze (1984) was a fast-moving action adventure about the ruthless struggle between organized crime syndicates.

The movie was filmed on location in several countries, including Egypt. I have already written in the preceding pages how since childhood I was mad about the mysteries of the ancient inhabitants of the Nile valley. Later I read widely about the Egyptians and was captivated by the legends surrounding them, especially about the curses. *La vengeance de la momia* is there to prove it.

I set off for Cairo with my DP Julito Burgos, my assistant Andrés Vich and the actress Julia Saly. We had obtained all the necessary permits from the Egyptian embassy and we boarded the plane bound for the land of the pyramids with high hopes. Little did we know what we were in for.

We arrived at Cairo airport at dusk. I don't know if the cheap and nasty facility is any different today but back then it was utterly depressing. We filed down a dark corridor flanked by men wearing grubby tunics and looking like something from a George A. Romero movie. Their eyes seemed to bore through us and they lecherously ogled Julia Saly, a pretty woman with long blonde hair. Eventually we reached the baggage claim hall and waited for our luggage, including the movie material. Only our cases turned up. Two sinister looking policemen dressed in black watched us closely, both clutching submachine guns. Time went by and the gear still didn't appear. Be-

One of the many characters I portrayed in *El último Kamikaze.*

coming impatient, I addressed one of the guards. The shady looking character smiled at me, revealing rotten yellow teeth and told me in poor French to follow him. I smelled danger but I had no choice.

We went into a small office ventilated by a revolving fan hanging from the ceiling. Behind a cluttered desk sat an officer who looked me up and down with a sarcastic expression. His badges of rank were attached to his black uniform by safety pins and a deep scar adorned his cheek. From his belt hung a huge pistol. The office smelled of sour sweat and hashish. With a certain vehemence I demanded an explanation and the fellow, who kept picking at his rotten teeth with a toothpick, answered with menacing politeness, "For the time being we will hold on to the film material. These are not happy times and espionage must be kept under control." Then there was the problem of the blonde woman. "There is a big traffic in high class prostitutes and we have to check with our superiors." My nerves got the better of me and I lost my temper because all our papers were in order and, if the situation wasn't cleared up, we could have provoked a serious diplomatic incident. The guard brutally shoved the barrel of his submachine gun in my ribs and roughly pushed me aside; I was reminded of the incident in Hungary.

The sinister official stood up and put his dark face close to mine: "We are in Egypt and here your papers don't mean a thing. The Nile is very deep my friend and it swallows up many people." As he spoke he fingered the butt of his pistol. "Be careful with the blonde woman. The sheiks pay fortunes for them." Humiliated and frightened I thought there was only one thing to do, to go to the Spanish embassy. At passport control we were relieved of much money. I passed a sleepless night.

In the morning we went to the embassy and explained what had happened. The ambassador, a likable man, frowned and promised to do all he could, although he acknowledged that it wouldn't be easy. We didn't understand anything. We were assigned a man called Fromistra, the consul, who happened to be Greek, to act as our liaison. He was a tall, gray-haired man and he explained things to us thus:

> It's crazy to come to shoot a picture in this country without a big team and without protection. The cameras and film equipment are a great temptation. Not to mention blonde women. Not long ago four young Basque girls wanted to sail down the Nile so they hired two river craft. The sailors raped them. They went to report it to the police and the policemen raped them again. Two of them practically lost their mind. That's what Egypt is like away from the tourist circuits.

While the equipment was still retained, Fromista recommended a popular and influential taxi driver to take us scouting for locations. He was an expert at the job, having undertaken the same task for several American film companies. Yusuf, for that was the driver's name, was a friendly and canny fellow and faithful at all times. His help proved providential although even so we would have a hard time.

Our odyssey began and my dreams started to come true. Besides the taxi, Yusuf had two old all terrain vehicles which allowed us to visit some pretty inaccessible places. We visited the pyramids and the Sphinx at Gizeh. We also went to Sakkara, where we later filmed the famous third dynasty pyramid, surrounded by desert dogs. In Medinet-Habú we saw the great sanctuary of Ramses III and at Deir-el-Bahari we took a tour around the unusual structure of Hatshepsut temple. A plane journey took us to the present location of the Abu-Simbel colossus and we viewed the famous triad and reliefs of Ramses the Great. But the greatest moment came when I entered into the tomb of Tutankhamon in the Valley of Kings. It was as though I were dreaming.

After following a long and arduous procedure, the minister of culture, an inept individual dressed in a blue tunic, stamped a pile of papers which would allow us to film wherever we wanted, after handing over a goodly amount of money to the local bigwigs, of course. Eventually, thanks to the efforts of the embassy, we recovered our equipment and overcoming one difficulty after another we set to work. We filmed on location in Mem-kan-ka, Gizeh, Menfis, Sakkara and in the alleyways of Cairo itself. The resourceful and faithful Yusuf proved to be of invaluable help. In addition, the Egyptian government put at our disposal a polite young civil servant. Through the offices of our influential taxi driver we were able to purchase some highly valuable objects which had been obtained through obscure dealings with grave robbers.

While visiting the Cairo Museum and having been dazzled by the sight of the fabulous treasures found in the tomb of the legendary Tutankhamon, I entered a dark gallery, flanked by huge display cases where hundreds of sarcophagi were stored. One of those sinister policemen in black uniforms approached me, barking, "Dollar! Dollar!" while his right hand gripped the butt of his pistol. Luckily there came the sound of the voices of a group of tourists and the corrupt cop hurried away.

One night the receptionist at the hotel offered me the services of a pretty teenage girl. Although I replied that I wasn't interested, he sent her to me anyway. I repro-

El último kamikaze, once again distributed by CIC, received its premiere at Madrid's Gran Duque Cinema.

duced the incident in the film. We also witnessed a savage shoot out in the street when the men in black shot down two suspected fundamentalists. One of the policemen was also shot dead and the truth is that we were pretty scared. At the time it was feared that Libya would launch an attack and everywhere you looked there were sandbags and machine gun emplacements.

When we boarded the plane to fly back to Spain, despite all that had happened, I felt that the mystery of ancient Egypt had taken a hold of me and I knew that sooner or later I would return. And so I would, years later, although the truth is that with *El último kamikaze* my life took a sharp turn and I was plunged into a dark tunnel. I've often wondered if the curse of the Pharaohs had reached me as well.

El último kamikaze, once again distributed by CIC, received its premiere at Madrid's Gran Duque Cinema.

Many years had passed since the distant days of 1967 when I had made *La marca del hombre lobo*. As I have described, I had experienced many ups and downs. I had known the success, the bitterness, the joys and the sorrows of this tough profession. It was as if each movie was a baptism of fire. What's more, it was clear that my convictions and way of interpreting cinema set me apart from the hackneyed and unimaginative formulas predominant in Spanish filmmaking.

For José Frade I made a parody of my most emblematic character, the Wolfman. This time it wasn't the legendary Waldemar Daninsky, but a creature called HL (*Buenas Noches Señor Monstruo*, 1982). It was directed by Antonio Mercero in his usual efficient style and my colleagues in the cast were Luis Escobar as Dracula, Guillermo

As you can see, state-of-the-art special effects were used on the creature called HL in *Buenas Noches Señor Monstruo* **(1982).**

Montesinos as Quasimodo, Andrés Mejuto as Doctor Frankenstein, Fernando Bilbao as the Monster and the then famous *Piranha* from the popular children's series *Verano Azul*. The unimaginative story related the exploits of a group of retired classic monsters and their encounter with a bunch of unbearable child singers (the juvenile pop group Regaliz). However the film benefited from high production values and was a big hit with the kids. It's still often shown on TV.

Like Boris Karloff, Bela Lugosi, Lon Chaney and Christopher Lee, I had been forced into self-parody, although I had to face Regaliz instead of Bud Abbott and Lou Costello. The film angered my fans who practically accused me of prostituting their beloved Waldemar Daninsky.

Next we come to *Operación Mantis* (1984) and the biggest mistake of my life. This film came about in an odd way, in which Augusto Boué's opinion was a deciding factor. A new production for Acónito Films was broached and Boué, who always had an odd love-hate relationship toward me, for the first time commissioned another writer to write the screenplay, although based on an idea of mine. It was to be a spoof of the adventures of the famous James Bond. The final draft of the script was the work of Joaquín Oristrell and a big name cast was assembled for the film. The leading characters were played by José Luis López Vázquez, José Sazatornil Saza, Fedra Lorente, Antonio Gamero, Julia Saly, Yolanda Farr and myself, among others. It was the most costly production of my movie career, requiring huge sets and plenty of action sequences.

Operación Mantis (1984) was the biggest mistake of my life.

The story tells of the sinister schemes of a female criminal organization which, under the leadership of the cruel and ruthless Mantis, plans to exterminate all males. This criminal organization was known as Matriarch and was the equivalent of Spectre in the Bond movies. I played Sam, the daring Bond-style hero. The spectacular battle scenes and explosions required the services of a host of stuntmen and specialists and my unforgettable armorer, José Luis Chinchilla, did an impressive job. Years later José Luis inexplicably committed suicide. I was very upset by his tragic end.

The Japanese also had a hand in the production and one of their most famous clothes designers, the prestigious Chiji, king of fashion in Japan, came up with a number of luxurious creations exclusively for the film. The movie was made on location in Tokyo and Madrid. In the Japanese capital an expensive set was built in the form of a huge catwalk for a spectacular fashion parade of haute couture models. One of the dresses, a handmade number embroidered with gold thread, cost the exorbitant sum of 15,000,000 pesetas.

Unfortunately, *Operación Mantis* was a total box-office flop, leading to the downfall of Acónito Films and causing a rift between us and the Japanese who had never been very keen on the project.

The film had its premiere at Madrid's Coliseum cinema. I've always thought that our type of almost surreal humor was too far ahead of its time, when most people were still limited to the type of crude and lewd comedies made by Mariano Ozores (akin to the British *Carry On...* movies). Although this ill-fated production sold well abroad later on, disaster had already overtaken us. It was the beginning of a veritable martyrdom for me. However my final downfall was still to come and it would be linked to the death of my father.

Paul Naschy

Augusto Boué was a pusillanimous fellow, always afraid of trouble and worried about losing his pension. He liquidated Acónito as fast as he could and made me sign documents that I wasn't even able to read. My family bereavement had left me in the grip of a deep depression. I remember the scandalous situation of a 2,000,000 peseta debt with Sincronía studios that had been allowed to grow to 6,000,000 thanks to the totally abusive compound interest charges. The two Enriques who ran the studio in those days were cunning devils indeed. To be sure, they split their roles perfectly: one was the hard bargaining, intransigent type while the other was apparently conciliatory and warm-hearted. To make sure the debt was settled, Augusto struck a deal with

Unfortunately, *Operación Mantis* was a total box-office flop, leading to the downfall of Acónito Films.

them. We would concede 50% of three films to them. Then, according to a "gentleman's agreement," they would return the percentage once the debt had been cleared. As was to be expected, the debt was duly paid off but Sincronía still retained the percentage. These two sly customers certainly took advantage of the weakness of one and the illness of the other.

But that wasn't the full extent of the debacle because Boué sold *El último kamikaze* to a Belgian buyer. This individual asked him for the negative so as to avoid the costs of making an internegative in order to strike new copies in Brussels. I smelled a rat but Augusto was so adamant that once again I gave in; the truth is that I wasn't fit for much. The material was sent but the fellow never returned the negative. In short, everything was sold off in record time and the work of years was gone in short order. In those days we were easy prey for vultures.

My only consolation is that there is a copy of *El último kamikaze* in the vaults of the National Film Library, ensuring the preservation of this wonderful action movie featuring a priceless turn by José Bódalo as a cruel Mafia boss.

Farewell to My Father

As often as I could I used to visit my father at his furrier's establishment in Calle Princesa where I'd find him clad in his white coat and smoking his inevitable cigar. We chatted about many things and it was comforting for me to know that the shadow of the patriarch was still far reaching. Strength and optimism oozed from this open-minded, likable and humane Basque. He was now 74 but looked 15 years younger. He still went out hunting with his dog and used to take long hikes along the river banks where, as a skilled angler, he used to catch trout. He continued to go horseback riding and was still a great marksman.

One morning we recalled the time when at the Gavilanes game reserve I shot an enormous stag with an extraordinary set of 14-point antlers. This hunting prowess of mine delighted my father but put me off hunting for life. The sight of the magnificent creature, almost the size of a horse, glassy-eyed and with blood streaming from a huge wound in its side was enough to turn me away from hunting for good. The animal's head presided majestically over the living room of our house in Lozoya for many years.

Some mornings Jaime de Mora y Aragón used to drop in. He had been a great friend of our family since the days when we used to spend our holidays at the Golf Hotel in Guadalmina. Jaime was quite a character, fun-loving and easy going, as flamboyant as you like but intelligent with it. Often he'd tell me about his days as a taxi driver or the tremendous bouts he'd fought as a wrestler! I remember him saying: "I'm not Laurence Olivier, but I play the part of Jaime de Mora y Aragón better than anyone." Actually, this brother of Queen Fabiola occasionally acted in movies, albeit only in banal domestic comedies. Then again, he never had great ambitions to be a movie star. He sometimes invited me to the nightclub where he played the piano.

We laughed as we recalled the exploits of Jimmy, the gigantic great Dane which Jaime had given us. For example, the time he had eaten Carmen Polo's gloves. [Carmen Polo was the wife of Spain's dictator, General Franco.] She had come into the shop with the wives of several other bigwigs to look at mink coats. My father put things right by making her a gift of a fur rug. Then there was the time some thieves broke into the shop, unaware of the great Dane's presence. In the morning when the shop was opened a hammer and chisels were found on the floor and there was blood all over the place.

I was saddened by the death of Jaime de Mora some years later, and recalled those happy times with melancholy.

In my father's shop we would reminisce about the famous people who used to visit the establishment to purchase diverse garments. Sofía Loren ordered a red velvet dress which was so tight that my father pointed out that if she sat down it would split. The actress smiled and told him that she was only going to wear the dress once, to greet the crowds from the door of the plane on her arrival in Rome. Stephen Boyd—the protagonist of *Fall Of The Roman Empire*—had a complex because he believed his arms

My father, my son Bruno and my mother pose together on the set of *La Historial de Espana A Traves del Palacio Real de Madrid*.

were too short and his back too narrow and they had to come up with the most ingenious arguments to convince him that a garment fitted him properly. On one memorable occasion Frank Sinatra and Cary Grant bumped into each other in the shop, each having come in to commission a chinchilla fur wrap, which happened to be for the same actress. John Wayne bought several leather and hide jackets with Indian style fringes which he actually wore in some of his films. Charlton Heston was another customer and he used to haggle like he was in an Arab kasbah. Other well known characters who made purchases in the shop were Jorge Negrete, María Félix, Danielle Darrieux, Anthony Mann and Orson Welles. We became quite friendly with Mario Moreno *Cantinflas*. At one stage in my life I even entertained the hare-brained idea of making a film with him. My father spoke to the actor on the phone but, although he seemed quite encouraging, nothing came of it in the end.

In short, the leather and fur retail outlet, which my uncle Emilio had decorated, lived through many years of splendor. However, happy memories always seem doomed to be cut short by some tragic destiny.

It was around the time when *Operación Mantis* caused the downfall of Acónito Films that something happened which I would never get over completely and which haunts me to this day. My father suffered a heart attack, which he survived by a miracle. He was a strong, healthy man and after several months he appeared to be completely recovered. But the sword of Damocles still hung over his head. He went off to fish in Manzanares el Real, driving his own car. Mid-morning on that ill-fated day we got a phone call. Elvira and I had been out and we heard the dreadful news on our return. Straight-away we got the car out and set off. After driving along some infernal dirt tracks we reached the spot by the river where two young lads confirmed my father's death. It was a brutal shock and I just broke down. The body had been taken to the Manzanares Hospital and there a nurse informed us that it was on its way by ambulance to Madrid.

On June 20, 1984, I entered into a dark tunnel. Thousands of images flashed by inside my brain like a movie. It was simply terrible. My father was dead, his protecting shadow was no more. To rub salt into the wound, I had to make all the funeral arrangements, including the purchase of the coffin. This time the grim reaper had struck a really hard blow.

I well remember the wake at the Ramón y Cajal Hospital. My mother was absolutely shattered and I had to thank so many people for their condolences, without really taking it all in. The worst would come later, when my father had been finally laid to rest in the San Justo y Pastor cemetery. My mother ordered the figure of the Virgin of Lourdes, which my uncle Emilio had sculpted, to be placed on his tombstone.

I was apparently still alive. I wanted to overcome this drama and I even started training at the gymnasium again. Prior to the awful event I had been able to shift impressive weights but afterward my strength abandoned me completely. Previously I had been lifting 160 kilos but now even trying to move 40 kilos taxed my strength to its limits. I hit rock bottom one day when, after showering, I found I couldn't even manage to towel myself. I had truly become one of the living dead.

Depression had taken such a hold of me that I had trouble even getting out of bed. I shut myself up at home and totally dropped out of circulation. I gave up sporting competitions and needless to say I gave up making movies. It got so bad that I couldn't even bear to hear anyone talking about the profession which had been the driving force in my life for so many years. My wife and my friend Takeda did their utmost to help me but I had become psychiatrist fodder. I only wanted to die and more than once I contemplated suicide. Something inside me had been shattered and putting me back together would be a tall order. Financial ruin and the death of my father had driven me to the edge.

I remember how whenever I was told that Augusto Boué was on the phone for me I would break out in a cold sweat because he always called to give me bad news or to get me to sign away the company. Once more the telephone had become an instrument of the Devil. I was treated by doctor Cullaut Varela, who gradually brought me back to the land of the living. I think I turned down some film work. Needless to say my relations with Japan were put under unbearable strain. Elvira had to go out to work to maintain the household. I was mentally blocked, and shut myself away, unshaven and clad in my dressing gown, chain smoking my way through an endless stream of cigarettes. I was locked in a prison, one I had created for myself in the depths of my own soul; it was far worse than any real prison with iron bars. I didn't write, I didn't draw, I just smoked and rotted inside.

A long time passed in this fashion, until the day when, still not fully recovered, I decided that I had to do something about it. Now, as I sit here in my study, it seems miraculous that I am able to write about all this and that I still go daily to train in the gym just like in the old days.

I sought help from Antonio Jiménez Rico, who seemed to me to be a good fellow, although I didn't know him personally. I thought he was kind-hearted, and what's more, he came from Burgos. I wrote him a letter, pretty pathetic I suppose, and he sent me one hell of a reply; according to him, I appeared to be wholly responsible for everything that was happening to me.

The other person I turned to was Juan Piquer Simón. I went to visit him like a shipwrecked man clinging onto a piece of wreckage. I had thought him more benevolent than he actually proved to be. He was polite enough, and I called at his office in Calle Pradillo many times. Looking back, I recall him as a facetious person with a superiority complex, who lectured me on the ins and outs of international markets. Talk about "coals to Newcastle." At the time he had two movies in the pipeline and had he employed me in any capacity whatsoever I would have been eternally grateful to him given my precarious economic situation. Thinking back on it I get really mad at myself. Paul Naschy was a star then. Why did I grovel so?

My father in a photo taken shortly before his death.

I have only ever asked two favors of people in the film industry and such were their replies. Never again!

Quite a few years later I bumped into Juan Piquer Simón again. He's aged a lot and needs to take care of himself.

Seeing how hard it was to get back to filmmaking, I decided to look elsewhere, although this turned out worse still. Those who recognized me, who were many, would exclaim with more than a touch of spiteful sarcasm, "Why, if it isn't Paul Naschy! I can't believe it, someone as famous as you asking for a job. Surely you must be rolling in it." For a lot of gray little men it was time for revenge. They now had the chance to humiliate someone who had done something different, someone who had surpassed a barrier which they, with their sheep-like adherence to convention, would never go beyond.

Two last straws broke the camel's back. First I went to see Rafael Mateo Tari in his office and after giving me a warm welcome he presented me with a book of religious texts to help me pray and, with a pat on the back, sent me on my way. The last straw of all was added by a cousin of mine who started putting me off all the time and eventually refused to come to the phone at all.

Yes sir, they were hard times and my outlook on life was ever closer to that of *El caminante*, the Devil defeated by mankind. I was living the parable in the flesh.

Two long years went by and I still hadn't thrown off the deep depression I'd been suffering. My wife was working on projects for Japan with Takeda and thanks to her the family was managing to make ends meet. On the other hand, genre movies, the cornerstone of the industry, had become a thing of the past. The State only granted advance subsidies, some of them astronomical, to serious films, as was only right and proper. I was amazed to read of money being advanced to productions which never got made. Spanish cinema had gone into a nose dive and box-office takings had fallen to really alarming levels. It was the end for many professionals in the business and consequently there were fewer pictures being made.

In 1986 I was approached by some Basque lads who offered me a part in a short film. These youngsters, captained by Luis Guridi, formed a team which was successively known as Escuadra Cobra, La Escuadlilla Amalilla and finally La Cuadrilla. I first worked with them in a short film shot in San Sebastián with the title *Pez* (1986). It was about a doctor who had to treat a strange patient, a sideshow diver who due to an accident was gradually mutating into a fish. I arrived in San Sebastián in pretty bad shape, I even had trouble memorizing my lines, but the truth is that the experience did me a lot of good because I was back among the cameras, lights and everything I had missed so much. I also took part in a film by Popocho Ayestarán, member of the great Javier Gurruchaga's pop group Orquesta Mondragón.

I worked with La Cuadrilla again on another short, *SSS* (1986), which was about a group of hooded men with the power to levitate. *SSS* was filmed in a studio in Madrid, and I was joined in the cast by Tomás Zori, Iñaqui Miramón, Maru Valdivieso, José María Cafarell, Luis Barbero and Carmelo Espinosa.

Just when it looked like I was making a recovery, I had a serious relapse and it was back to confinement, chain smoking, the dressing gown and the stubble and, of course, back to bed. Depression had sunk its claws into me once again. I couldn't sleep and I became a vegetable, with no stimuli and no goals.

At the time I was great friends with the actor Eduardo Fajardo, a friendship going back to the time we had worked together on the documentary about El Escorial monastery. Eduardo was a keen plate collector, and he had even managed to obtain pieces belonging to Napoleon, Elizabeth II and some painted by Picasso. He also kept in a heavy oak chest the skulls and parts of the skeletons of his father and brothers. Fajardo, who helped me out a lot, came to my house to persuade me to accept the role of the villain in a low-budget picture which was being directed by a flamboyant filmmaker from Mallorca by the name of Martín Garrido. I would play a ruthless murderer nicknamed *El Murciano*. Though he was bad through and through, he had one sentimental compulsion: to visit the grave of his favorite niece. *El Murciano* tended the grave himself, prayed and wept before the girl's last resting place.

We shot the film on the most sordid locations in Palma and a number of singular, picturesque low-lifes took part as extras or actors. One stood out in particular, a Fellini style prostitute with a huge pair of jugs.

In the end my character was gunned down by the brave and daring inspector played by Martín Garrido himself. Fajardo played a humane and weary chief of police whose patience and long experience offset the impetuousness of Garrido's young inspector. Two unpleasant things occurred during filming. A drug addict died of an overdose and a black councilor of the *Partido Popular* was knifed by a thug who was after the man's gold bracelet.

Mordiendo la vida (1986) was a film which obviously didn't do a great deal for my film career but helped lift me from a depression.

    Mordiendo la vida (1986) was a film which obviously didn't do a great deal for my film career but which I've dedicated a few lines to because it signaled the beginning of my escape from the Dantesque black hole of depression, something I'll always be grateful for. Eduardo Fajardo also included me in the group of competent actors and actresses he gathered together to work as dubbers. We dubbed a few films, including, funnily enough, one of Amando de Ossorio's, then for some reason he disbanded the team.

    Eduardo disappeared from my life suddenly, without a word, without a farewell. Years later I found out that he'd opened a fabulous restaurant in Almería and that he'd married a much younger woman. Later on my fondly remembered José Antonio Rojo, my best film editor, now unfortunately deceased, told me he'd seen Fajardo walking with some difficulty with the aid of a walking stick. Eduardo Fajardo is a person for whom I feel real affection, and who helped me out when times were hard. I don't know if we'll meet again but in any case I wish him all the best.

El aullido del diablo (*Howl of the Devil*, 1988) was like my own howl of anguish.

Paul Naschy

Another Decisive Year

So we come to 1987, a year in which several major events took place in my life, some almost as dramatic as the death of my father.

Fortunately I had overcome my depression and felt in pretty good shape. I decided to prepare a project about the life of my admired Gustavo Adolfo Bécquer to take to the Ministry of Culture in order to apply for an advance subsidy as so many others were doing. Naturally, beforehand I needed some advice since it was going to be a costly project. I had a long standing acquaintance who worked at the Ministry and much to my amazement and chagrin this person told me not to bother to apply because I would certainly be turned down. The script lies gathering dust in a drawer in my desk.

I can't understand it. Why do such things happen in our country? Why we have to put up with those who lurk in the shadows deciding who will receive handouts and who won't? There's always somebody pulling strings, those who prey on the fear of others; fear of losing a job, fear of not being given a contract, fear of losing future prospects, fear of not being able to earn a living: fear, fear, fear. Then there are the powerful clans who dictate their own unwritten laws which subvert and prostitute everything.

On TV, in the papers, in all the mass media, we see what a show the irritating, self-righteous, wisecracking, histrionic politicians put on for our benefit, but they are the only ones who actually show their faces. Those who hold real power will never be known to us. They are like creatures of the netherworld, lurking in the midst of an impenetrable darkness.

The following episode is revealing in this respect. A few years ago, before I was its president, the Spanish Film Writers' Guild (Círculo de Escritoires Cinematográficos de España, CEC) organized a tribute to the great filmmaker Ana Mariscal. The event took place in the Doré cinema, seat of Spain's National Film Archive, and at one point in the proceedings the director, writer and actress spoke about one of her novels which had been prohibited under the Franco regime and which had finally seen the light of day. She said the following words, which I'll never forget:

> The Franco regime eliminated artists by firing squad. Now we have a more refined and cruel way of getting rid of them, by neutralizing free thinking, giving work to certain men or certain women merely on the say so of some unknown who makes decisions in some hidden place. I'd rather face the firing squad, it's a lot quicker!

Ana hadn't directed a film for many years while others had worked non-stop. Will we ever be rid of these dark confabulations? In my opinion it isn't so much a question of the attitude of official bodies but rather the fault of the lurkers, the climbers, those who flatter and ingratiate, the smart guys who are skilled at wheeling-dealing in the corridors of power.

But let us return to my career in 1987. I had long been considering a pet project, namely a horror fantasy film with Olvido "Alaska" Gara [the flamboyant Spanish punk-pop singer who led various groups in the '80s and '90s, including one called Fangoria]. She's a person whom I've always liked and admired. Her peculiar personality appealed to me and I was also aware of her love of horror movies. I got in touch with her, we had several meetings and, together with Luis Murillo, we started work on the script, which was obviously a made-to-order vehicle for Alaska. Once the screenplay was finished I got in touch with a film company who agreed to make the movie. It was a film which had all the makings of a cult movie. But Alaska's agents demanded an astronomical fee which the film company were unwilling to meet. It was a crying shame. As it happens, I recently saw Olvido in *Sólo se muere dos veces* (*You Only Die Twice*), popping a ping pong ball with her well endowed bust. I still feel the same fondness and admiration for her.

When I was least expecting it, my old friend Ramón Planas called me. Ramón held me in esteem as a scriptwriter and it was thanks to him that I had written *Los monstruos del terror* and *Disco rojo*. There was the chance of making a movie and he wanted to introduce me to the producer, Juan Gómez. We met at the Cuzco Hotel and I showed him the script of *El aullido del diablo* (*Howl of the Devil*, 1988), which I had written years previously and which had been sleeping at the bottom of a drawer. It's worth taking time out to examine the history surrounding this script.

It all started with someone we might describe as a rather bizarre character who I had met years before at the Sitges Festival. The Bizarre One was fairly tall, pot-bellied, with acromegalic, Frankensteinish features and, to top it all, he was a stutterer. For many years this gentleman had written letters to the specialized press slagging me off, but on that occasion in Sitges we became friends, or so I thought. That's how I came to get mixed up with him in a filmmaking venture, and how I came to start writing this particular script.

A certain Catalonian lady showed an interest in producing the movie. She spoke to several actors and technicians and got in touch with various studios and things seemed to be on the move. But suddenly she turned 'round and said that there was no money available and, what's more, she was facing prosecution for her involvement in a particularly nasty affair: the attempted murder of the president of the Catalonian Boxing Federation. It all sounded like a cock and bull story to me but, in any case, that was the end of that and the script was put on ice.

The script had to wait until 1987, when Juan Gómez assured me that the film was going into production. I called up Augusto Boué and asked him to collaborate with Ramón Planas on the pre-production. I don't know what happened between them but a few days later Ramón left the project and Augusto remained as sole production manager.

The screenplay, which was pretty far out, told the story of a failed actor called Héctor Doriani who lives in an isolated chalet in the Sierra near Madrid. The sinister house is also inhabited by his nephew, whom he treats in a cruel and authoritarian fashion, and his brooding manservant, a one time mortuary attendant and Devil worshipper who's adept at the Black Arts. This servant wears a black glove to hide the

EL AULLIDO DEL DIABLO

PAUL NASCHY • CAROLINE MUNRO • HOWARD VERNON

Dirigido por: PAUL NASCHY

LORION

scars caused when some students poured sulfuric acid over him, after finding out he'd been practicing necrophilia with the corpses of dead women—shades of Diana Lorys' fetishistic prosthesis in *House of Psychotic Women.*

Carmen, a stunningly beautiful women from the nearby village, comes to work at the house. For a long time she'd been the mistress of the village priest, but she's ambitious and knows she has Héctor in the palm of her hand. The Dorianis are an old and distinguished family rolling in money. Héctor had a brother, Alex, also an actor, who had committed suicide by blowing his brains out. Alex, in his film career, had been a kind of Lon Chaney, Sr., a great star of horror films. On his death Héctor became sole beneficiary of his will and legal guardian of Adrián, Alex's son. The sadistic Héctor, bitter with envy, torments his unfortunate nephew by telling him that his father could only act when hidden behind a mask and had wasted his life churning out cheap horror movies. On the other hand he, Héctor Doriani, had played in works by Pirandello, Ionesco, Shakespeare and other great playwrights.

But Héctor tries to blot out his own true failure as an actor by playing out sadistic sexual episodes with women he picks up on the road. While he's in costume and made up as Rasputin, Fu Manchu or Bluebeard, someone spies on his perversions through the eyes of a portrait of Gilles de Rais. Meanwhile, Adrián has created a fantasy wonderland inhabited by the cherished monsters his father used to play—Quasimodo, the Frankenstein Monster, Mister Hyde, The Phantom of the Opera, and even Waldemar Daninsky the Wolfman.

Mysteriously, every one of the women who comes to the house and agrees to take part in Héctor's sado-erotic games is brutally murdered. Carmen, seduced by the power and wealth of her employer, gives in to his advances and so becomes his lover. This

In *El aullido del diablo,* Adrián has created a fantasy wonderland inhabited by the cherished monsters his father used to play such as the Phantom of the Opera.

provokes Don Damián, the priest, to a jealous frenzy and he vows revenge. To do his dirty work the clergyman utilizes Zacarias, a drunken tramp who used to be a schoolmaster but has been reduced to an alcoholic by a failed love affair. Eric, the devil-worshipping servant, uses Black Magic to summon up the specter of Alex. It turns out that Alex, Eric's friend and true master, hadn't committed suicide but had in fact been murdered by his brother and Adrián's mother, who were having an adulterous affair.

The film's climax is claustrophobic, unwholesome and sinister. Inside the cursed house time seems to have stood still.

The musical leitmotif of the film is *Dies Irae*—bringing back memories of Barbara Muller, Klaus Rabe and the supposed Black Mass in Munich—and an entire sequence unfolds to the strains of Albinoni's *Adagio*, the same musical background which had accompanied me when I was writing *La marca del hombre lobo* at my parents' home. Moreover, as can be seen from the reading of these memoirs, I included in the film all the things that had a special significance for me personally: old movie serials, terrifying fairy tales, the legendary Universal monsters, the scorn of certain critics towards my work, the many envious and spiteful characters who had had an adverse effect on my life. As a way of getting it out of my system I had the story conclude with a totally apocalyptic vengeance. It finally transpires that Adrián, the apparently innocent child, is in fact responsible for summoning up all the evil, as he is marked with the triple six, the sign of the Antichrist.

Howl of the Devil was like my own howl of anguish, a painful catharsis which finally liberated me from long repressed phobias and obsessions.

Suddenly the Bizarre One reappeared and, in a display of profound mental subnormality, started a smear campaign against me in several publications, claiming to have

As the Frankenstein Monster with my son Sergio in *El aullido del diablo*.

written the script himself. He went so far as to send a letter to my producer, continuing his attacks against me and offering his own services for the film.

This weird movie also gave me the chance to meet and work with Caroline Munro, a very beautiful woman, the prettiest of all the actresses I've ever known, a true professional and an extraordinary human being. She became a great friend and confidante to my youngest son Sergio and they were always together.

Caroline played the part of Carmen, while Sergio was the evil Adrián. We have kept in touch over the years and I'd like to work with her again.

Another enjoyable collaboration was that of Howard Vernon, a magnificent actor, and a wonderful person. I consider myself fortunate to have been able to work with him. I read his biography in Paris and I was moved by the admiration and affection with which he talks about me and the film. Howard, as I know you are listening to me up in heaven, thank you. Give my fondest regards to Boris Karloff and Peter Cushing. I once spoke to Vincent Price as well, try him too, maybe he remembers me.

Howl of the Devil also holds an extra appeal for me: Although it utilizes universal legends, it remains a totally domestic horror fantasy. During the incident-filled shoot, carried out almost entirely in my country house at Lozoya del Valle, we suffered a number of mishaps. The entire crew, except for Caroline and Sergio, came down with a stomach bug after drinking from a polluted water source. It was quite something to see the camera operator toiling at the camera, suddenly throwing up from time to time while the rest of us accompanied him in the ceremony. Then we had a visit from the Civil Guard after we blew up a dummy with explosives—they thought it had been a terrorist bomb.

Memoirs of a Wolfman

Howard Vernon in *El aullido del diablo*

I must also make mention of the wonderful performances given by Fernando Hilbeck as the priest, and Cris Huerta as the drunken tramp. Fernando Florido created the superb makeup aided by his wife, the lovely Loli, and what can I say about Julito Burgos whose photography was once again splendid. I did however have serious problems with the producers although luckily our paths haven't crossed since then. I exclude Juan Gómez who seems to me to be a decent sort.

A whole book could be written about this production because its trajectory was one long string of incidents, some tragic, some unusual, with something happening almost daily. For instance the film's distributor, whose name I don't recall, was driving back from Paris when he was involved in a crash and killed outright. This drama undoubtedly changed the course of the whole project.

A group of keen youngsters filmed a *Making of...* documentary but have been unable to show it because the owner of the movie's negative—I don't know who it is—demands an astronomical price for the rights to the excerpts from the film.

This is what critic Adolfo Camilo had to say about *Howl of the Devil*:

> The best cast Naschy has ever been able to
> assemble in his most way-out film, a summary
> of his movie career, and a summary of his life
> seen as a bitter chronicle of the progressive
> ostracism to which Naschy and all around him
> have been subjected. A cameo appearance by
> Waldemar Daninsky constitutes a self tribute.

Extraordinary acting, in their respective roles,
by Ms. Munro and Howard Vernon.

I have a few more things to add. Tony Pueo was the so-called art director. Although he was said to have won an Oscar, I say so-called because he took it as his *mission* to be blind drunk all day long. The day we shot the Quasimodo scene he hadn't brought any of the gear, the costumes weren't ready and neither were the sets. I had to improvise Quasimodo's hump with a large cushion. Things came to the point where one afternoon Fernando Florido and I had to dress the set for the butler's Black Magic ceremony ourselves. Finally Juan Gómez had enough and he sacked Pueo.

El aullido del diablo, shot in English in four weeks, was a real *tour de force* for me as an actor. I played 12 characters, each well-rounded and all believable. I really had a ball. Today in the USA and other countries it's a cult movie.

This was the last film I made at the family's country home where such productions as *El Espanto Surge de la tumba, Jack el destripador de Londres, Los crimenes de Petiot* and *Todos los gritos del silencio* had also been filmed. Shortly after the film was finished my mother sold the place. One night long ago the steaming corpse of Alaric de Marnac rolled down those steep stone steps and Eric the sinister butler stumbled down

them to finally be blown to smithereens by the unleashed forces of evil. Lozoya: The End. A major part of Paul Naschy's world disappeared with it.

Now I'm going to speak about a very special woman with whom I was reacquainted after a gap of several years, just as *El aullido del diablo* was starting to come together. I refer to the actress, journalist and writer Isabel Pisano.

I met Isabel in producer Jaime Prades' office in 1968. She was a breathtaking beauty who was working as a secretary in the office of Samuel Bronston's old partner. It's even possible that she was the one who had typed up the manuscript of *Los monstruos del terror*, who knows? Prades had just finished *Pampa Salvaje* with music by Waldo de los Ríos which is probably how the composer met Pisano, and eventually they married. Waldo was an extremely

As Fu Manchu in *El aullido del diablo*

With Caroline Munro in *El aullido del diablo*

talented musician who had such memorable hits as the famous "Ode to Joy." He also composed countless film soundtracks including *Curro Jiménez*.

Somebody suggested Isabel for *El aullido del diablo*. At that time she was quite well-known for having appeared in the Bigas Lunas movies *Caniche* and *Bilbao*. I thought it wasn't a bad idea and Pisano flew from Rome to Madrid to discuss the project. Of course she had changed somewhat but she still possessed that rare animal magnetism that she had all those years before. She invited us to dinner at her luxurious chalet, the home she had shared with Waldo, and she showed me the white grand piano her husband had used for his compositions. We became friends and I used to visit her often. She knew all about the Italian film business and was friendly with Fellini, Sordi, Gassman and Mastroianni, among others. We talked about writing a script together based on an old idea of mine for an original thriller but we never finished it.

She told me all kinds of interesting things about her assignments as a journalist, some of which had been pretty dangerous. I was particularly impressed by the tribulations she'd gone through in order to interview Muammar El Gaddafi. She told me that he was a natural born seducer and she had spent several nights in his *jaima* in the desert. She made me a present of a book of interviews with Italian filmmakers and a weird little novel called *Los diabólicos de Blois*. She was undoubtedly a comely and ambitious woman, but also talented. The idols of her youth had been Sartre, Simone de Beauvoir and, above all, Camus—as shown by her somewhat existentialist musing: "I am destined to love the dead." She appeared to me to be obsessed by Waldo's suicide and she showed me the bedroom in which he'd shot himself. I seem to recall that Isabel had been in Rome when the tragedy happened, making the blow all the harder to take. She was writing a book about her life with the musician, undoubtedly as a kind of therapy.

Sometimes I would take her to see movies of mine. We saw *El huerto del francés, El retorno del hombre lobo* and she was particularly fascinated by *El caminante*. One morning she got really angry because she claimed that the music accompanying the title credits on one of my pictures was ripped off from a Waldo de los Ríos soundtrack.

One day she told me she was going to Montevideo because her mother was not well. I warned her to be back in time to make the movie. I never heard from her again and naturally we started shooting with Caroline Munro. When shooting had been completed and the film was being edited Isabel returned. We had a cool meeting in a Madrid hotel and I then saw her again on a radio show with Emilio Romero and later at a dinner party given by a journalist friend. I never met her again in person but I saw the photos of her posing totally naked in a magazine and more recently I saw the newspaper notices on the occasion of the presentation of her book about Waldo de los Ríos, *Obsession*. Such was Isabel Pisano, quite a character.

But 1987 still held another awful experience in store for me. Death was once again lurking amid the shadows of Destiny. Masurao Takeda, my faithful friend, my brother, the one who never let me down, was working tirelessly to restore our lost prestige in Japan and his efforts were starting to pay. Once more doors were opening and the future looked rosy. He had worked hard and well, like all Japanese, and coming from Samurai stock his tenacity, courage and patience made him a force to be reckoned with.

One evening he called me up in a state of some excitement, having just returned from Tokyo bearing excellent news. The following day at noon we had to go to the notary public's office to formalize the constitution of a new company. But February 17, 1987, Takeda failed to arrive at the notary's office. It was the first time in his life that he'd missed an appointment. I realized straight away that something serious must have happened to him. Elvira and I tried to call him but the phone just went on ringing. He was my only friend and in my heart I knew that he was dead. We went straight round to his home but nobody answered the door. Elvira was unwilling to accept what I kept telling her:"Takeda's dead! He's dead!" When the police broke into the flat they found the body. It was dreadful, another blow that I just couldn't take.

At the autopsy it was discovered that he had advanced pancreatic cancer. I put two and two together and a lot of things became clear. He hadn't touched a drop of alcohol for almost a year when previously he'd never ended a meal

My dear friend Masurao Takeda

Competing at the Powerlifting Championships in Sydney

without a small glass of Patxarán liqueur. He'd been following a strict diet, which I had assumed was part of his fitness training program. Above all, he'd said some enigmatic things which, although not out of keeping with the man's character, now suddenly made sense. He'd said, "One day I shall have to leave. I will go away but I'll leave everything fixed up. You won't have any more financial worries. Everything will be just fine." Unfortunately the illness prevented all his plans from coming to fruition. We made all the arrangements and his brothers came to take the body home. He was 46 years old. The Spanish Judo Federation held a memorial service in his honor. They placed his kimono and his red and white belt on the altar. I cried bitterly, inconsolably. A unique and wonderful part of my life had gone with him. My friend had gone.

I returned to darkness and oblivion. I needed to get away from movies, at least for a while. Maybe I'm saying this because deep down I don't want to acknowledge the fact it was I who had been abandoned by the film world. I needed to get back to something that would keep me totally absorbed and I thought of painting but, marvelous activity that it is, it would only have kept me even more shut in and I would probably have gone over the edge again. Eventually I settled on sport and returned to weightlifting.

I went in for powerlifting which requires more strength than suppleness. I qualified for the over 40s master category. Despite their age, most of my competitors were still pretty tough and I had my work cut out to keep up with them. Luckily they later started an over 50s category. In any event I was champion of Spain in 1989.

At that time I was going to a gym where a lot of hard guys used to hang out, low-lifers all, but they could lift weights like cranes, providing me with good competitors to measure my progress by. The fauna that frequented this gym deserve a few lines. Most of them were professional bully boys, bodyguards or nightclub bouncers. They would discreetly carry out certain services such as collecting debts, roughing up anybody who had a score pending with certain clients, breaking bones in unfortunate accidents and, for more money, even going on to more serious stuff. They could also take a hand in cases of adultery. All this was done with remarkable professionalism. One of these thugs, whom we shall call El Picado, used to tell me in great detail about the techniques they employed. They would find out all about the target's routines, find out which market his wife shopped at, which school his children went to and everything else that could be used to "put the screws on" before resorting to actual physical violence. Re-sults were usually obtained once the family came under threat. I remember that El Picado used to wear a couple of stilettos taped to his legs.

These characters respected me because, to their way of thinking, I was a living legend. After a few months I decided to leave that gym and go and train elsewhere. Some time later I read in the paper that two of them had been arrested for burning down a disco. Another was found dead at his home. It was a fellow for whom I had found work as an extra in some film or other.

Then somebody entered my life whom I wish I had never met. His name was Sidney Ling and he was a Dutchman. He told me he was a film producer and he was keen to promote me abroad. We had a first meeting and he showed me photographs of several fairly renowned international actors and actresses whom he claimed to repre-sent. I needed to believe in something which would restore my lost self-esteem and agreed to go along with him because, as I imagined, I had nothing to lose.

Later on Ling organized a lunch date with Amando de Ossorio. He had some idea about us making a film together. It was such a flimsy project that neither of us was convinced, Amando even less than me. I didn't see Amando again but unfortunately I did see Sidney Ling again.

One fine day he called me up and asked me to fly out to Amsterdam to star in a film he was going to direct. It didn't sound very promising but I agreed and off I went to Amsterdam to shoot a thing called *Shadows of Blood* (1989). It was a crazy story about two serial killers who compete with each other to see who is the greater sicko and who can murder the most people. That's all I want to say about that.

Following my appearance in the ineffable Sidney Ling's oddity I decided to go away to Egypt with my wife. In spite of all the unpleasant things that I had experienced during the making of *El último Kamikaze,* I felt a genuine nostalgia for the unique, enigmatic Land of the Pharaohs. This time we weren't taking any chances and we booked through a well-known travel agent. We went on an unforgettable cruise along the Nile, stopping off to visit Karnak, Abidos, Edfu, Luxor, the three great pyramids and the Sphinx at Gizeh, the mosques and the bazaars.

Later we flew to Abu-Simbel and made trips out to visit ancient monuments, stop-ping off at the nearby villages. In one of these places something happened to us that sounds like a gag from a comedy film.

We disembarked and, surrounded by children, made our way towards the place where the temple we had come to see was located. We wound our way through the

A photograph taken at the Temple of Amon on our trip to Egypt.

narrow streets where the owners of souvenir shops offered us everything under the sun: T-shirts, phony antiques, papyrus scrolls. In one of these shops Elvira spotted some tablecloths and went over to have a look. As it was so hot I was wearing a short-sleeved shirt, and my arms are not exactly what you'd call skinny. There were two men dressed in typical Egyptian tunics, the younger of the two kept looking at my arms and making gestures which I didn't understand. When he took me by the hand and led me to a table it dawned on me—he wanted a bout of arm wrestling. Although I refused, the man made certain gestures implying that I was too scared to accept the challenge. This was too much for me and I decided to do it. My opponent wasn't very well built but he had one hell of a grip. I eventually beat him, after a mighty struggle. The Egyptian went crazy and jumped me as if he wanted to bite my jugular. We fell to the ground and rolled around like two lovers in a passionate embrace amid piles of tablecloths, shirts and rugs. The bugger was doing his utmost to kill me and things were starting to look really nasty. In the end the spectators who'd been attracted to the scene pulled us apart. I was dripping sweat and the other fellow had a bloody nose. Elvira hadn't bought any tablecloths but she'd got two or three T-shirts. She had been unaware of the whole episode. When we left my challenger looked at me with murder in his eyes while the others were all smiles.

Later we went to visit Cairo Museum where Elvira was dazzled by all the wonders on display: the priceless treasures of Tutankhamon and the perfection of the statues of Ra-Hotep and his wife. She insisted that he looked just like Clark Gable—it must have been the moustache. We also went to see the tombs in the Valley of Kings and we both went down with "the curse of the pharaohs." Despite this last minute indisposition it was an unforgettable trip, a fortnight away from reality which seemed to have taken all my stress away.

Little did I know what was in store for me.

Working on Low Budgets

Luis Guridi and Santiago Aguilar, aka La Cuadrilla, asked me to star in *La hija de Fu-Manchú* (*Daughter of Fu Manchu*, 1990), this time calling themselves La Escuadlilla Amalilla. It was an entertaining action-adventure comedy involving the cruel mandarin cum scientist king of crime created by Sax Rohmer. It was a well-funded short film and I had a great time shooting it. What's more I was very fond of the boys of La Cuadrilla. This was the second time I'd played the cunning Chinese arch criminal.

Apart from this repeat performance with La Cuadrilla, Alvaro Sáenz de Heredia offered me a guest starring part in *Aquí huele a muerto* (1989). I wasn't too keen to tell the truth: I read the script and naturally it turned out to be a vehicle to the greater glory of José María Yuste and Millán Salcedo, the comic duo known as Martes y Trece [*Tuesday the Thirteenth*, the equivalent in many European countries of the Anglo-Saxon *Friday the Thirteenth*]. I quickly realized that Alvaro intended, to some extent, to follow in the footsteps of the famous *Abbott and Costello Meet Frankenstein*. I met the director and he seemed to be a very nice person. He said something about using masks and tests were made but it wasn't working out at all well. I advised him to find a good makeup artist and surprisingly he took my advice.

The film (one of the biggest grossing in the history of Spanish cinema, amazing but true) featured Frankenstein's Monster, Dracula and the Wolfman. The original touch was that it was all phony, the monsters were nothing but a scheme hatched up by a gang out to get their dirty hands on the inheritance of some Marquess or other, played by Josema. In short, Sáenz de Heredia was making a cross between the American comedians' picture and *Mark of the Vampire*. He didn't have a Bela Lugosi or a Glenn Strange or a Lionel Barrymore. Neither did he have Abbott and Costello, just Josema and Millán. Right now he's breaking box-office records with the ineffable stand-up comedian Chiquito de la Calzada in a Dracula spoof (*Brácula: Condemor II*).

I have never understood why television producers haven't called on me more often. I believe many people in Spain who have a lot to offer are under employed while certain really mediocre individuals are on all the time.

Following *Aquí huele a muerto*, I played a professional assassin in an episode of Pedro Maso's series *Brigada Central*. The title of the episode was "Desde el pasado" ("Out of the Past," 1990). I portrayed an Argentinean named Chaves who, in the name of revenge, went around murdering members of policemen's families with a single bullet between the eyes. At the end of the episode, just as Chaves is about to gun down the family of El Gitano, the police officer played by Imanol Arias, he is himself shot dead by El Gitano with, of course, a single bullet between the eyes. Two great friends of mine worked on this series, the brilliant DPs Alejandro Ulloa and Julio Burgos, both unfortunately now retired.

I had previously appeared on the small screen in the series *La Máscara*, in an episode called "Una bala en el camino" (1982). I played an Italian named Sandro

Coltini, aka *El Angel Negro*, the inventor of a parabolic trajectory cannon who sets off to bombard the city of Zaragoza into submission, planning to hand it over to Napoleon Bonaparte. Naturally it ended up with a duel to the death between Coltini and La Máscara (Sancho Gracia). Both characters were well-rounded and I enjoyed playing them.

I was absolutely mortified when a series of horror shows was made called *El quinto jinete* (*The Fifth Horseman*) and every Tom, Dick and Harry in the Spanish film business got in on it—except the only horror star this country has ever produced, who didn't get so much as a guest star spot. Had it been made in England, for example, Christopher Lee and Peter Cushing would have been bound to head the cast. But over here, we all know how it is—prejudice, lack of imagination and, above all, string pulling and nepotism rule supreme.

In 1990 I got together with Director of Photography José Enrique Izquierdo (*Las cuevas de Altamira*) with the idea of making a new horror fantasy movie on video. Wax museums had always appealed to me as a good setting for a horror story and so I wrote *Horror en el museo de cera* (1990). The story tells how a group of Media Science students decide to spend a night locked in the Madrid wax museum as an initiation test for the Alpha fraternity. As a clear homage to Boris Karloff, the film starts with a showing of *Tower of London* which the students have to study for an assignment.

Later they all meet up at the museum after the public have all left. A psychology professor (played by me) goes with them in order to study their reactions to the experience and to analyze the possibilities of collective psycho-suggestion. He's a seedy character who gives good grades to those of his female students who agree to sleep with him.

The most terrifying of all the horrible figures on display in the museum is a hooded medieval executioner armed with a huge double-headed ax, a character known as the Headsman of Fredesval who was supposed to have lived in the 16th century. All's quiet until midnight when somebody uses Black Magic to bring the waxworks to life. Even Gary Cooper comes out of the saloon with his pistols blazing. The Horrible Headsman goes on the rampage and the bloody crimes begin.

There are several beheadings as the students are ruthlessly stalked down one by one in an orgy of blood and horror. Finally, after a number of gory shock scenes the baffling mystery is unraveled and it turns out that the Black Magician responsible for the whole nightmare of horror is none other than the professor.

During filming several incidents occurred, one of which nearly had dire consequences. The stunt double was brandishing the ax with such force that the huge steel blade flew off the haft and rocketed across the set straight towards José Enrique Izquierdo. It missed him by a hair's breadth and embedded itself with a loud thud in a metal window shutter.

Filming was completed and the footage was edited but unfortunately it still hasn't been dubbed.

I continued to take part in powerlifting competitions and in spite of the occasional injuries I once again became Spanish Champion and entered the European Championships held in Orosatza, Hungary, where I came in fifth.

I was getting hardly any work and it was my wonderful, self sacrificing wife Elvira, who took on the burden of working in my cousin José Luis' fur and leather store as well as doing all the housework and domestic chores. As if she didn't already have enough on her plate, she was still organizing cultural events and fashion shows for the Japanese as well. It was her idea to make a high definition TV documentary about the House of Alba, spanning from the time of the first, legendary Duke up to the present heirs. The Japanese state TV channel NHK named me as its delegate in Spain and I was in charge of the complex job of organizing and coordinating filming. This was further complicated by the attitude of the Japanese production manager, a real pigheaded individual who put one problem after another in my way. I was having a tough time and was almost tempted to give it all up but eventually the stubborn, incompetent oaf was replaced and from then on everything went like clockwork. We made countless trips to film on location in the historical places associated with the Albas and after several months the film was completed.

The people at NHK then suggested we make an epic historical film about the exploits of the first Duke of Alba. It came at a bad time for me as I was stressed out and I failed to write the rough draft of the script which they had asked me for. Gradually the whole project fell through. I was getting closer to disaster than I knew.

One night I had a very unpleasant experience. After leaving the gym where I had been working out I had to walk down a number of narrow, poorly lit side streets near the Plaza de Toros. I recall that it had been raining and the damp pavement reflected the yellowish light of a solitary street lamp. Suddenly three scruffy youths appeared in front of me. They looked like they were out for trouble. Two of them whipped out hunting knives and I knew what I was in for. I don't know exactly what thoughts flashed through my mind at that moment, I just reacted instinctively. Dropping my sports bag to the ground I quickly unzipped it and got hold of the thick protective belt used for power lifting. I could feel the rage boiling up inside me. Maybe it was the pure anger of frustration that I'd had to hold back so many times in my life or maybe I saw those thugs as a symbol of all the bastards who've had it in for me down the years. The fact is I just went for them with a vengeance and left two of them in a really bad way.

It looked like I wasn't going to be so lucky with the third assailant but, fortunately, the headlights of a passing car put the wind up them and they made a run for it.

This episode was followed a short time later by another violent incident; a pretty young friend of ours was raped and brutally beaten one night on her way home.

These two terrible experiences were the inspiration for *La noche del ejecutor* (1993). It has been said that this film is a copy of *Death Wish*, the film starring the ever impassive Charles Bronson. There's a grain of truth in that statement but I approached the film from a totally Spanish viewpoint, with the Madrid criminal underworld in mind. I wanted to make a movie that reflected the sordid side of certain parts of the capital.

The bitter, brutal story is about the revenge of a doctor who witnesses the rape and murder of his wife and daughter at the hands of a gang of thugs who then tortures the man and cuts out his tongue. Miraculously he lives and, once physically recovered, his sole motivation is to exterminate the vermin who slaughtered his family and to get rid of as many delinquents as he can along the way. To achieve this he has to learn to handle all types of knives and firearms while building up his muscles and increasing his all-around physical fitness. Eventually he becomes a lethal killing machine.

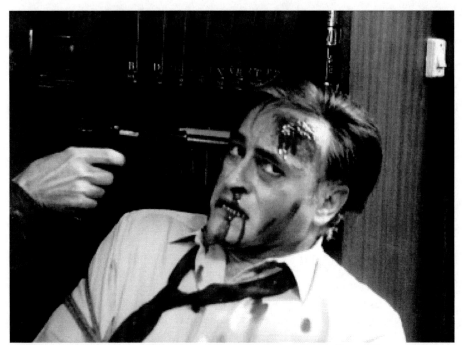

With *La noche del ejecutor* (1993), I wanted to make a movie that reflected the sordid side of certain parts of Madrid.

He starts to act, ruthlessly executing small time criminals and delinquents. He can throw knives with deadly precision and has become a cunning and bloodthirsty predator. A veteran police inspector (Manolo Zarzo) tries to capture him although at the same time he admires him for clearing the streets of the scum of society. A beautiful lady lawyer discovers the avenger's identity and, as her own father and brother were also murdered, decides to help him. The film was made for just 6,000,000 pesetas and was completed thanks to the many people who were willing to work on the film for free.

The superb actors who appeared in the film were the aforementioned Manolo Zarzo, Paloma Cela—for whose support on this project I'm especially grateful—Loreto Valverde, Marta Valverde, José Àlvarez, Pepe Ruiz, and Adriana Vega. The Production Manager, as always, was Augusto Boué and José Enrique Izquierdo was the DP.

Filming had several disagreeable and awkward moments. While in the Parque del Oeste to shoot a number of scenes we became fed up with the continual harassment by all the prostitutes, transvestites and nocturnal weirdoes who hang out in the area. I was amazed at José Enrique Izquierdo's good humor and patience because they really were a pain in the arse.

Another night we were filming in an out of the way place, in front of a building which had been abandoned before it had even been finished. As we were setting up our gear a great crowd of beggars and vagabonds came streaming out from among the broken red brick walls. All of them were old men, clutching the pieces of cardboard and tattered blankets under which they had been sleeping. It was as if Goya's painting *La Corte de los Milagros* had suddenly come to life. Not even Santiago Segura in his

La noche del ejecutor **was made for just 6,000,000 pesetas.**

most pathetic characterization could have done them justice. They demanded money to let us carry on filming and some of them even started to get violent. They all held cartons of rough wine in their sinewy hands. It was a pitiful scene and I thought to myself that we were in the '90s, not in the post-war years. We gave them some money and they left us alone.

Once editing and dubbing had been completed on this, the most modest film of my career, I went away to Almunécar for a holiday. I spent two or three weeks down at the beach and I really needed it. One day as I was buying the papers I bumped into Juan José Portos, still as overweight as he had been when I went to Granada to film *El último guateque II* (1988) with him. He told me about a multitude of projects in which, of course, I was included. Naturally I didn't believe a word of it.

Near our apartment block there was a modestly equipped gym which was enough for me to keep fit. I intended to take part in the powerlifting World Championship to be held in October. I remember a huge bull mastiff, an exceptionally affectionate and noble creature, who was my only companion many mornings while I was working out. On one of those mornings I first started to notice a dull pain in the middle of my chest. I didn't worry about it, thinking I'd simply pulled a muscle. What's more, before the beginning of the summer, I had performed remarkably well in an official competition, breaking the Spanish record by lifting 202.5kg in the 80kg category. As if that were not enough, a first class cardiologist had given me a thorough cardiovascular check up and proclaimed me to be in excellent shape. But the black bird of Death was hovering over me. This time the Grim Reaper would do his best to try and carry me off.

A Shot in the Heart

Back in Madrid I returned to the Argüelles gym to get into training for the upcoming World Championships in Montevideo. It was the morning of August 27, 1991. I was about to execute a lift when I suddenly felt as if I'd been stabbed in the middle of my chest, an excruciating, incredibly agonizing pain. I got changed and went straight home. I'm amazed that I made it. Only my two sons Sergio and Bruno were at home, as my wife was visiting her parents in Burgos. I got to my bedroom and the pain became unbearable, now shooting through my shoulders and along my arms too. I was convinced I was dying. During those critical moments a lot of thoughts raced through my mind like snapshots of my life: the struggles, the love affairs, the envy, the contempt, the successes, the failures and the terrible feeling that the only worthwhile thing in my life had been my family. Then the ambulance arrived and I stopped thinking. My life was all behind me and there wasn't going to be any future.

In the ambulance I was given oxygen. I looked up at my son Sergio, then 15 years old, and remembered working with him on *Mi amigo el vagabundo*, *El aullido del diablo* and *La noche del ejecutor*. We arrived at the Ruber Hospital where Sergio was told that they didn't have the necessary equipment available to deal with the extreme gravity of my condition. Without a second thought the boy had me taken to the nearest

clinic, Clinica de la Princesa, where the doctors and nurses got to work on me with commendable diligence and coordination. At the hospital I had been diagnosed as suffering a massive heart attack. Time was precious and it was running out for me.

I heard voices giving hurried commands and saw men and women in white coats leaning over me, while others rushed to and fro busying themselves with various pieces of equipment. That extraordinary team must have put up a titanic struggle against death. Sometimes I saw lights, other times faces and others just darkness. It was touch and go for an hour and a half, when finally they were able to take me up to the intensive care unit. I was awake when they took me into the glass-fronted room which is so often the last stop before death. They stripped my clothes off. The

Paul Naschy

At the time of my heart attack I'd completed three episodes of *Olla de grillos* and had a lot more left to do.

nurses appeared to be very young and instinctively I held on to my underpants. Here I was at death's door but I still retained an absurd sense of propriety.

I was soon lying in bed with all sorts of tubes in me and wired up to a number of monitors. I realized that, just like in the movies, it was the machines that were keeping me alive. The terrific pain, far worse than any I had ever experienced before, had now passed, in large measure thanks to the morphine I'd been given.

Following the initial crisis, during which to all intents and purposes I'd been practically dead, I rallied just when they were about to give me up as a lost cause. I spent that first night wide awake and thinking things over. I became preoccupied with a totally trivial matter, namely the children's program that I had been recording at Television Española. It was called *Olla de grillos* and I'd completed three episodes and had a lot more left to do. These programs were recorded live with the participation of the children in the audience. What bad luck, for once when I'd got some television work my heart had to let me down!

I reflected that I had given almost 30 years of my life to the movies and looking back on it, maybe it hadn't been worthwhile. I would have probably been much better off as an architect. I thought of all the petty and unjust people I had known and also about my friends, my parents and my sister, my wife and my sons. My mind was filled with memories of my childhood, of my youth and of my adult life. I wished I had done everything better, but maybe I hadn't been able to or just hadn't known how.

After some two or three hours the alarms on the machines I was connected to went off. The nurses and the cardiologist who was on duty rushed in and once more the air was filled with tension and hurried orders as they started to inject me with God knows what drugs. Eventually the crisis passed and all was calm again.

I was deeply moved by the affection with which the women in white cared for me. I learned to appreciate the goodness in people, people who go out of their way for others, who get involved, who share the sorrows and joys of their patient. The alarms went off several more times but they were always there to pull me through, to save my life which hung by the finest of threads.

The time came for me to be catheterized. Shivers ran down my spine and I felt an acute sense of dread. A young bearded doctor and two nurses were waiting for me and the process began. The catheters were inserted through my groin and I could see them advancing across the screen in search of the damaged arteries. Funnily enough I was now perfectly calm, as if the arteries and the battered heart which I could see beating didn't belong to me.

When the probe was over I looked at the young consultant. He had a serious expression on his face and glanced at the nurses. There was a tense, awkward silence which I finally broke by asking the inevitable question, regardless of what the answer might be. The doctor hesitated, but he must have seen something in my eyes because he told me the truth: "You have a case of advanced heart disease with serious damage to three major blood vessels." I was wheeled back to intensive care.

The next day they took me for a scan. When I got back to bed I started shaking like a leaf. I felt chilled to the bone and my teeth were chattering so hard that I had to have a sort of bit placed in my mouth. I was having a terrible fit and it felt like all my bones were going to break. I was given more dope, including morphine, and the fit passed.

On my fourth day in hospital I could make out my wife and my mother-in-law on the other side of the glass partition. Luckily the nurses very rarely left me on my own. I saw the bodies of two men wheeled away along the corridor. Both had been in intensive care with me. My turn soon, I thought.

The head surgeon, a well-built, bald, ginger-bearded man, visited me often. He was circumspect and distant, but everyone said I'd been lucky because he was one of the best. The head nurse was also a marvelous person. She had an actress daughter and she was always asking me to remember her once I got back to making movies again. And I did. I recall another pretty young nurse who tried to spend as much time as possible with me in order to cheer me up.

Everybody knew me, some because they had seen my films at the cinema or on TV, others because my name was familiar. Everyone in the Hospital de la Princesa knew that Paul Naschy was dying there. My sense of hearing had become as sharp as a wolf's and when the doctor and his team stood around whispering I could hear everything, absolutely everything.

I had been in that glass cage for eight days when the ginger-bearded surgeon gathered his people around him and said in hushed tones: "He's been here a week and he still shows no signs of making a recovery. There's not much hope but we'll operate on him tomorrow morning at eight. He can't hold out much longer. We've got to try it." That evening a priest came. I confessed, took holy communion and was given the last rites. Then, for the first time in days, I slept.

In the morning a male nurse shaved my torso and soon I was being wheeled to the operating theatre. I felt quite calm because I was resigned to my fate. Besides, death brings an end to a lot of bad things: incomprehension, injustice, envy, depression, tragedy—but on the other hand there were my loved ones, my wife and sons, my love of painting, the six or seven of my films which I hope will never be lost and so many other things I still might have enjoyed. But now nothing was up to me.

As they wheeled me out of the intensive care unit, my family were waiting there, together with Augusto Boué. I raised my hand and waved them all good-bye, convinced that this was the end. They took me into the theatre with all its dazzling array of paraphernalia and started getting me ready for the operation. The head anesthesiologist leaned over me, only her lovely blue eyes visible above the surgical mask and in an incredibly gentle voice she said to me with a marked Argentinean accent: "We'll pull you through. You'll live, we're all here to make it happen, you've no need to worry." She put the mask over my face and soon I felt myself falling into a dark, bottomless pit.

I know the operation lasted seven hours and it was highly complicated. Before it started my wife spoke to the surgeon who told her quite bluntly not to get her hopes up since the odds on my coming out of it alive were practically nil.

I did come up from the bottomless pit, regaining consciousness little by little. I saw standing before me the big man with the ginger-beard who, for the first time, was looking at me with the hint of a smile. He certainly wasn't God or Saint Peter, and he didn't look like Charlton Heston—anyway, the beard was a giveaway. Shortly afterwards my dear ladies from intensive care took charge of me once more. I wouldn't be out of danger for another 48 hours and they took turns to watch over me, never leaving me alone for a second. There were one or two dodgy moments but I came through all right. After two or three days I was taken out of the intensive care unit and moved downstairs where I shared a room with a relatively young man who was in for observation pending an operation. He looked healthy and was accompanied at all times by his dedicated wife.

I was feeling terribly weak and just couldn't eat. Every day I had check ups, I was weighed, washed and dosed up to my eyeballs with pills. My post-op was not going at all well. Every day at visiting time my wife and my mother-in-law came to see me and sometimes they brought Sergio and Bruno along.

I started to improve slightly and one day, much to my surprise, the toughs from the gym came to see me, led by El Picado. They brought me a present and I knew they were totally sincere when they expressed their best wishes for my recovery.

The press treated me with consideration. They came in turns to get their story, so as not to tax me too much. I got a great shock when I saw the photos in the magazines. I looked like death warmed up. However, I had survived and was still in one piece. I knew then why Death's shot in the heart hadn't been fatal. It had been on target sure enough but there had been one vital error; the bullet wasn't made of silver, an unforgivable blunder.

One of the team of surgeons explained the operation to me and it made my hair stand on end. They had cut through my sternum and held the ribs apart with huge forceps. Then they had taken out my heart and replaced the damaged arteries with three other arteries taken from my own body; luckily these were all perfectly healthy. I pictured myself laid out and sliced open like a pig on a butcher's slab. Talk about gore!

The days dragged by and the only thing that relieved the boredom were the visits of my family, my best friend, doctor Carlos Rodríguez Jiménez and Fernando Zamora, producer of the children's TV show *Olla de grillos*. With only two exceptions, absolutely nobody from the film industry came to see me! I didn't get a single phone call to find out how I was. The wonderful solidarity of my fellow showbiz workers was demonstrated by the extent of their *affection* and *desire* to help me out. Thank you, dear colleagues, thank you. To be sure, if somebody who's in the limelight dies, you all rush to the funeral with your eyes hidden behind trendy dark glasses and your faces a picture of grief for the benefit of the press photographers. Not very long ago I went to the funeral of dear old León Klimovsky, a man who had worked with everyone in the film business in the course of his long career. There were scarcely 20 of us present to bid him a final farewell. Truly pitiful.

The exceptions I mentioned were the producer and exhibitor Primitivo Rodríguez who, as soon as he heard the news, journeyed all the way from Galicia to Madrid to be by my side, and a visit from my dear friend, the actor Vidal Molina. Later on Primitivo continued to lend me his support. Every morning during my long, slow convalescence he would put aside his multiple business obligations and come to fetch me and take me out for laborious walks. I'll never forget such generous, humanitarian behavior especially since I had only met him once before at a meeting of the Film Writers' Guild.

One afternoon I had the stitches removed. As I glanced at the TV I saw they were showing my film *Los cántabros*. Naturally I was unable to watch it. At long last I was able to get out of bed by myself, although still with some difficulty. I went to the bathroom, took off my pajama top and saw myself in the mirror for the first time. My muscles had wasted away and I now looked like a victim of a Nazi concentration camp. I had gone from weighing 82.5 kilos down to 56 kilos. I felt wretched.

Fan magazines like *Fangoria* set the record straight about my illness and false reports of my demise.

A few days later, when I was discharged, I felt lousy. In fact, though I didn't know it, I had liquid in my left lung. This whole dramatic episode left me with a triple bypass and the memory of the affection of my nurses and all the ordinary folk at the clinic who used to stop by to chat, to cheer me up and to ask for autographs. I saw for myself the warmth and admiration which so many people held for Paul Naschy.

Augusto Boué and my family came to fetch me and, with the premature discharge form in my pocket, I returned home. The outpatient doctors wrote me off as almost totally incapacitated. *Adios* to practically everything; in their opinion I was finished. For them and for many other people too.

But the torture wasn't over yet. There were serious complications due to the liquid in my lung. Once again I was in the vice-like grip of the Parcœ. But, as I said, the bullets weren't made of silver and that was the big mistake.

The character from Reus whom I call the Bizarre One, the fellow who went around accusing me of stealing other people's scripts, was at that time, unbelievably, the correspondent in Spain for the French magazine *L'Ecran Fantastique*. This individual was so anxious to see me dead that he sent news of my death to the magazine. *L'Ecran Fantastique* has a considerable international readership and the news spread like wildfire. Luckily, although the damage had already been done, the influential American magazine *Fangoria* set the record straight about this macabre lie. In spite of this, whenever Primitivo traveled to New York, Los Angeles or Cannes, many producers and distributors were still convinced I'd kicked the bucket. Naturally *L'Ecran Fantastique* gave this spiteful customer the boot for being both a lousy correspondent and a rotten liar. I found all this out from the magazine's current correspondent. *Variety* had also prepared an obituary for me but they were informed of the truth in time to stop publication of the false information.

One night I had a phone call from Steven Spielberg in person. The phone rang some time after midnight. My wife, thinking it to be a hoax, hung up. It rang again with the same result. The third time Sergio answered it and, still unable to credit it, he brought the phone through into the lounge where I was lying on the settee. I took the receiver with a great deal of skepticism but it actually was Steven Spielberg himself. He spoke quickly and I couldn't understand him. Eventually I realized he was telling me that he would phone me back. The following night he did indeed call again, this time with the aid of an interpreter. By coincidence, this young lady happened to be the daughter of an actor I had worked with years before, Victor Alcázar (Vic Winner). She explained to me that Mr. Spielberg wished to obtain information about me and my films as well as tracking down three titles which were missing from his collection of my movies (he had 40 films on video). Besides this, he wanted me to go to Los Angeles so we could meet in person. Obviously this was out of the question. I gave some excuses about being unable to travel due to work commitments and told him that at a later date, when it suited him, I would have no objections to traveling to Los Angeles. We left it at that and I still got a few more calls requesting further information.

Enter one Santiago Cobos, who claimed to be the representative of Spanish Cinema in the United States. "I can get a pile of money out of him. So he wants information? Well let him pay for it and pay damned well!" I begged him not to interfere since Spielberg had contacted me personally, and it was none of his business. But he evidently did interfere and Spielberg never called again.

A short time ago I was in Seville (the trade union U.G.T. were having a do in my honor) and I spoke to Victor Alcázar who advised me to get in touch with Spielberg and explain what had happened. His daughter no longer worked for this Cobos fellow and he admitted that the representative of Spanish Cinema had screwed up the whole business. I really didn't understand a thing.

Following these calls, which could have meant so much, my long and arduous convalescence followed its course. To take my mind off things I started to write a Waldemar Daninsky script entitled *Licántropo* (1996). It was just to kill a little of the nostalgia I felt. I still had no intentions of returning to the film business.

Once I could see that I was improving I decided to get back to the gym. I started gradually, at first just doing benchwork and before I knew it I was able to lift considerable weights. The Spanish championships were coming up and I decided to give it a go. Surprisingly I didn't tire easily and I was building up my muscles and regaining my strength day by day. I went into training without telling my cardiologist who would probably—no, who would certainly—have forbidden it. My weight had gone up from 56 kilos to 78 and was still increasing.

The eagerly awaited day came at last, my great trial. I had been written off as just being along for the ride—at the very most I'd be able to wander down the road, sit on a bench and maybe read the paper before shuffling back home. At six in the morning I was up and about. I conscientiously prepared my kit—I was still using the old blood-red singlet from my weightlifting heyday—my boots, the thick leather and metal belt, etc. Then I lay down awhile thinking it over. What could go wrong? Perhaps the new tubes of the triple bypass through which my blood was flowing would be torn apart by the tremendous exertion. What hadn't happened in the Clinica de la Princesa could well take place on the podium of a powerlifting championship. I dismissed these thoughts from my mind, had breakfast, stuffed a box of pills in my pocket and set off.

At about noon I stepped up to execute my first lift, I think it was 130 kilos. I looked up and felt grateful to be living this moment once more. I didn't break any records but I became Spanish champion again. Some time later I traveled to Budapest to take part in the European championships. By now I weighed in at 82.5 kilos. I took seventh place. I'd regained my confidence and I started to train in earnest.

In 1992 Sidney Ling reappeared on the scene. He offered me a guest star part in a

film called *State of Mind* (1992). Obviously this wouldn't add anything worthwhile to my filmography but I accepted and went out to Belgium to film my scenes together with Lisa Gaye and Fred Williamson.

Primitivo Rodríguez called me up asking to see the script of *Licántropo*. He liked it and he told me he'd try to get it off the ground. At first I was to direct it.

I continued to train and made good progress. Once again I became Champion of Spain and I competed both in the European Championships which were held in Bratislava in Slovakia and the World Championship in Sydney. I took with me a gift from the Madrid City Council for the Mayor of the Australian city. In Sydney I met the Spanish Consul and it turned out to

During the Championships I was visiting the Sydney Spanish Residents' Social Club and there, in the television lounge, they were showing *El retorno del hombre lobo*!

be quite a coincidence—he was the brother of a good friend of mine, the late Alfonso Chicharro y Lamamie de Cleirac, aka the wrestler Hércules Cortés. The Consul showed me every kindness and he took me in his car on a tour of Sydney's most interesting places, including its dangerous Chinatown.

The Consul took me to the Sydney Spanish Residents' Social Club and by another coincidence, there, in the television lounge, they were showing *El retorno del hombre lobo*! I couldn't believe it: I'd come all this way, to the very antipodes, and here I was seeing one of my own films on TV. Together with some South American *compadres* (*Carajo!*) I sat down to enjoy the movie with considerable nostalgia.

When the day came for me to compete I didn't have much luck. I realized that the cycle had come to a close. I had done it all both in regular weightlifting competition and in powerlifting and, seeing as I'd started out back in 1957 and here I was in 1992, with a major heart attack behind me, I decided it was time to call it a day.

Although I was beginning to be forgotten by the Spanish film business, a lot of things still awaited me in 1993.

The Scorpion's Sting

A well known legend says that if a scorpion is trapped by a wall of fire it will take its own life by stinging itself in the head. Eventually I was going to imitate the scorpion. Presently I shall explain why.

In 1993, as every year, we had a family Christmas at home. Elvira was still working in the fashion industry and I was now completely recovered from my heart attack, although, to tell the truth, I didn't expect much from the Spanish film business, television or theatre. On the other hand, the public at large, the *aficionados*, the fans did miss me and I was continually getting letters and phone calls both from home and abroad inquiring about my health and asking the reason for my lengthy absence from the screen. They loved my films and there were some really moving appeals from people who were ill, including paraplegic marines and others who were confined to wheelchairs, even from alcohol and drug abusers' support groups, all requesting autographs and signed photos. I was also contacted by some gay associations.

Fan clubs from the U.S., France, Japan, Germany and Belgium were keener than ever to know about my activities. I traveled to these countries several times to lend my wholehearted support to these dedicated fans. I fondly recall the warm tribute put on for me in London at the beginning of 1992. Caroline Munro, Herbert Lom, Christopher Lee and Peter Cushing were all there and the cinema was chock-a-block every day. They showed *El espanto surge de la tumba*, *El jorobado de la morgue*, and *El gran amor del conde Drácula*. At the end of each session there were prize draws for videos and signed posters of my movies and I gave a few talks. I was delighted by the admiration and affection people had for me.

Two press conferences were organized at my hotel, and my stay in London gained a much greater coverage than I had expected. The land of Jack the Ripper smiled on me.

In Spain the enthusiasts of the Barcelona Independent Film Festival were the first to hold an event in my honor. There were a number of memorable moments. For example, I had

Fanzines in the United States such as *Videooze* helped keep the memory of Paul Naschy alive.

many of my restaurant bills paid for me, rather to my embarrassment, and there was a constant show of friendliness from people who had enjoyed my films. I was touched by the gesture of several beggars who shook my hand with a sincere display of affection while refusing to accept any alms whatsoever. I am held in extremely high esteem in Catalonia, a fact which makes the hostile attitude of the Sitges Festival towards me even more absurd. The Generalitat [the autonomous regional government of Catalonia], a symbol of sobriety and national identity in Catalonia, should look into whether the peculiar Gorina and his gang, paradigms of poor taste, are fit to run such an illustrious event.

Shortly after this, the Spanish Film Writers' Guild held its General Assembly. This prestigious body was formed in 1944 by a group of eminent critics and specialized film scholars with the aim of protecting and promoting film culture. Among the international celebrities who have been members are Federico Fellini, Ingmar Bergman and Mario "Cantinflas" Moreno. At a time when the SFWG was about to embark on a number of new, highly-challenging projects, I stood for the office of chairman and was elected. The awards given by the SFWG are highly coveted by professionals in the sector. In the most recent general assembly, held last month, I was once again voted chairman. As I'm ambitious and surrounded by an excellent team, I hope to accomplish many new goals for the good of culture in general and the cinema in particular.

Some time previously I had myself received a medal of honor from the Guild in recognition of my lengthy film career. Who would have thought at the time that I was to be a future chairman? I remember that when I started out in the film industry I used to dream about winning the famed SFWG medal. And now I've got two, including the medal of honor. At least that's one dream which has come true.

At the International Film Festival of Oporto

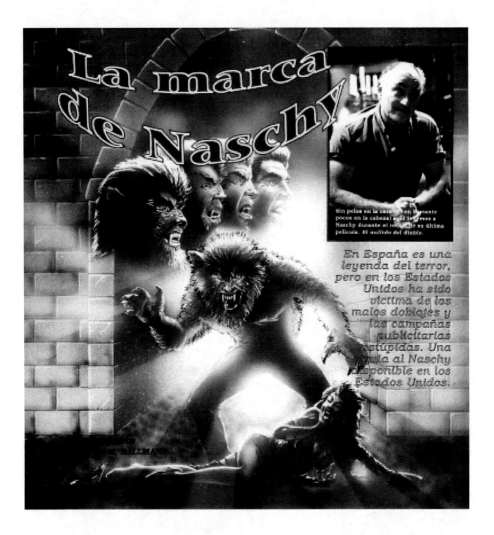

Before the Guild first elected me as chairman, the National Film Archive (*Filmoteca*) rendered me an unexpected and much appreciated tribute by showing a lengthy season of my films which comprised 45 top quality prints of such cult classics as *La noche de Walpurgis, El retorno del hombre lobo, El caminante, El jorobado de la morgue, El gran amor del conde Drácula, El huerto del Francés* and *El espanto surge de la tumba*.

I recall the half envious comment of the fondly remembered León Klimovsky, who never missed a single showing: "You're lucky, the *Filmoteca* has organized a terrific season of your movies and you're not even dead." I replied half-jokingly, "Just as well, otherwise I'd never have known."

The season was a resounding success with showings that attracted both rebellious youths and middle-aged citizens: audiences of many and varied types of viewers, just as it should be. It was absolutely unforgettable and it made up for a lot of the injustices perpetrated against me. I remember that, when introducing one of the films, I claimed with some feeling that I had to "seek refuge abroad to lick the wounds inflicted on me

Paul Naschy

in Spain." I thank the *Filmoteca* for their recognition through a wonderful season which attracted a lot of new young fans to my work. To coincide with the season a book was published titled *Paul Naschy, The Cycle of the Full Moon*, written by Ignacio Armada and the singular Guzmán Urrero.

All of this was enormously gratifying of course, but obviously I desperately needed to work. Then something happened that was so ludicrous that I can well understand that it takes some believing.

Sidney Ling got in touch with me. He wanted to work with me once more and claimed he had already found an American co-producer and distributor for two new projects, a thriller and a horror-fantasy film which would resurrect one of the classic monsters as its main character. I was to write the scripts. Apart from this I would have to provide the film stock for both movies as well as playing the lead parts in each.

I was keen to go ahead with the project and wasted no time in setting pen to paper coming up with two scripts called *El regreso de Dracúla* [*The Return of Dracula*] and *Cuando las luces se apagan* [*When the Lights Go Out*]. I still remember the line which appeared on the first page of the screenplay of the latter, between the title and the cast list: "The serial killer never calls at your door by chance."

Anyhow, I finished the scripts and sent them posthaste to Sidney Ling. In the meantime, by mentioning my name, he had managed to involve the Belgian producer Johan Vandewowstijne in the project. Johan was to provide the cameras, the power plant, the lights and, in short, all the equipment necessary for the shoot, including dollies and cranes if need be. Everything else, cast, crew, transport, accommodation, catering, etc., would be the responsibility of Sidney Ling and his American co-producer. I would direct the films and post-production would be carried out in Paris. The Dutchman was so convincing that I was completely taken in and the same thing happened to the Belgian.

Quite a long time passed, during which Ling was supposed to have scouted for locations, cast the principal roles and generally set the machinery in motion. I bought the film stock which cost me some 6,000,000 pesetas. Finally it was time to set off for Paris to start work on pre-production. Ling informed me over the phone that we would sign the contracts in the French capital and that for the time being I would be staying in an apartment that he had found for me. It was agreed that I would pay my own travel expenses.

Without the slightest suspicion of anything untoward, I left Barajas airport bound for the most demented adventure of my whole life. It was a miserable, rainy day when I touched down in Paris where Ling and his American co-producer, a horse-faced, hunchbacked octogenarian, were waiting for me in a clapped out old Chevrolet. I started to smell a rat, but as I'd started out on this undertaking, I had to see it through.

A terrific thunderstorm broke out as we drove to Paris in the old banger. We arrived at the apartment which turned out to be the strange old man's offices and dwelling combined. This was what Sidney Ling had arranged for me. For the time being, of course. The old man showed me to my room which was furnished with an old iron bedstead, a rickety old table, TV monitors, tape recorders and diverse items of sound equipment. It was evident that everything had been improvised at the last moment. That evening we had dinner in a nearby restaurant and, naturally, I had to foot the bill. Ling tried to set my mind at rest by telling me that he was on the verge of obtaining the necessary financing thanks to a loan arranged through his girlfriend who was a top executive at the bank, and although I was becoming increasingly suspicious, I could only bide my time. Johan was due to arrive in a couple of days' time and I was waiting to see his reaction.

Meanwhile I asked Ling to introduce me to the cast and crew. A number of odd characters who were clearly amateurs were duly summoned to the old hunchback's office and I realized things were going from bad to worse; the situation bordered on the surreal. As scheduled, Johan arrived with all the equipment and we had a meeting. Although the Belgian wasn't too enthusiastic at how things were shaping up, he left all the stuff he'd brought and went back to Brussels. The cameras were stored in my pseudo-bedroom.

Time passed and no cast or crew members were contracted, no locations were scouted, not the slightest progress was made on the project. I fell into a deep depression and spent the long, empty hours lying on my bed listening to the soundtrack music from Francis Ford Coppola's *Dracula*. Ling boasted that he would be out of Paris for a few days to clinch a deal with Omar Sharif who was joining the project, so I was lumbered with the deformed old man and his two dogs; these were affectionate mutts but they stank something rotten. The sinister looking "American producer" asked me for money to buy food, including dog biscuits. I handed over the francs and went to eat out in restaurants. In all this time it hadn't stopped pouring with rain. The whole thing was becoming a nightmare and I cursed the day I let myself be persuaded to have anything to do with it.

At last Ling returned, although he hadn't solved anything. He assured me that it would be a question of a few days and everything would be OK. I'd had enough and I took myself off to my room where there was a phone and called Primitivo in Madrid for some advice. My friend was quite clear: "You've already made a big hole in your patrimony. Give it up, the whole thing's a con, and come on back." The incredibly ill-mannered and discourteous Ling had actually listened in to my conversation from the office and had the gall to accuse me of double-crossing him. That was just too much, I flew off the handle and landed him a couple of good hard punches.

The following day I took a taxi to the airport. It was still pouring down. I bought a Spanish newspaper and was surprised by the sad news of the death of Mario "Cantinflas" Moreno. The journalist added that "Cantinflas" had been dead for quite some time, in fact; ever since the day when plastic surgery had turned his hitherto expressive face into a mask. Maybe he was right.

Although I brought the unexposed film stock back with me, with the passage of time it had became clouded and useless. The whole crazy affair had cost me over 7,000,000 pesetas. I returned to Madrid with my tail between my legs and utterly defeated. My future in the film industry seemed bleaker than ever. I was going down-hill.

Shortly afterwards I had a call from *Flashback*, a magazine based in Valencia and edited by someone named Busquets. They wanted to organize an event in honor of Jack Taylor, Carlos Aured and myself. The tribute wasn't what I had expected and once again I found myself the target of the same old derision, this time from the mouth of the aforementioned magazine editor. I will never understand why events are organized to pay tribute to someone whom the organizers don't hold in the slightest esteem.

It's absurd. Another case in point is the 1996 Sitges Festival. The good thing about it was that I met a lot of genuine fans and some really nice people. That's what encourages me to carry on the fight.

In 1994 I spent part of the summer in Burgos and as usual I met up with my old friend Antonio Gregori. Antonio is a journalist and he produced the film *Soldados* which was directed by Alfonso Ungría. I was very fond of Gregori and we had been trying to set up a horror film festival in Burgos for several years. We had even submitted a detailed proposal to the city's previous mayor, a certain Sr. Peña, who left it to gather dust among a pile of forgotten old documents.

Antonio had recommended me to the newspaper *Diario 16* in Burgos and I started to write a column for them

called *Chronicles of Evil*, which became famous. The column continues to be published in the magazine *Cinerama*. So, there we were, Gregori and I, sitting in the café Grana on Calle Victoría, in the city of El Cid, when Valentín Niño, current mayor of Burgos and a wonderful fellow, happened along and sat down to have a beer with us. We started to chat and suddenly I had a bright idea. I told him all about our old project for a horror film festival. He thought it was a great idea. Burgos was the very place; a wonderfully Gothic city with a totally unique cathedral, brimming with old monuments and ancient traditions, excellent hotel accommodation, fine new cinemas and a host of historical sites to visit. Not to mention the fabulous local cuisine. Undoubtedly it was the ideal location.

We got to work and the project went before the town council, receiving the support of all parties, especially the PSOE (Spanish Socialist Workers' Party), even though the mayor belonged to the conservative Partido Popular.

I had the idea of giving awards in the form of metal reproductions of cathedral gargoyles. One icy winter's morning we set off with a photographer to take some pictures of the gargoyles. We had to wait for the fog to disperse and then we covered the whole of the marvelous edifice which had been built on the orders of Fernando III, *El Santo*. I finally selected one of the gargoyles as the model for the award which would be cast in Madrid—the necessary resources weren't available in Burgos. The trophy was sculpted from a drawing I had made, while the official festival poster was a strange painting by a famous naïf artist.

However, the project ran into trouble because Antonio Gregori neither understood nor cared for the horror genre and, what's more, for some reason his odd wife hated me more than the very Devil. In any case, Gregori kept coming up with weird ideas which had little to do with the genre, such as organizing round tables with filmmakers from Castille and León who had nothing whatsoever to do with the cinefantastique, arranging cultural outings, food tastings and so on, which were all very well and good, but again had nothing to do with horror fantasy cinema.

Depression began to take a hold on me once again. I started to smoke three packets of cheroots a day and my mental health took a dangerous turn for the worse. To make matters worse, few genre movies had been produced that year and I had my work cut out trying to find films that hadn't yet been released. It was the year of *Wolf*, but unfortunately that film had already had its premiere shortly before the Festival was scheduled to begin. Antonio arranged the jury, among whom was Jiménez Rico. The Festival hardly attracted any media attention at all and I returned to Madrid taking my despondency with me.

I didn't have any projects, I didn't have any money, I didn't have any will to carry on. I was trapped by the flames of despair so I imitated the scorpion which stings itself in the head. I pulled out of the Festival.

Later on Antonio Gregori didn't even bother to call me for the second edition. I found out quite by chance, thanks to two letters I received from people in Barcelona who thought that I was still running the Festival. Antonio Gregori, with malice aforethought, had taken it upon himself to give me the cold shoulder and leave me totally out of it.

A little while back, while attending an event which had been organized in my honor at the Málaga International Film Festival, I ran into Antonio Gregori again. I'm not one to bear a grudge and I behaved as if nothing had happened. He told me how his wife had exerted an unbearable influence over him and almost driven him 'round the bend. Fortunately he was now separated from her. Although I was sorry about the way the Burgos event had ended up, I consider that a friend is worth far more than any festival.

Following the Burgos fiasco I was so despondent that I even stopped writing. One fine day in 1994 I had a call from La Cuadrilla, from Luis Guridi to be precise, and naturally I was delighted. They were about to start filming *Justino*, their first feature film and of course they had a part for me. I awaited the script eagerly, but when I read it my hopes were totally dashed. They had only included one brief scene with me in. I thought that was a bit thick. I had appeared in their short films for free, I had helped them out as much as I could and they respond by giving me a single miserable scene which was not so much a small cameo as a big insult. In spite of this I asked Guridi if there wasn't something—something a bit better. I never got a reply. The SFWG gave them that year's award in the Most Promising Newcomers category. I think they deserved it.

Some time after this I was reacquainted with José Antonio de las Heras who had interviewed me many years before on several occasions for a newspaper named *Pueblo*. Now José Antonio was working as manager and agent for film and television personalities. He kindly offered to take over the running of my future career in showbiz. It seemed a good idea. He'd been a journalist, he had a lot of contacts and he'd probably make a good manager. I must say his first film project came as something of a surprise; it was a story about the building of a cathedral in the Middle Ages and the stars were to be David Carradine and Torrebruno [a pint-sized circus ringmaster who worked on

With Hammer star Ingrid Pitt at the International Film Festival in Brussels.

several Spanish children's TV shows]. The director would be Antonio del Real. It's true that you must expect the unexpected in show business, but David *Kung Fu* Carradine co-starring with Torrebruno! It takes some getting used to. Anyway this was quite some time ago and as far as I know the cathedral's foundations have still to be laid.

José Antonio had a lot of things in the pipeline and had me writing material non-stop for the aforementioned Torrebruno, and well known Spanish comedians such as Pepe Rubio, Bigote Arrocet and others. Needless to say, none of these ventures ever came to anything, although he did use to phone me up and we'd spend hours talking about nothing at all. Meanwhile my name once more started to appear with increasing frequency on TV, in newspapers and magazines. The mass media in general remembered Paul Naschy and numerous tributes to me were held at festivals in Zaragoza, Alcalá de Henares, Salamanca, San Sebastián, Málaga, Seville, Bilbao, Estepona, etc. However, not one single article or interview was signed by José Antonio de las Heras. Eventually one day he came clean. He told me there was nothing he could do for me. He had found work for all his clients except for *moi*. He'd even found work for Nadiuska whom he'd only known for three weeks and who was now co-starring with Chiquito de la Calzada [a short, chubby, middle-aged nightclub comedian who after 20 years doing clubs had achieved an unexpected and short-lived fame following a TV appearance] and Bigote Arrocet in the horror comedy titled *Brácula* or something of the sort. José Antonio had spoken to the film's director, Sáenz de Heredia, about the possibility of a part for me but he was told that I only knew how to play the Wolfman and I'd already done that with Martes y Trece.

Needless to say, if Bela Lugosi, Christopher Lee, John Carradine, Gary Oldman or Max Schreck could see Chiquito de la Calzada as the vampire count, their blood would turn to ice!

Back from the Dead

Why have I always been so fond of the horror-fantasy genre? Perhaps because it is the genre which comes closest to the true essence of the cinema, which is in itself a phantasmagorical phenomenon. Horror-fantasy films deal with the terrible frontier between life and death, with a terrifying universe populated by creatures which have troubled men's dreams since the dawn of creation, creatures which remind us that we carry evil within ourselves.

My own first-hand brush with death has allowed me to adopt a broader perspective on the subject. I have come back from the dead and I've begun to understand why certain people turn their backs on the genre, why some people laugh at these movies. This type of cinema is purely phantasmagorical and the omnipresent reminder of what comes to us all sooner or later, the reminder of death, is something which many people find hard to take, which they find too disturbing to contemplate, even within the realms of fiction.

I've always been amazed how people I've worked with, people I've shared unforgettable moments with, and who have since passed on, can, at the touch of a button, be magically brought back to life up on the screen. For example I put on *El huerto del francés* and I see José Nieto, Carlos Casaravilla or Nélida Quiroga, I recall that Miguel Agudo is behind the camera and I totally forget that they're now all dead. I'm drawn into the film and I relive the story, I see them move, speak, look at each other, express feelings... For a time Man's wizardry vanquishes death itself. It's no wonder that there are so many fan clubs, genre addicts, specialized magazines, doctoral theses, fanzines and so on, for the horror fantasy genre evokes so strongly the fascination with tragedy which appeals irresistibly to the transcendental nature of the individual. Legends never die.

This is why, just as Prince Vlad the Impaler screamed at Jonathan Harker in his eerie castle in darkest Transylvania, I scream at the false critics who dare to scribble the history of cinema any way they please. Critics are the pathologists of the imagination. If only they'd forget their prejudices and not try to set boundaries to the total freedom of this wonderful, practically unknown genre, they would uncover values they'd never imagined and discover totally different perspectives. I hope that all those who read these memoirs do so in a spirit of goodwill and with a certain complicity. Right now I feel the loneliness of the goalkeeper before a penalty. Which way will the ball go? Will they shoot high, low, or chip it in off the woodwork? This humble book will be like the goalie's hands. In any event, I have an ancient amulet on my chest which will protect me against any forked tongue or evil eye, whichever quarter they may come from.

As well as those abroad, there have been people here in Spain who have had an enormously positive view of my work. I'd like to mention three of them who have championed my work over the years: Luis Gasca, Luis Vigil and Adolfo Camilo.

Gasca and Vigil have been important figures in the world of film and comics in Spain and it would be an arduous task to list in detail their countless invaluable contributions to these fields. It comforts me to know that they are around, for the good of those of us who love to journey into the ghostly world of the unknown, trying to cross, in our imaginations, the dreadful and enigmatic frontier which separates life from death.

I can't resist the temptation to reproduce here part of the prologue which Gasca wrote for Adolfo Camilo's thesis, published under the title *An Examination of the Horror-Fantasy Genre in Spain Through the Films of Paul Naschy*.

Paul Naschy shares with Peter Lorre, Bela Lugosi and Lon Chaney something more than a great skill for playing the most diverse fictional characters—all of them evil. His secret, his magic, lies in his disturbing screen presence, the twisted, penetrating look with which he fixes and traps his victims, doomed to be impaled on the pins in his particular butterfly collection.

He has brought to life the whole gallery of cinematic horrors over the 20 years since he made his first film *La marca del hombre lobo*. He doesn't need to speak to have the audience squirming in their seats, both captivated and repelled by his portrayals. And, just like Boris Karloff, he knows how to bring to life, within the strictures of the most modest resources imaginable, all the monsters of literature or of brutal historical reality, as well as contemporary villains: terrorists, serial killers or criminals forged in the arid wildernesses of Spain.

Paul Naschy, a self-taught filmmaker who can write, produce, direct and star in a feature length movie for what it costs to produce a French student short, has become a cult actor in Japan, the United States, Belgium, France and in the temples known as fanzines which have followed his humble career for many years. With their support and admiration he fights alone against the establishment, periodically pulling off another minor miracle, a new film as straightforward as his own human personality, a work which is never lacking in thrills.

Adolfo Camilo Díaz, historian at the University of Oviedo, has written a fascinating book, a superbly well researched study, the first of its kind. It brilliantly analyses the works of Naschy seen as a resumé of Spanish cinefantastique cinema which is overdue for rediscovery. This book is an indispensable work.

FANTOOM 5

KING KONG 1933 & 1976 · MAD LOVE
HET GROTE PAUL NASCHY INTERVIEW

Unfortunately Adolfo Camilo's book is out of print. His own vision, sometimes concurring, sometimes divergent, joins the contributions which Gasca and Vigil have made over the years. These three have steadfastly presented a very different view of me to the almost always malicious opinions and very often deliberately distorted picture purveyed by a number of self-proclaimed *experts* who write in our country's media.

Neither must I forget, for that would be unjust, the extraordinary labor carried out in their day by Francisco Muntaner and Pedro Yoldi through their magazine *Terror Fantastic.* I treasure my copies of this unforgettable periodical, which was serious, well-researched and absolutely unbiased and made an invaluable contribution to the history of Spanish horror fantasy cinema. Later on Pierrot also did his bit with his peculiar publication *Vudú.*

As an example of the opinions my films merit abroad, here's the judgment of Gilbert Verschooten, president of the International Fantastic Film Association, critic, writer, founder of the Brussels Fantasy Film Festival and editor of *Fantoom* magazine:

> Spanish literature, Spanish thinkers, the overall Spanish cultural tradition proclaim that Realism is one of their most deep-rooted, fundamental values, and this is partly true, partly false. What this proclamation falsifies, or at least ignores, is the definite existence of Spanish legends of a fantastic nature. The whole of the northern part of Iberia is brimming with horror stories and tales of terror every bit as suggestive as English or German ghost stories. There are ghosts in Spain too, as well as apparitions, demons, bogeymen and werewolves. Moreover the Romantic Movement, although somewhat later than elsewhere, also found adherents in Spain, such as the poets Espronceda and Gustavo Adolfo Bécquer.
>
> For this reason the appearance of Paul Naschy is all the more surprising. Spanish cinema was rather slow to utilize the country's centuries-old

legends as movie material. Up until *La marca del hombre lobo* the national film industry had never properly dealt with the fundamental mythology of the horror genre, such as lycanthropy and vampirism. What's more, although the film was partially financed by German capital, it is a totally autochthonous movie. In my opinion this is not a mere imitation since Jacinto Molina's script approaches the subject from a personal angle reflecting the influence of his own roots.

Universal, Hammer and even German Expressionism are as mere scaffolding to his love of Gothic. In other words he recreates the classic mythologies, endowing them with a rare kind of magic which surpasses mediocre—or at best workaday—directors, often limited resources (although there are exceptions) and a hostile environment, quite apart from troubles with censorship, critics or other factors inherent to the film industry. Maybe his projects wouldn't have come to fruition under other circumstances.

The fact remains that he is one of the few Spanish filmmakers to have transcended their national boundaries, becoming a true star, a legendary movie maker written about in countless books, encyclopedias, magazines, etc. I must add that his strange though coherent career provides us with valuable information as to the social, religious and even political circumstances which his troubled country has traversed. Sometimes much more revealing messages are conveyed under the guise of fantasy than through reality based stories.

It is also obvious that to my mind the best pictures in his filmography are those he directed himself, perhaps because those which were directed by others only give us glimpses of the vision of Jacinto Molina, scriptwriter.

I soon discovered his charisma as an actor when I first saw *El jorobado de la morgue* at the International Fantasy Film Festival in Paris. The film *La bestia y la espada mágica* is one of his best works.

I'm writing these lines on September 6, 1997, a red letter day for me since it's my birthday and, one way or another, I've managed to survive the Civil War, the Franco dictatorship, the turbulent political transition and the years of democracy. I'm not so sure that I've done the same in the film world. In his doctoral thesis Adolfo Camilo wrote about me:

> Apart from a longing to be a wolfman, life has given Paul Naschy a good deal of incomprehension from the critics and a triple bypass, on top of which he has been increasingly forgotten over the last few years. But Paul Naschy bides his time and trusts in the full moon...

Adolfo is quite right, but it's not the public who have forgotten me. For over 12 years I have had constant proof of that. I still live on in the memories of ordinary people. What can I say? That unfair and unjust laws have prevented me from doing practically anything while others, either smarter or more influential than me, have had a field day? That Spanish producers and directors have typecast me as "the horror man" and can't envisage me in any other roles? As if my 30 years in the business, the more than 20 international awards I've won and the countless different roles I've played count for nothing. I've been everything from a Roman general to a priest, a desperate father, a terrorist, a policeman, a newspaper boss, a *Death Wish* vigilante, a trapeze artist and a secret agent. In short, I've worked in every genre—melodrama, comedy, historical drama, thriller, action, adventure, documentary and, of course, horror fantasy. In all these different genres I have years of experience not only as an actor, but also as a director and a producer.

I currently have several scripts lying on my desk. They are all recent offers. The call of the movies is as strong as ever. All the awards, the tributes and above all the support of my fans have helped me to fight against the bitterness I still feel inside. I hope these memoirs will serve as a final catharsis and I will be able to lay the past to rest once and for all.

My dog Lon (named after Lon Chaney, of course) is here stretched out at my feet. You see, the Wolfman's most faithful, understanding and affectionate friend is a floppy-eared golden Cocker Spaniel with the sweetest, saddest and most intelligent expression you could imagine.

My dog Lon (named after Lon Chaney, of course)

My role has always been like that of some wizened old villager, recounting tales of terror in front of a blazing log fire inside a darkened kitchen while the wind howls and screams outside. To quote Lord Dunsany: "Men tell tales and the smoke rises. The smoke departs and the tales are told."

Paul Naschy bides his time and trusts in the full moon...

We are not descended from apes. Sorry Mr. Darwin.
We are wolves without fur, walking upright through the world
with cruel, bloodshot eyes and jaws full of razor sharp teeth,
wolves prowling the Forest of Chaos, cunning devourers of children.
Along with the vampire, our most ancient mythologies
are inhabited by the hirsute Wolfman. Just as Hyde dominates Jekyll,
So the beast that lurks in our own inner darkness eventually overcomes the angels
we once were, I know not when (or it could be that we were never really angels at all),
And although we disguise ourselves in sheep's clothing or
as sweet little grannies, just for fun,
Deep down we are predators,
Wolves howling at the moon in the terrible night of reason,
Refuge of black nightmares where monsters dwell. Hobbes was in no doubt and,
as an avid fan of the werewolf film, I am bound to agree: homo homini lupus.

—Luis Alberto de Cuenca
Madrid, 21st January 2000

Last Moon

Since these memoirs were published in Spain in 1997 a lot of things have happened, some good and some bad but all of which I have to relate in order to bring my story up to date. I have written this final chapter especially for all my dear friends and fans in the United States. I'll never forget the warmth and affection with which I was greeted at the Fangoria convention in New York where I had the chance to meet my American friends for the first time, an event I'll never forget as long as I live. My heart and that of Waldemar Daninsky are yours forever. Thank you *Fangoria*, thank you Mr. Timpone. In return I am going to be totally frank. I feel that you, my readers, who have proved that you know and understand my modest work, deserve to be told exactly what goes on behind the scenes and what I have had to contend with to get my films made. Not a great deal has been written about me up till now and in most cases what there is has been penned by biased individuals who know nothing about either Paul Naschy the man or Paul Naschy the filmmaker. So I consider this final part of my memoirs to be the most important, since it will shed light on many dark places—although not all, because there are some recesses of the human soul which remain totally inaccessible. But when it comes down to it, just like anyone else, I am what I am by virtue of my circumstances. I originally titled this chapter "Black Moon" because this is a black time for me and I fear Waldemar Daninsky will never return to howl at the full moon. A treacherous silver bullet has left him mortally wounded somewhere in the heart of a dark forest where fantasy has no place... or rather where a bunch of evil, venomous dwarves have done away with it. My film career is in the shadow of eclipse. This country of mine where envy, corruption, oafishness, absurdity and vulgarity go hand in hand with the wonderful, the magical and the marvellous is very rarely benevolent towards her own sons. That's why I can't help feeling a certain satisfaction in the knowledge that my films are there for posterity, in spite of everything.

I think it was the great Groucho Marx who said something like: "Starting from nothing I've scaled the heights of absolute poverty." I could say more or less the same about myself. My long odyssey through the film world has reached a most ungratifying conclusion, my bitter struggle seems to have come to an end and I find myself adrift in the middle of nowhere. After three decades dedicated to genre cinema I have no money and precious little glory (in my own country, I mean. I probably should have been born elsewhere). I have to recognize that here, right from the start, I was faced with incomprehension and downright contempt. To use the simile so appropriately suggested by the great Luis Alberto de Cuenca, I was like the dog swimming against the current in the famous Goya painting which hangs in the Prado Gallery in Madrid. In retrospect I realize that it was hopeless to stand alone against the kingpins of the monolithic, official cinematic establishment who, for some reason which I'll never understand, had it in for me ever since *La marca del hombre lobo*. Some of them just ignored me, while others attacked me with the utmost impudence and in the grossest terms. I could write a long list of such individuals but I prefer to deny them the satisfaction of seeing their names in print.

To achieve anything at all in the Spanish film industry it's not enough to be talented, hard-working and dedicated. You have to know how to be an opportunist, a bootlicker, a hustler, you have to learn that "politics is what counts" and that to swim against the tide is like banging your head against a brick wall. So it's really quite a miracle that the horror fantasy genre ever made an appearance in Spain and then only because a madman called Jacinto Molina or Paul Naschy pulled it out of his hat like some arcane, heretic magician. To be sure, the docile, domesticated Spanish film industry never forgave him for it. The outcome of the recent general elections in Spain will make not the slightest difference to the situation of what is pejoratively known as genre cinema which will remain in the ghetto while the all powerful producers' circle of friends will be guaranteed plenty of rich pickings. New directors, most of them still wet behind the ears, will be elevated to star status through the complicity of those who hold the reins of power. There will almost certainly be no place for me. To their narrow-minded way of thinking, I am just "the horror man." All my years of experience directing and starring in comedies, historical epics, political and social dramas, thrillers and children's films count for nothing with them.

Here are a couple of examples which illustrate the extent of the animosity to which I have been subjected. In 1982 Pilar Miró, an intelligent and tremendously charismatic screenwriter and movie director, was appointed to the post of "General Director of Cinematography" by the Socialist party, subsequently drawing up her new, and infamously biased, laws for the regulation of Spanish cinema. These clearly erroneous laws brought about widespread corruption within the Spanish film industry thanks to the perverse system of nonreturnable subsidies and handouts which led to the appearance of influential "clans" within the film world who lined their pockets (and continue to do so) at the expense of the Spanish taxpayer. These powerful families, firmly ensconced for all time in the Hell's Kitchen of Spanish cinema, are the ones who decide who will work and who won't, who will live and who will die, who will triumph and who will go under, who will get the awards and the prizes—in short, who can make movies and who can go to blazes. The explanation is simple. Over the last few years these "capos" have completely taken a hold over film distribution and exhibition in this country, as well as getting their hands on all the subsidies going. That's why everything is subject to manipulation and a barbaric policy of excluding (and effectively ruining) many fine creative talents who are far more gifted than the "clans'" prôtegés. The Spanish film business today is based on barefaced nepotism. Since those in power openly despise genre cinema (especially horror fantasy), my future couldn't be bleaker.

But, coming back to Pilar Miró. This intelligent, charismatic lady was a great artist and always remained true to her beliefs. In 1997 she put my name forward for an Honorary Goya Award (the Goya is the Spanish equivalent of the Oscar). All the other members of the Academy's voting committee seconded her nomination but unfortunately Pilar died and they lost no time in withdrawing my nomination. They didn't show the slightest respect for Pilar's wishes and committed a gross injustice—I believe that my humble work deserves such a recognition. So the "capos" struck again. Who can believe in the integrity of the members of the Spanish Motion Picture Academy after that? Just like today's new young directors, they are in thrall to "their master's voice." In any case, wherever you are now Pilar, my heartfelt thanks. In spite of our differences you tried to see justice done.

The second example of the "esteem" in which I am held by the "barons" of the Spanish film business is quite similar. One of this country's most eminent writers and a foremost figure in the world of culture nominated me to receive the Medallion of Fine Arts, the highest accolade an artist can be awarded in Spain. The voting committee were all agreed; I deserved it. All except one one, who happened to be the current General Director of Cinematography and who duly overturned the nomination. It's more than likely that if he had agreed to my nomination he'd have been sacked. Just as I'd been denied the honorary Goya, so I was robbed of the Medallion of Fine Arts. "El Pernales," José María "El Tempranillo," Curro Jiménez and Luis Candelas ride again! The wolf had to be put to flight. So you see, I have very little for which to be grateful to the current despots of Spanish cinema.

The chronicle of misfortunes which have befallen since 1997 continues with the deaths of three people who were close to me. The first was that of the director José Luis Madrid who died from a massive heart attack at the age of 65. I was terribly upset by his passing, he was a good friend. He directed me in *Jack el destripador de Londres*, *Los crimenes de Petiot* and *Comando Txiquia, muerte de un presidente*. Rest In Peace José Luis. My father-in-law, the Italian diplomat Giovanni Primavera, also passed away recently. The best epitaph for him would be quite simply to say that he was a warm-hearted person and a man of absolute integrity. Another blow was the recent death of my nephew Javier who was killed in a tragic motorcycle accident at the age of 23. I once again felt the icy touch of the Grim Reaper at my shoulder. I had to go back into hospital for an emergency gall bladder operation. Despite the gravity of my condition, the fortitude of the ex-weightlifter held me in good stead and pulled me back from the brink. I am glad to say that I've made a total recovery and now feel fit as a fiddle once more.

As for the Spanish Film Writers' Guild, that was taken over by "Opus Dei" and after I had been its president for six years I was ousted from the post by Primitivo Rodríguez (producer of *Licántropo*). Some friend he turned out to be. The behavior of the members of Opus Dei is totally unethical and I'm glad that I no longer form part of the Guild.

I have also resigned as General Coordinator of the Lumiere Cultural Association after holding the position for three years. I consider the conduct of its president, Señor Mayorales, most unfitting. I found him to be the most unsuitable person to carry out any type of cultural projects, much less the promotion and advancement of Spanish cinema. His only interest is in making money and he doesn't care how he does it. I can't go along with that.

However, there have also been many gratifying events, such as the homage I received at the International Fantasy Film Festival in Oporto (Fantasporto) where I won another award, and a book about my life, written in Portuguese by Fernando Alonso Barahona, was published under the title *Paul Naschy*. I spent a marvellous 10 days there.

As well as other tributes in various Spanish cities like Albacete, Madrid and Cáceres, the latest homage to date took place at the International Comic Fair in Madrid over the weekend of March 18-20. Special T-shirts were printed and there were round tables, book signings and an exhibition dedicated to my film career.

I must also make special mention of last October's Horror and Fantasy Film Festival held in San Sebastián. This edition featured a special tribute to Spanish Horror Fantasy and was accompanied by the publication of an excellent book titled *Cine Fantástico Y De Terror Español 1900-1983*. This is the first serious study ever undertaken on this topic in Spain and I believe it is an excellent resource, paving the way for future research. Incidentally, the cover is illustrated with a famous scene from *La noche de Walpurgis*. The Festival also brought together for the very first time (and possibly the last) Jesus Franco, Narciso Ibañez Serrador, Juan Piquer and myself. Only Amando de Ossorio was unable to attend due to health problems. José Luis Rebordinos and his team have a real respect and love of the horror fantasy genre and as usual they ensured that a wonderful time was had by all.

Another important event I attended was the ceremony at which the first stone of the future Actors' Hospice was laid. The act was presided over by Elvira's good friend the Countess of Siruela with all her usual grace. At this event I met Antonio Banderas, the international megastar who, in the space of our brief encounter, proved that apart from being a great actor he knows how to give others their due. Our short conversation can be summed up as follows: "Paul, you're not just a film star, you're a living legend and I know what I'm talking about; when I made *Interview with a Vampire*, I got more fan reaction than I've ever had, even after *The Mask of Zorro*, you're one of the greatest in the genre, something unheard of for a Spaniard..." We embraced and he left for Jerusalem. Thank you Antonio, thank you for your esteem and your sincerity. The Actor's Hospice is a great social work—maybe someday I'll have to seek refuge there myself, if I live that long. You see, dear fans, Spain doesn't treat her artists well and after all my years in the film business, I don't even get a pension! So if I don't keep working, and when my health fails, I could end up on the streets. Like the old tourist slogan said "Spain is different"—and how! Antonio also told me that Paul Naschy has long been a respected name all over the world and that Waldemar Daninsky represents more than just a charismatic character of the silver screen. As well as being a fierce, persecuted, erotic, ambiguous hero/antihero who is forever seeking deliverance in death, Daninsky is a kind of Don Quijote of the netherworld and only those who love him can comprehend him. Really he has little in common with Lawrence Talbot or León Carido. Waldemar is the Sir Percival of Darkness, the result of a unique set of circumstances, at once real and unreal. Gracias Antonio, you're one of the greats.

I recently had the chance to get to know the Oscar winning José Luis Garci, probably Spanish cinema's greatest director. We met at a dinner given for leading intellectuals by Spain's president [the Conservative] José María Aznar. I must point out that all political tendencies are represented at these occasions. I would also like to say that, coming from the world of culture, I am only interested in politics in so far as they affect the arts. Just as I attended this gathering at the Palace of Moncloa (the President's official residence), I would equally have gone to (his Socialist predecessor) Felipe Gonzalez's informal get-togethers or those of (current Leader of the Opposition, Joaquín) Almunia. In my opinion the world of culture has no other idealogy than to educate and to fire men's imaginations.

On the professional front, since 1997 I have appeared in two short films, two TV series and two feature films, details of which are included in the relevant sections of the accompanying filmography. In the hit TV series *Querido maestro* (*Dear Teacher*) I had the role of soccer coach Rafael Montero, a character who was head over heels in love with a lady teacher played by that marvelous and distinguished Spanish actress Amparo Soler Leal. Following appearances on several chat shows (on one of which Sonia Braga was a fellow guest) I was honored on Television Española's prime time show *Version Española*, presented by the beautiful and talented actress Cayetana Guillén Cuervo. I was accompanied by my much admired Terenci Moix, a truly brilliant writer, and by my longtime friend and oracle of Spanish Horror Fantasy, Luis Vigil. Two films were shown, the disappointing *Licántropo* and the legendary *El jorobado de la morgue*. I later worked on a new TV series which is currently showing in Spain on the Antena 3 network. In *Antivicio* (*Vice Squad*) I have the role of a treacherous General of the Spanish Armed Forces involved in illegal espionage activities. My next TV assignment will be a part in another successful cop show, *El comisario*.

I starred in a short film made in Asturias called *Rondadores Nocturnos II (Night Prowlers)*. This was directed by Aure Roces and set in the 10th century. It tells the story of a redeeming spirit (played by me) who has to educate and prepare a disciple called Anaid to combat the evil spirits named Apocalypse, Dominion and Slaughter.

The latest completed feature film I have appeared in was Juan Pinzás' *Erase otra vez* (*Once Again Upon a Time*), released in Spain at the beginning of April this year. This was the first ever Spanish Dogma film. Dogma refers to a decalogue of rules to be followed during shooting thought up by a group of innovative European film makers headed by the Danish director Lars Von Trier—artificial lighting is forbidden, so is indirect sound and soundtrack music, only hand held cameras may be used, no dollies or cranes are allowed and so on. The film was made in the Galician language and stars a cast of rising young Galician actors. My part was that of a menacing Anarchist gardener. Filming with Juan was a real joy and I hope to have the chance to work with him again soon.

Two other films yet to be released are *La gran vida* (1999) and *Mucha Sangre*. The first is an international, big-budget production which tells the story of a man who has to spend 100 million pesetas in just one week. I play a Madrid taxi driver in a cast including Salma Hayek, Carmelo Gómez and Tito Valverde. *Mucha Sangre* is an entertaining Tarantino-style action comedy about a group of aliens who adopt the guise of gangsters in their bid to spearhead an invasion of Earth. Co-producers Cinecito, S.A. pulled out of the project when shooting was nearly completed, leaving the film unfinished. Hopefully production will be resumed soon on this feature in which I play the protagonist and Rodolfo Sancho the antagonist.

Unfortunately the Spanish film industry remains unwilling to produce horror movies which means I have been unable to get backing for *Los ojos del lobo* and it looks highly unlikely that Waldemar Daninsky will ever return to the big screen. Still, in spite of having the odds heavily stacked against me, I shall keep trying. I believe my films are more Anglo Saxon than Iberian. America was always my filmic point of reference and maybe if I'd made the movie overseas my life would have worked out in a totally different way. Now without work and without even a pension to subsist on, I ask myself: "Was it all worth it? Was it worth giving the best years of my life to a lost cause?" The obvious answer is no, I was wrong, I made a mistake and if I had been an architect instead I wouldn't now find myself in such dire straits. But what's done is done. The only deep-rooted consolation I have is the knowledge that a lot of people all around the world have been happy and forgotten their everyday troubles watching my movies. I hope that all you fans in the United States will always have a place for me in your hearts and that you will continue to cherish the memory of Waldemar Daninsky howling at the full moon. And so my dear American friends, as I come to the end of these memoirs, I look forward to getting to know you at our forthcoming meeting in Washington. With the hope that Paul Naschy will be able to go on making movies for you all, I take my leave. Hasta pronto de corazón.

—Paul Naschy, Madrid, April 2000

Filmography

by Adolfo Camilo and Luis Vigil

The early part of Paul Naschy's filmography comprises Naschy's work as an extra or very brief on-screen appearances and, as such, holds no interest for anyone but completists. This phase merely served as a kind of introduction to the medium for Naschy, a medium in which he has remained for almost 30 years.

AGONIZANDO EN EL CRIMEN (1967)
Production Company: Logar Films; Director: Enrique López Eguiluz; Script: Juan Logar; Music: Juan Logar; Released: January 5, 1970
Starring: Juan Logar, Irene Gutiérrez Caba, José Rubio, Tomás Blanco, David Molva (Jacinto Molina) and Yelena Samarina

A surgeon loses his fiancée in an operation. The tragic event unhinges him and he turns into a psychopath, committing cruel ritual murders and cutting off the hands of his victims. The film has the odd point of interest—the first murder, the appearance of Naschy, here calling himself David Molva, and not much else. The director, a graduate from film school, does a merely acceptable job of work. The future Paul Naschy plays a young inspector at the Sûreté who ruthlessly hunts down the killer and dies in the final showdown. Much of the film was shot in Paris.

LA MARCA DEL HOMBRE LOBO (1968)
Production Company: HI-FI STEREO 70 (München)—Maxper PC; Director: Enrique López Eguiluz; Story and Screenplay: Jacinto Molina; Music: Angel Arteaga; Director of Photography: Emilio Foriscot; Released August 17, 1970
Starring: Paul Naschy, Dianik Zurakowska, José Nieto, Carlos Casaravilla, Julián Urgarte, Aurora de Alba, Manuel Manzaneque and Rosana Yanni

A legend is born with the first public appearance of Waldemar Daninsky. Two basic sides stand out from among his thousand facets: ambiguity and a compelling perversity. Eguiluz achieves the best, most significant film of his short career. Supported by a well crafted script, the film is a homage to German expressionism and the American Universal Studios. Within this film we find the embryo of the imaginative proposals which Naschy would develop throughout his career. There's a succession of tributes to the legendary monsters played by Lugosi, Lon Chaney or Boris Karloff: the Gypsies who plunder Imre Wolfstein's tomb, vampires and werewolves locked in combat, the exaggerated Gothic atmosphere, which is enhanced by viewing in black and white (there is an excellent French monochrome version).

The film has moments of a great visual beauty and the underground labyrinths create a claustrophobic and phantasmagorical atmosphere. The scene showing the arrival of the pair of vampires, Wandesa (Aurora de Alba) and Janos de Mialhoff (Julián Ugarte), at the lonely railway station is wonderful. Despite a certain showiness evident in Eguiluz' direction, Naschy is magnificent in his first performance as the Wolfman, and the late Julián Ugarte gives the best portrayal of a classic vampire in the history of Spanish cinema. Makeup artist José Luis Ruiz set a high standard as did Emilio Foriscot with his subversive lighting.

Naschy's savagely sexual iconography is present in the movie, exacerbated by the almost textural utilization of the four elements. Thus water becomes sex and liberation, fire represents quasi-metaphysical cleansing, earth stands for degradation and air for damnation. *La marca del hombre lobo* is a historic milestone in the horror fantasy genre since it kick-started the unprecedented boom of Spanish cinefantastique productions. It was highly successful abroad and today it stands as a genuine cult movie.

LAS NOCHES DEL HOMBRE LOBO (1968)
Production Company: Kin Films (Paris); Director: René Govar; Screenplay: Jacinto Molina, René Govar and C. Bellard
Starring: Paul Naschy, Monique Brainville, Helen Mattel and Peter Beaumont

Joan Pratt, co-author of the splendid book *Las raíces del miedo* (*The Roots of Fear*), claims that he saw *Las noches del hombre lobo* in Spain. We have only managed to unearth a few stills but we are familiar with the film—suffice to say it had a troubled history. The plot centres on the attempts of an evil Parisian scientist to control and carry out research on Waldemar Daninsky.

PLAN JACK 03 (1968)
Director: Cecilia Bartolomé
Starring: Paul Naschy, Charo López

Cecilia Bartolomé was a graduate of the old Official School of Cinematography based in Madrid. She had a short career although recently she directed a film called *Lejos de Africa* which recreated the days of Spain's decolonisation of Equatorial Guinea. *Plan Jack 03* is a spoof of the American film noir in which Naschy plays a gangster à la Bogart. The film ends with a very funny Harold Lloyd/silent movie-style sequence.

LA ESCLAVA DEL PARAISO (1968)
Production Company: Dominó; Director: José María Elorrieta; Screenplay: José María Elorrieta and Navarro; Released July 27, 1970
Starring: Raf Vallone, Jeff Cooper, Luziana Paluzzi, Paul Naschy, Rubén Rojo and Perla Cristal

An Oriental fantasy made on a fairly lavish budget with a good cast, large sets and reasonably accomplished direction from the workmanlike José María Elorrieta. Although not too inspired, the movie is worth a look for its camp appeal. Paul Naschy plays Chantal, evil lieutenant to the Grand Visir (Raf Vallone), in a tale of revenge, lamps and genies. Made as a US-Spanish co-production.

LOS MONSTRUOS DEL TERROR (EL HOMBRE QUE VINO DE UMMO)(1970)
Production Company: Prades P.C. (Spain), HI-FI STEREO 70 (Germany), Italian International (Italy) and Dichberg PC (Germany); Directors: Hugo Fregonese and Tulio Demicheli; Story and Screenplay: Jacinto Molina; Music: Franco Solima; Director of Photography: Godo Pacheco; Editor: A. Isai Isasmendi
Starring: Michael Rennie, Paul Naschy, Karin Dor, Craig Hill, Ferdinando Murolo, Gene Reyes, Patty Shephard and Ängel del Pozo

An alien from the planet Ummo (Michael Rennie) attempts to take over Earth by exploiting mankind's ancestral fear of legendary monsters—the Wolfman, the Vampire, the Mummy and Frankenstein's creature. This was a fairly expensive film but it had a troubled production history—and it shows. Still, this comic book on film has its moments, such as the materialization of the vampire after the stake has been removed, the fights between the various monsters (particularly the one between the Mummy and the Wolfman), the scenes in which the elaborate labyrinths become filled with gas and the final explosions. Robert Taylor who had just filmed *Pampa Salvaje* with Prades was set to play Odo Varnoff but in the end the role went to Michael Rennie. A strange mix of science fiction and horror fantasy.

EL VERTIGO DEL CRIMEN (1970)
Production Company: Argos PC SL-CEA; Director: Pascual Cervera; Screenplay: Pascual Cervera, Heriberto Valdés, Manuel Suárez and Santiago Peláez; Music: Antonio Valero; Director of Photography: Francisco Sánchez; Editor: José Luis Matasanz; Released December 3, 1973
Starring: Paul Naschy, Jaime Toja, Mara Laso, José Marco, Barta Barry, Sun de Sander and Víctor Israel

This story of a vendetta between rival drug trafficking crime syndicates in France stars Paul Naschy in the role of Lolo, a cruel and sadistic gangster. The film's highlight is the final shoot-out between Naschy and Mara Laso, who shoots him from her bathtub. The film's original title was *Bombones para Petulia*.

LA FURIA DEL HOMBRE LOBO (1970)
Production Company: Maxper PC; Director: José María Zabalza; Story and Screenplay: Jacinto Molina; Music: Angel Arteaga; Director of Photography: Leopoldo Villaseñor; Editor: Luis D. Alvarez; Makeup: Carlos Paradela; Released May 28, 1973
Starring: Paul Naschy, Perla Cristal, Michael Rivers, Diana Montes, Mark Stevens, José Marco and Verónica Luján

A Nazi professor's daughter attempts to control the mind of Waldemar Daninsky with some scientific apparatus called chemiotrodes in order to use both man and beast to further her evil schemes. Her sinister manipulations lead to a confrontation under the full moon between Waldemar and his own wife (Diana Montes), both transformed into ferocious lycanthropes. This is the first European on-screen appearance of a female werewolf. The film was started by Enrique López Eguiluz who, for some reason, was replaced by José María

Zabalza. It's a weird film, kitsch and quasi-surreal, but of a much lower quality than the previous outings directed by Eguiluz and Fregonese-Demicheli. In spite of the poor direction it has become a semi-cult movie.

LA NOCHE DE WALPURGIS (1970)
Production Company: Plata Films SA (Spain), HI-FI STEREO 70 (Germany); Director: León Klimovsky; Story and Screenplay: Jacinto Molina; Director of Photography: Leopoldo Villaseñor; Music: Antón García Abril; Editor: Antonio Jimeno; Makeup: José Luis Morales; Art Director: Ludwig Orny; Released May 17, 1971
Starring: Paul Naschy, Gaby Fuchs, Bárbara Cappel, Andrés Resino, Yelena Samarina, Julio Peña and Patty Shephard

The biggest Spanish Horror Fantasy hit of all time. An indisputable cult movie, it lead to a worldwide revival of the genre. Klimovsky pulled off the greatest triumph of his career, breaking box-office records and creating what could almost be described as "Walpurgismania." The late Russo-Argentinian director conjured up a phantasmogorical atmosphere reminiscent of Dreyer and utilized slow motion to great effect in portraying the shadowy world of the vampire (a "trick" which was subsequently much imitated). Waldemar confronts the terrible and powerful Countess Wandesa Dárvula de Nadasdy. Naschy's iconography is consolidated and elaborated in this picture to include the cross of Mayenza, the knight's tomb, black masses, the spectral monk and the terrifying Bathory in the guise of the beautiful and disturbing Patty Shepard, who could have become the new Barbara Steele. A genuine milestone of international horror fantasy cinema. It was filmed in 70mm.

DOCTOR JEKYLL Y EL HOMBRE LOBO (1971)
Production Company: Arturo González PC; Director: León Klimovsky; Story and Screenplay: Jacinto Molina Director of Photography: Francisco Fraile; Makeup: Miguel Sesé; Music: Antón García Abril; Released November 13, 1972
Starring: Paul Naschy, Shirley Corrigan, Jack Taylor, Mirta Miller, Luis Induni, Elsa Zabala, Barta Barry and Jorge Vico

A surprising blend of the legend of the werewolf and Stevenson's *The Strange Case Of Dr. Jekyll and Mr. Hyde*. Waldemar Daninsky leaves the ancient castle in the Carpathians which had been his refuge and travels from the legendary Transylvania to London in search of a cure for his condition through Dr. Jekyll's formula, now in the possession of his grandson. Waldemar has an injection of the formula, resulting in a strange case of triple personality. Waldemar becomes Mr. Hyde whose evil cunning will vanquish the beast, after which the application of the antidote will eliminate Hyde and Waldemar will finally be free of the curse of the werewolf. Unfortunately Dr. Jekyll's assistant murders him in a fit of jealousy and the experiment goes out of control, leading to a spiral of death and horror.

There are several standouts, among which we may list Waldemar's transformation inside a lift; the death of Hyde's assistant, impaled on metal spikes and, above all, Naschy's superb portrayal of the evil Mr. Hyde. His simple characterization recalls that of the great John Barrymore and also brings to mind *El testamento del doctor Cordelier*. Unforgettable are the scenes which show a drunk thrown into the river Thames, the murder of a prostitute in a murky Soho dive—a glimpse of the murderer's cruel, yellow eyes seen through silk stockings—and the terrific struggle of the three-personalities-in-one inside a night club.

This is a surprising, Gothic movie which intelligently combines two great horror legends. Klimovsky doesn't quite achieve the same magic as in *La noche de Walpurgis* but, then again, that would have been a pretty tall order.

JACK, EL DESTRIPADOR DE LONDRES (1971)
Production Company: Cinefilms (España), Edmundo Amatti (Italy); Director: José Luis Madrid; Story and Screenplay: Jacinto Molina and José Luis Madrid; Directors of Photography: Diego Ubeda and Enrique Salete; Music: Piero Piccioni; Editor: Luis Puigbert; Released July 10, 1972
Starring: Paul Naschy, Orchidea de Santis, Renzzo Marignano, Patricia Loran and Andrés Resino

Updating the legend of the enigmatic Ripper, Madrid's directorial flair and the well written screenplay manage to catch the viewer completely off guard. The surprise ending is particularly well done. The scene of an extremely drunk Naschy is also memorable. Shot entirely on location in London, the film delivers an excellent pay-off.

Awards: IV Sitges International Festival of Horror and Science Fiction Films. Special mention for Paul Naschy for his important contribution to the genre.

DISCO ROJO (1972)
Director: Rafael Romero-Marchant; Story: Jacinto Molina; Screenplay: Jacinto Molina and Antonio Vilar;
Released March 26, 1973
Starring: Antonio Vilar, Paul Naschy, Mara Cruz, Antonio Casas and Hugo Blanco

A high-budget, action packed thriller revolving around the world of drug Mafias, filmed in Lisbon, the
Algarve, Estoril and Madrid. Naschy wrote the script as a vehicle for his good friend the superb Portuguese
actor-star Antonio Vilar. Here Naschy plays an important Hungarian gangster (Sergio Meleter) who controls
not only the illegal drugs business but also high class prostitution and gambling rackets. The final show
down between the journalist (Antonio Vilar) and the Mafioso (Paul Naschy) is highly memorable.

Awards: Best Director, Best Screenplay and Best Female Lead at the 1973 National Show Business Syndi-
cate awards.

EL GRAN AMOR DEL CONDE DRACULA (1972)
Production Company: Janus Films SL (Manuel Leguineche); Director: Javier Aguirre; Story and Screen-
play: Jacinto Molina, Alberto S. Insúa and Javier Aguirre; Director of Photography: Raúl Pérez Cubero;
Producer: Francisco Lara Polop; Editor: Petra Nieva; Camera Operator: Miguel Agudo; Released September
22, 1975
Starring: Paul Naschy, Haydee Politoff, Rosanna Yanni, Mirta Miller, Ingrid Garbo, Vic Winner, Julia Peña,
Susan Latur, Alvaro de Luna and José Manuel Martín

The Transylvanian prince Vlad III *The Impaler* is known to have been well built, very strong and a skilled
wielder of the heavy double headed battle ax and chain mace and easily able to bear the weight of a suit of
battle armor. The historical basis for the legendary Count Dracula was a far cry from the popular image of an
extremely tall, almost skeletal figure, and so it seems fitting that Paul Naschy decided to change the stereo-
type. The terrible aristocrat probably resembled Naschy more than Christopher Lee (although we're aware
that conventionalisms are highly effective too).
    Coppola gave us his own superb, overwhelming vision of the fascinating Dracula legend which, in our
opinion, is second to none, not even *Nosferatu*. But his *Dracula* does not reflect Stoker's—it merely trans-
poses and interprets the book—and neither is his the first aged screen vampire—Murnau got there first.
Neither is his excellent movie the first film to make love the central leitmotif of the story. Paul Naschy beat
him to it by 20 years with his own important screen version.
    Can you imagine Dracula committing suicide for love? Can you imagine him resisting the urge to bite
the neck of the woman he loves? Can you imagine such a sacrifice? You don't have to, you can see it. *El gran
amor del Conde Drácula* is considered a mythical picture among genre fans. As an expression of Gothic
Romanticism the film is highly thought of in England and the USA, descending directly from the English
ghost story tradition. Aguirre didn't hit the heights of *El jorobado de la morgue*, but he certainly came close.

EL JOROBADO DE LA MORGUE (1972)
Production Company: Eva Film SL, Francisco Lara and Manuel Leguineche; Director: Javier Aguirre; Story
and Screenplay: Jacinto Molina, Alberto S. Insúa and Javier Aguirre; Director of Photography: Rául Pérez
Cubero; Music: Carmelo Bernaola; Makeup: Miguel Sesé; Art Director: Cubero y Galicia; Special Effects:
Pablo Pérez; Editor: Petra Nieva; Released July 13, 1973
Starring: Paul Naschy, María Pershy, María Elena Arpón, Rosanna Yanni, Vic Winner, Alberto Dalbes, Manuel
de Blas, José Luis Chinchilla and Antonio Pica

Whale and Lovecraft, Guy de Maupassant, Poe and Jones, among other creators of cinematic, literary or
pictorial works, all the phantoms, the social beliefs, the intense Gothicism, the macabre; in short the entire
cultural and metaphysical paraphernalia which characterize the astonishing *auteur* Paul Naschy come together in this film which refuses to fit into any established category. The new "Man Of A Thousand Faces"
inhabits, with absolute credibility, an appalling world of necrophilia, sadism, and evil, permeated by the
stench of graveyard corruption. At the same time and without falling into contradiction, he demonstrates a
love which transcends death, an exaggerated romanticism, a loyalty to the bitter end, all handled with a
gravity and visual flair which was as surprising at the time as it is now.
    This story of an ostracized and self-marinating creature, whose attempts to justify his existence with
acts of selflessness are undone by other acts of extreme cruelty, reaches unforgettable heights of cinematic
excellence. His portrayal of Gotho, the wretched hunchback, was one of the highlights of Paul Naschy's

acting career. Scenes like the savage fight against the rats, the hunchback's cruel stoning, the sensitive scene with the lady doctor and the deformed wretch's various displays of kindness hark back to the best of Chaney, Sr. or Charles Laughton. One of the very best Naschys, and by far the best film to come from Aguirre who, in two horror fantasy movies, proved that he could have been so much more than just the director of mediocre vehicles for teeny bopper pop group Parchís or crooner Raphael.

Awards : Special George Méliès Award for acting at the 1973 International Fantastic and Science Fiction Film Festival in Paris. Award for Best Screenplay at the Festival of Antwerp in 1976.

LOS CRIMENES DE PETIOT (1972)
Production Company: Cinefilms S.A.; Director: José Luis Madrid; Story: Jacinto Molina; Screenplay: Jacinto Molina and José Luis Madrid; Director of Photography: Felix Mirón; Editor: Angel Arteaga; Released June 24, 1974
Starring: Paul Naschy, Patricia Loran, Fernado Marín, Quique San Francisco, Vicente Haro, Antonio Campoy, Lucía Prado and Mónica Reich

A sinister thriller filmed in Berlin. A serial killer leaves a Tötenkopf on the corpses of his victims. The phantom of the Nazis hovers over this dark tale. Naschy versus Naschy in a grim struggle with a surprise ending. José Luis Madrid's adequate direction makes the most of the magnificent locations.

LA ORGÍA DE LOS MUERTOS (1972)
Production Company: Petruka Films and Prodimex SRL.; Director: José Luis Merino; Screenplay: José Luis Merino and Enrico Calento; Director of Photography: Modesto Rizzoli; Released September 29, 1975
Starring: Stan Cooper, Gerard Tichy, María Pía Conte, Dianik Zurokowska and guest starring Paul Naschy

Another turn of the screw on the mad doctor theme in which the evil scientist conjures up a homicidal monster. Paul Naschy, in a brief but leading role, plays his part to a "T," first as a depraved necrophiliac, later transformed into a lethal zombie. His extraordinary Igor bears a strong similarity to his inimitable Gotho. This is the best film by José Luis Merino, a fairly inconsequential director.

EL ESPANTO SURGE DE LA TUMBA (1972)
Production Company: Profilmes S.A.; Director: Carlos Aured; Story and Screenplay: Jacinto Molina; Director of Photography: Manolo Merino; Executive Producers: Ricardo Muñoz Suay and José Antonio Pérez Giner; Music: Carmelo Bernaola; Makeup: Julián Ruíz; Special Effects: Molina; Released April 30, 1973
Starring: Paul Naschy and Emma Cohen

Now we come to one of the greats, a venerated cult movie and a fundamental title in the history of Spanish gore cinema. Paul Naschy demonstrates his unstoppable creative talent. The terrifying and fascinating evil entity that is Alaric de Marnac returns from his putrefact sarcophagus as a decapitated warlock brought back to life. Feeding on living hearts and warm blood he seeks to visit vengeance, extermination and death upon the hapless desecrators of his secret and his treasure. Notable points are the claustrophobic atmosphere, the ever latent horror and the exact co-ordination of the malignant plot machinations paying homage to the totem-like figure of Giles de Rais. Emma Cohen was seldom so lovely or sensual and the whole film is possessed of a character that forms a solid blueprint for Spanish horror fantasy. It is a cryptically Gothic, mysterious and shocking picture. Written in a one and a half days and shot in under four weeks, it inaugurates the superbly horrific cycle of films about the terrifying knight of Marnac, inspired, as previously noted, by Giles de Rais, who appears in all of Jacinto Molina's most personal works. The music by the great Carmelo Bernaola sets just the right tone and the work of the great makeup maestro Julián Ruiz is exceptionally good. Directed with gusto by Carlos Aured who understood perfectly the depths of Naschy's screenplay.

LA REBELION DE LAS MUERTAS (1972)
Production Company: Profilmes S.A.; Director: León Klimovsky; Executive Producers: Ricardo Muñoz Suay and José Antonio Pérez Giner; Story and Screenplay: Jacinto Molina; Director of Photography: Francisco Sánchez; Music: Juan Carlos Calderón; Makeup: Miguel Sesé; Art Director: Gumersindo Andrés; Released June 27, 1973
Starring: Paul Naschy, Romy, Mirta Miller and Vic Winner

A highly enjoyable zombie film, a strange, esoteric blend of Devil worship and ancient voodoo rituals leading to the resurrection of terrifying female zombies. Naschy gives a remarkable double performance as the monstrous Kantaka and his brother Krisna. He also appears as the Devil during a delirious Black Magic ceremony. It's a highly personal and macabre film which has the look of a comic book, and the flavor of a recurringly rabid sepia vignette. Juan Carlos Calderón's music is a major letdown. Here we have another example of León Klimovsky's masterly use of slow motion to reflect the shadowy world of the living dead. In the final analysis, a nightmare within a nightmare.

EL RETORNO DE WALPURGIS (1972)
Production Company: Lotus (Spain) and Escorpión (Mexico).; Director: Carlos Aured; Story and Screenplay: Jacinto Molina; Director of Photography: Francisco Sánchez; Music: Angel Arteaga; Makeup: Fernando Florido; Released September 21, 1973
Starring: Paul Naschy, Fabiola Falcón, María Silva, Eduardo Calvo, Maritza Olivares, Vidal Molina, José Manuel Martín, Inés Morales, Elsa Zabala and Ana Farra

The title is deceptive: There is no return to the first, great, classic Walpurgis movie in this film, which is one of the finest from the early part of Naschy's film career. Aured's direction is spot on and, except for the odd narrative hiccup, he manages to build this film into one of the fundamental cornerstones of Naschy's filmography. Standouts include the excellent medieval prologue (which Naschy is so fond of) in which Maria Silva wears the skin of the evil Elizabeth Bathory de Nadasdy and indulges in human sacrifices, witches' Sabbaths and Black Masses.

Memorable moments include the scene in which Waldemar Daninsky, the ambiguous, shadowy hero, offers coins in compensation for the death of a Gypsy whom he has shot from the top of his castle's staircase—a clear allusion to the overbearing arrogance of the landed gentry. In another brilliant sequence we share the unbearable anguish of a blind woman who senses the presence of the werewolf in her parlor. Another notable point is the climax with the mob of villagers' bearing flaming torches, very much in the style of Universal's horror pictures. There is also a great final narrative twist, as Daninsky's widow visits her husband's grave and we discover that the mark of the beast will cause the evil curse to continue through the Wolfman's son.

LOS OJOS AZULES DE LA MUÑECA ROTA (1973)
Production Company: Profilmes S.A.; Director: Carlos Aured; Executive Producers: Ricardo Muñoz Suay and José Antonio Pérez Giner; Story and Screenplay: Jacinto Molina; Director of Photography: Francisco Sánchez; Music: Juan Carlos Calderón; Makeup: Miguel Sesé; Editor: Javier Morán; Released August 5, 1974
Starring: Paul Naschy, Diana Lorys and María Perschy

This title marks the birth of the genuine Spanish thriller. It's a cruel, savagely erotic tale which transfers the story of a literal lady-killer from Siegel in the south of France to a stifling and unwholesome setting. Based on real events [according to Aured, very loosely] which happened in Madrid the film tells of a serial killer who gouges out the blue eyes of his victims, also paying homage to those legendary wax museum movies. There's an element of undisguised fetishism in the shape of Diana Lorys' revolting orthopedic hand. In all, a fine film with well-paced action, a great climax and an excellent plot. One of Aured's very best.

LA VENGANZA DE LA MOMIA (1973)
Production Company: Lotus Film; Director: Carlos Aured; Story and Screenplay: Jacinto Molina; Director of Photography: Paco Sánchez; Makeup: Miguel Sesé; Released October 27, 1975
Starring: Paul Naschy, Rina Otolina, Eduardo Calvo, Helga Liné, Jack Taylor, María Silva, Fernando Sánchez Polack and Luis Dávila

A brilliant comic book of a movie which plumps for home grown exoticism in a menacing recreation of Universal's Mummy, although its blatant sadomasochism brings it closer to Hammer than to the former puritanically bandaged 3,000-year-old codger. It also carries a message of protest with regard to the pillaging by Western archeologists of the Pharaohs' mysteries and treasures. A terrible vengeance from beyond the grave ends with a final apotheosis of fire and the stench of corruption. Naschy is convincing in the double role of the accursed Pharaoh Amenhotep and his scheming descendant Assad Bey. Aured rises to the challenge with highly creditable results. Luis Gasca considers this to be one of the best Mummy films ever made. The period detail is excellent, as is the directing. [If we overlook the fact that in one scene Aured treats us to a close up of the crest over the gates of Scotland Yard on which we see the letters ER (Elizabeth Regina) when it should be VR (Victoria Regina); another location insert has a modern office block in the background and, worst of all, as Jack Taylor looks out over the Thames we can see (repeatedly) cars driving over Tower Bridge behind him!]

LAS RATAS NO DUERMEN DE NOCHE (1973)

Production Company: Antonio Liza, Mezquiriz Film—Eurocine (France); Director: Juan Fortuny; Screenplay: Juan Fortuny; Director of Photography: Jaime Biadu; Music: Daniel J. White; Distributed by: Metro Goldwyn Mayer; Released June 7, 1976
Starring: Paul Naschy, Silvia Solar, Carlos Otero, Olivier Mathot, Yul Sandres, Evelyn Scott, Gilda Anderson, Victor Israel and Ricardo Palmerola

This is an interesting thematic potpourri—a gangster movie with shades of *Frankenstein*. The best thing is Naschy's death scene; his character, Surmett, is shot to pieces against a barbed wire fence. Fortuny's direction is run of the mill.

TARZAN EN LAS MINAS DEL REY SALOMON (1973)

Production Company: Profilms Plaza; Director: José Luis Merino; Screenplay: José Luis Merino; Director of Photography: Manuel H. Sanjuan; Music: José Luis Navarro; Art Director: Gonzalo García; Editor: Antonio Ramírez; Released December 4, 1973
Starring: David Carpenter, Nadiuska and guest starring Paul Naschy as Stanley

Paul Naschy here plays a ruthless villain who attempts to get his hands on the treasures from King Solomon's mines. Unfortunately this one was made strictly for the money.

UNA LIBELULA PARA CADA MUERTO (1973)

Production Company: Profilmes—Astro Films SA; Director: León Klimovsky; Executive Producers: Ricardo Muñoz Suay and José Antonio Pérez Giner; Story and Screenplay: Jacinto Molina; Director of Photography: Francisco Sánchez; Makeup: Miguel Sesé; Released November 17, 1975
Starring: Paul Naschy, Erika Blanc, Angel Aranda, Eduardo Calvo and María Kosty

This unfairly forgotten *giallo*, better than most of Dario Argento's efforts, is a surprising precursor of *The Silence of the Lambs* involving necrophilia, cross dressing and dragonflies in a most interesting thriller. Naschy gives a highly convincing performance as Milan police inspector Paolo Scaparella, a hard, smart Italian cop who also is sentimental and extroverted, showing off another facet of this chameleonic actor.

EL ASESINO ESTA ENTRE LOS TRECE (1974)

Production Company: Bermúdez de Castro (Picasa); Director: Javier Aguirre; Screenplay: Alberto S. Insúa and Javier Aguirre; Director of Photography: Francisco Fraile; Art Director: Eduardo Torre de la Fuente; Released July 5, 1976
Starring: Fernando Guillen, Carmen Maura, Eusebio Poncela, Paty Shephard, Simón Andreu, Gemma Cuervo, José María Prada, Eduardo Calvo and guest starring Paul Naschy

This somewhat rushed and fragmented update on the old cliché of a number of characters locked in a claustrophobic setting and being stalked by a murderer is full of dialogues which slow down the action to a snail's pace. The extraordinary cast suffers from anarchic directing by a Javier Aguirre who is light years away from *Dracula* or *El jorobado*. In a brief appearance Naschy plays a butler, but he's not the killer. The murderer is in fact another butler; Ramiro Oliveros does what he can with the role but this remains a totally forgettable film.

TODOS LOS GRITOS DEL SILENCIO (1974)

Production Company: Daga Films (César Gallego); Director: Ramón Barco; Screenplay: Jacinto Molina, J.J. Porto and Juan José Daza; Director of Photography: Emilio Foriscot; Music: Angel Arteaga; Released August 16, 1976
Starring: Paul Naschy, José María Prada, María Mahor, Máximo Valverde, Mirta Miller, Blanca Estrada and Damián Rabal

An unlucky film for an unlucky director, this thriller is well thought out but badly made. The only decent part in the film is what was shot on location in Paris. Paul Naschy plays a journalist investigating the exploits of a serial killer.

LA DIOSA SALVAJE (1974)

Production Company: Profilmes SA; Director: Miguel Iglesias Bonns; Director of Photography: Jaume Deus;

Music: Alberto Argado; Released March 24, 1975
Starring: Eva Miller, Paul Naschy, María Perschy, Ricardo Merino and Luis Induni

A female version of the Tarzan legend, fairly well made by a director of limited talent who set out to give his movie a comic book flavor. Notable performances include Paul Naschy as the kindhearted villain, sometime Hollywood actress María Perchy and the evil predator played by the huge Italian actor Luis Induni. The last scenes in which Naschy and Induni, locked in mortal combat, are swallowed by quicksand are technically impressive.

EL MARISCAL DEL INFIERNO (1974)
Production Company: Profilmes SA (Spain) and Orbe PC (Argentina); Director: León Klimovsky; Executive Producers: Ricardo Muñoz Suay and José Antonio Pérez Giner; Story and Screenplay: Jacinto Molina; Director of Photography: Francisco Sánchez; Art Director: Oscar Escomarsino
Starring: Paul Naschy, Guillermo Bredeston, Norma Sebre, Graciella Nilson, German Kraus, Vidal Molina, Eduardo Calvo, José Luis Chinchilla

The second screen outing for the Knight of Marnac, this time under his real name, Gilles de Rais, *The Marshall from Hell*. The film is a splendid pastiche of all the clichés of sword and sorcery movies and rousing adventure yarns, with magnificent imagery and outstanding sword fights. A really emblematic title, one of Klimovsky's very best.

LA CRUZ DEL DIABLO (1974)
Production Company: Bulnes; Director: John Gilling; Screenplay: From an Original Idea by Jacinto Molina based on three of the *Legends* by Gustavo Adolfo Bécquer—*La cruz del diablo* (*The Devil's Cross*), *El monte de las ánimas* (*The Mount of Lost Souls*) and *Maese Pérez, organista*; Released March 29, 1975
Starring: Adolfo Marsillach, Carmen Sevilla, Emma Cohen, Ramiro Oliveros, Mónica Randall, Eduardo Fajardo and Tony Isbert

A marvelous original story (a combination of Bécquer's *Legends*, Castillian folk tales and Naschy's own literary-cinematic tradition) completely ruined by unscrupulous producers and dreadfully miscast performers—especially Marsillach.

EXORCISMO (1974)
Production Company: Profilmes SA; Director: Juan Bosch; Story and Screenplay: Jacinto Molina and Juan Bosch; Director of Photography: Francisco Sánchez; Music: Alberto Agudo; Makeup: Adolfo Ponte; Released March 10, 1975
Starring: Paul Naschy, María Kosty, María Perschy, Luis Induni, and Grace Mills

This production cashed in on the success of Friedkin's *The Exorcist* (although in actual fact the story had been written some years before). The highlight is the encounter between the priest and a wolfhound which is possessed by the spirit of the main character's dead father.

LOS PASAJEROS (1975)
Production Company: Gregor PC; Director: José Antonio Barrero; Screenplay: José Miguel Hernan y José Antonio Barrero; Director of Photography: Francisco Sánchez; Music: Luis Eduardo Aute; Released June 2, 1980
Starring: Aurora Bautista, Paul Naschy, Eva León, Loreta Tovar and Henry Gregor

A forgotten film if ever there was one (but worthy of rediscovery) on the appalling theme of snuff movies. The travelers of the title arrive at Mr. Akenaton's mansion where after being wined and dined they are murdered in front of the camera. Shades of the Michael Powell classic *Peeping Tom*.

MUERTE DE UN QUINQUI (1975)
Production Company: Gregor PC; Director: León Klimovsky; Story and Screenplay: Jacinto Molina; Director of Photography: Miguel F. Mila; Art Director: Cruz Beleztena; Music: Phonorecord; Released September 19, 1977
Starring: Paul Naschy, Carmen Sevilla, Julia Saly *La Pocha*, Henry Gregor, Pedro María Sánchez, Fernando Hilbeck, Eva León and Mabel Escaño

This thriller was loosely based on the escapades of Eleuterio Sánchez (a Spanish criminal famous for repeated jailbreaks who finally took advantage of a prison rehabilitation scheme to study law and graduate as a lawyer), with shades of James Cagney in *White Heat*. It's a well written story in which amorous passions are unleashed inside a claustrophobic mansion house, including a struggle between mother (Carmen Sevilla) and daughter (Julia Saly) for the tainted love of the crook (Naschy). There is something dreamlike in the relationship between the mother and the criminal. In the harrowing finale, tragedy and vice bring about the destruction of the participants in this twisted game.

There are several stunning sequences, such as when the motorcycle cops who are chasing the delinquent are shot down in slow motion, the shoot-out between the protagonist and his gang, and the dramatic ending when the daughter shoots her lover dead to save her mother's life.

The film expertly conjures up a stifling world permeated by revenge, sex, violence and man's darker nature, Oedipus complex included. A great story superbly handled by the Russo-Argentinian director.

LA MALDICIÓN DE LA BESTIA (1975)
Production Company: Profilmes SA; Director: Miguel Iglesias Bonns; Story and Screenplay: Jacinto Molina; Director of Photography: Tomás Pladevall; Makeup: Adolfo Ponte; Editor: Carmen Fábregas; Released January 9, 1978
Starring: Paul Naschy, Grace Mills, Gil Vidal, Luis Induni, Silvia Solar, Verónica Miriel and José Luis Chinchilla

Another fascinating comic on film, the eighth chapter in the Waldemar Daninsky saga, this time opting for an out-and-out exotic action-adventure scenario. On this occasion the legendary lycanthrope comes up against all manner of perils including female werewolves, Tibetan bandits, ancient curses and, above all, the Mongolian tyrant Sekkar-Khan. Just when it looks like it's all over bar the shouting, the Wolfman has to fight it out with the mythical Yeti.

Awards: Silver Carnation award for Best Actor at the International Cinefantastique Film Festival in Sitges (1975).

AMBICION FALLIDA (1975)
Production Company: Productions Belles Rives (France), Talia Films (Spain); Director: Christian Jaque; Screenplay: Raphael Marcello, Jean Ollivier, Robert Jacques and Christian Jaque, Based on Characters from the comic book *Docteur Justice*; Director of Photography: Michael Kelber; Music: Pierre Porté and Angel Arteaga; Released February 26, 1982
Starring: John Philip Law, Gert Fröbe, Paul Naschy, Nathalie Delon, Hugo Blanco and Eduardo Fajardo

A movie extravaganza, based on a comic book, narrating the power struggle between two rival gangs for the control of the international drugs and arms markets. Action, intrigue and elegant locations were filmed in South Africa, Belgium, Germany and Spain.

INQUISICION (1976)
Production Company: Ancla Films (Italy), Anubis PC (Spain); Director: Jacinto Molina; Executive Producer: Rafeael Martínez de Azcoitia; Story and Screenplay: Jacinto Molina; Director of Photography: Miguel F. Mila; Music: Máximo Baratta; Makeup: Fernando Florido; Art Director: Gumersindo Andrés; Camera Operator: Julio Burgos; Released January 9, 1978
Starring: Paul Naschy, Daniella Giordano, Juan Luis Galiardo, Mónica Randall, Julia Saly, Antonio Casas, Eduardo Calvo, Tony Isbert, Ricardo Merino, Antonio Iranzo, Eva León and Tota Alba

Following his long experience as an actor, Naschy decided to take on directing, choosing for his *opera prima* the difficult subject of the trials, tortures and executions carried out under the auspices of the Holy Roman Catholic Church. However he didn't choose the Spanish Inquisition but instead went for the French one, basing his screenplay on real events. Instead of Torquemada's trials, the story centers on the cruel French judge Bernard de Fossey, the scourge of witches and heretics, who condemned thousands of people, accused of practicing Black Magic and Devil worship, to the gallows or to be burned at the stake. His final comeuppance gives him a taste of his own medicine. He falls in love with a beautiful woman accused of being a witch and ends up burned at the stake, the victim of a Machiavellian plot which is partly orchestrated by one of his own henchmen.

The film is held together by a well-written script and the direction is handled with professionalism. This was a fairly costly production, shot almost entirely on specially constructed sets. Gumersindo Andrés' period detail is magnificent, faithfully reproducing the historical period in which the story is set, the end of the 16th century. An efficient cast helps ensure the success of this ambitious project, a well researched study into Inquistional demonology and all the sinister paraphernalia surrounding its bloodthirsty machinations. There are good special effects in the scenes depicting merciless tortures and an excellent atmosphere is sustained throughout the film. Jacinto Molina's visual flair is already in evidence here.

SECUESTRO (1976)
Production Company: Azor; Director: León Klimovsky; Screenplay: Jacinto Molina and Antonio Fos; Director of Photography: Miguel F. Mila; Released June 20, 1977
Starring: Paul Naschy, María José Cantudo, Máximo Valverde, Luis Prendes, María Luisa Ponte, Gemma Cuervo, Tony Isbert, Teresa Gimpera and Manuel Tejada

The Patricia Hearst case transferred to a Spanish context in a well-paced intrigue which unfolds within a claustrophobic setting, leading to the Stockholm Syndrome. The direction is acceptably workmanlike.

PECADO MORTAL (1976)
Production Company: Laro Films SA; Director: Miguel Angel Díez; Screenplay: Miguel Angel Díez, Juan José Daza, J.J. Porto; Director of Photography: Polo Villaseñor; Music: Angel Arteaga; Released July 15, 1977
Starring: Sara Lezana, Yvonne de Sentis, Mari Carmen Prendes, José Nieto, Pedro Díez del Corral, Paul Naschy and Sandra Mozaowski

Unambitious direction, poor script and a brief appearance by Naschy as a 1940s police inspector.

ULTIMO DESEO (1977)
Production Company: Trefilms; Director: León Klimovsky; Screenplay: Vicente Aranda and Joaquín Jordá; Director of Photography: Miguel F. Mila; Music: Miguel Asins; Makeup: Tony Nieto; Released November 28, 1977
Starring: Paul Naschy, Teresa Gimpera, María Perschy, Alberto de Mendoza, Julia Saly, Nadiuska, Ricardo Palacios and Emiliano Redondo

This film is an amazing rarity. It starts off like *Saló,* continues like *Day of the Triffids*, turns into *Night of the Living Dead* and ends up like *The Great Escape*. The world's population has been blinded by an atomic explosion with the exception of a handful of upper class survivors who had been indulging their sexual and drug vices in the cellars deep below a stony mansion house. Unluckily for them the newly blind have become zombie-like creatures who surround the house, intent on attacking the upper crust degenerates inside. This is the starting point for a chain of horrifying events with a surprise ending. Naschy plays the part of Borne, an unscrupulous gangster with a refined streak of cruelty. By the time the dramatic plot has run its course, all the characters are dead. This movie is a must-see. With this film the long and fruitful partnership of Naschy-Klimovsky was drawing to an end.

COMANDO TXIQUIA (MUERTE DE UN PRESIDENTE) (1977)
Production Company: Servi; Director: José Luis Madrid; Story and Screenplay: José Luis Madrid and Rogelio Bahón; Director of Photography: Enrique Salete; Music: Angel Arteaga; Released April 3, 1978
Starring: Juan Luis Galiardo, Paul Naschy, Tony Isbert, José Antonio Ceinos and Julia Saly

This film is a painstaking recreation of the terrorist bomb attack which took the life of Admiral Carrero Blanco [one of the Franco dictatorship's closest collaborators] which, although lacking pace, is dramatically superior to Pontecorvo's film on the same subject. Several scenes were shot at the actual locations where the events happened, which lends the film an added documentary value. The film's ideological fence-sitting is something of a drawback. This last Naschy-José Luis Madrid collaboration is possibly their weakest.

EL FRANCOTIRADOR (1977)
Production Company: Laro Films S.A.; Director: Carlos Puerto; Screenplay: Jacinto Molina, Carlos Puerto and J.J. Porto; Music: Carlos Laporta; Released January 18, 1978
Starring: Paul Naschy, Elisa Montes, Blanca Estrada, José Nieto, Carlos Casaravilla, Carmen de Lirio and Antonio Vilar

The dramatic story of a failed assassination attempt against General Francisco Franco, very well told and full of intrigue, leading to an excellent denouement in which the terrorist (Naschy) is shot down during the Annual Trades Union Parade in the Santiago Bernabeu soccer stadium. Naschy gives a memorable performance as a humble Basque watchmaker who attempts to assassinate the dictator in revenge for the death of his daughter. The terrific photography is complemented by the skillful use of documentary footage. At the time it was made this film raised a lot of hackles due to the controversial nature of the subject matter.

EL TRANSEXUAL (1977)
Production Company: Laro Films S.A.; Director: José Jara; Story: Jacinto Molina; Director of Photography: Leopoldo Villaseñor; Released October 24, 1977
Starring: Paul Naschy, Agatha Lys, Vicente Parra, Eva Robin, Paco España, Yeda Brown and Sandra Albertí

In 1977 there were still a number of semi-taboo subjects (which have since completely lost their forbidden status), among which was the gay and transvestite scene. Around that time the so-called Lorena Capelli scandal was making the news as the consequence of one of the first sex-change operations to be carried out in Spain. These operations were performed clandestinely since Spanish laws were particularly repressive in this regard. Unfortunately Lorena Capelli died during surgery and soon there was talk of medical Mafias controlling the lucrative market of illegal sex-change operations, often putting their patients' lives at risk. The plot of the movie is centered around the investigation undertaken by an aggressive and unscrupulous journalist (Paul Naschy) in order to uncover the truth behind Cappelli's death. The investigation turns out to be a much tougher assignment than he'd bargained for, exposing him to danger and physical violence. Some of the scenes were shot at the old Gay Club in Madrid. *El Transexual* was a painstakingly researched film which preceded by several years one of Vicente Aranda's most personal movies, *Cambio de Sexo*. Agatha Lys played Lorena Capelli and Vicente Parra was the professor of theology who fell in love with her. There are several outstanding scenes, such as the wedding of two transvestites, the birth of their first child (a doll) and the routines performed by resident artists of the Gay Club. In short, *El transexual* put on show the whole psychological and moral background of the slightly pathetic world which these misunderstood individuals were forced to inhabit in those less enlightened times. José Jara, who had only made two feature films previously, did a praiseworthy job. *El transexual* caused more than one riot during its original theatrical release and certain sectors even tried to halt the film's distribution.

EL HUERTO DEL FRANCÉS (1977)
Production Company: Laro Films S.A.; Director: Jacinto Molina; Story: Jacinto Molina; Screenplay: Jacinto Molina and Antonio Fos; Director of Photography: Leopoldo Villaseñor; Music: Angel Arteaga; Makeup: Angel Luis de Diego; Released June 5, 1978
Starring: Paul Naschy, María José Cantudo, Agatha Lys, Pepe Calvo, José Nieto, Carlos Casaravilla, Nélida Quiroga, Silvia Tortosa, Manuel Pereiro, Luis Ciges and Julia Saly

One of the best films in Paul Naschy's filmography is also one of the best ever documentaries in the history of Spanish cinema. Here we have a homegrown serial killer more chilling than any *American Psycho*. A perfect flashback showing the murderer's execution by garroting bookends the main narrative. *El huerto del Francés* is a bloody portrait of depravity which splendidly recreates the turn of the century period. The climax is perfect, complete with a highly critical social commentary reflecting on the darker side of Spanish society in the setting of deepest Andalusia. The abortion scene is simply stunning.

Paul Naschy gives a superb performance in the role of one of the coldest and cruelest killers in the annals of crime in Spain. Everything works like clockwork in this movie which cries out for rediscovery and deserves to be championed wholeheartedly. Each scene, each frame, each single image are like impressions of Goya and Solana come to life, while the film's unrelenting realism makes it at once compelling and stomach churning. The strength of Naschy's personality and his maturity as a filmmaker shine through.

MADRID AL DESNUDO (1978)
Production Company: Horus Films S.A.; Director: Jacinto Molina; Story and Screenplay: Jacinto Molina and Eduarda Targioni; Director of Photography: Alejandro Ulloa; Music: Angel Arteaga; Released March 5, 1979
Starring: Fernando Fernán Gómez, Paul Naschy, Agustín González, Silvia Aguilar, Rosanna Yanni, Paloma Hurtado, Pastor Serrador, Pepe Ruiz, Yolanda Rios, Blaki, Julia Saly and Rafael Hernández

A slap in the face for so-called VIPs, this scathing comedy makes fun of the high society of the day while delivering a mocking but caustic social commentary. The film is peopled by an eclectic array of bankers, film directors, property developers, M.D.s, private eyes, spoiled brats, government ministers, millionaires, bartenders, chauffeurs and maids. It's a brilliantly made picture, shot on magnificent locations with a top-notch cast. The film's theatrical release stirred up a fair amount of trouble. The *creme de la creme* saw themselves reflected in a celluloid mirror and evidently didn't like what they saw.

EL CAMINANTE (1979)
Production Company: Horus Films S.A.; Director: Jacinto Molina; Story and Screenplay: Jacinto Molina; Director of Photography: Alejandro Ulloa; Music: Angel Arteaga; Released April 21, 1980
Starring: Paul Naschy, Sara Lezana, Irene Gutiérrez Caba, Silvia Aguilar, David Rocha, Blanca Estrada, Adriana Vega, Rafael Hernández, Taida Urruzola, Paloma Hurtado, Pepe Ruiz, Eva León, Javier Gamboa and Antonio Durán

Satan walks the Earth—we witness his rise, his triumph and his downfall, by men defeated, in the most impressive and quintessentially Spanish fantasy film ever made, photographed in the colors of ancient Grimmoire parchment. In this jovial, rollicking but nonetheless scathing medieval frieze, the characters are motivated by lust, pride, wrath, envy and greed. This particular Naschy-created world casts echoes of literary works like *El lazarillo de Tormes* and *El diablo cojuelo* as well as distilling all of the author's personal obsessions into a cry of anger and desperation. The fast moving camerawork mockingly underscores the excesses of vice on show, especially gluttony and lust for beautiful and submissive women. All this is counterpointed by the apocalyptic vision of a future full of injustice, war and executions and culminating with the image of the sinister mushroom cloud of a devastating atomic explosion. This is a visually beautiful film with a terribly pessimistic tone, the moral of which must give Satan an inferiority complex—Man is worse than the very Devil! By virtue of both its intent and its content, *El caminante* is an essential title in the filmography of Paul Naschy, auteur.

Awards: At the 9th edition of the International Fantastic Film Festival in Paris 1979 Naschy took the Best Actor award and also a special award for his "cultural contribution to fantastic cinema"; at the International Festival of Imaginary and Science Fiction cinema in Madrid (Imagfic '79) Naschy received a special award for his labor in favor of the renewal of Spanish fantasy cinema.

EL CARNAVAL DE LAS BESTIAS (1980)
Production Company: Hori-Kikaku-Seisaku (Japan), Dálmata Films S.A.(Spain); Director: Jacinto Molina; Story and Screenplay: Jacinto Molina; Director of Photography: Alejandro Ulloa; Editor: Pedro del Rey; Released July 8, 1985
Starring: Paul Naschy, Azucena Hernández, Silvia Aguilar, Eiko Nagashima, Lautaro Murua, Kotji Moritsugu, Roxanna Duprey, José Ruiz, Luis Ciges, Ricardo Palacios, Rafael Hernández, Tito García and guest starring Julia Saly

The first Hispano-Japanese co-production ever made is a perverse tale of crime, erotic fantasies, sadomas-ochism and cannibalism. A contract killer cheats, robs and murders his way out of Japan with the terrorist gang he's double-crossed hot on his heels. A beautiful Japanese girl, the gang leader's sister, has had an affair with the mercenary and is expecting his child. The Oriental terrorists manage to track down the traitor in Spain and a spectacular gunfight ensues in an old Templars' sanctuary (the same imposing ruins can be seen at the end of *El caminante*). The bloodthirsty fugitive shoots his lover's brother dead and escapes, himself badly wounded. Luckily, when he is at death's door he is found by the inhabitants of an isolated chalet in the mountains and in this cozy though claustrophobic dwelling he is nursed back to health. The intriguing and enigmatic plot gradually leads the ruthless mercenary into a dark pit where the frontiers of reality merge into nightmare. He starts to soften and become more human after falling in love with one of the beautiful daughters of Don Simón, the owner of the house. Just when it seems that we know which way the story's going, the plot takes a sudden savage turn, ending up with the terrorist being chopped to pieces as the main ingredient for Don Simón's celebrated stew, to be served at a fancy dress birthday party. Don Simón himself attends the celebration in the uniform of a Nazi colonel. The whole film is possessed of an unwholesome atmosphere. Among many shocking scenes, one which stands out is a sequence set in the murky pig sties where the hapless vet is devoured by a number of huge pigs. *El carnaval de las bestias* is an amazing movie which constitutes another turn of the screw in the peculiar film world of Paul Naschy. The title credits play over

Brueghel's "The Triumph of Death" accompanied on the soundtrack by "Dies Irae." A vein of macabre black humor runs through the whole film. Rarely has Naschy been so Naschy.

Awards: In 1980 the Spanish Film Writers' Guild presented Paul Naschy with an award for raising the prestige of Spanish cinema abroad.

MISTERIO EN LA ISLA DE LOS MONSTRUOS (1980)
Production Company: Almena and Fort Film; Director: Juan Píquer; Screenplay: Juan Píquer; Director of Photography : Andrés Berenguer; Music: Alfonso Angulo; Released April 3, 1981
Starring: Terence Stamp, Peter Cushing, Paul Naschy, Ana García Obregón and Blanca Estrada

Peter Cushing, Paul Naschy and Terence Stamp are in this Jules Verne adaptation, although it has to be said that they hardly appear. It is only mentioned here in the interests of making this filmography thoroughly comprehensive.

EL RETORNO DEL HOMBRE LOBO (1980)
Production Company: Dálmata Films S.A.; Director: Jacinto Molina; Story and Screenplay: Jacinto Molina; Director of Photography: Alejandro Ulloa; Music: Ennio Morricone; Makeup: Juan Luis de Diego; Editor: Pedro del Rey; Camera Operator: Eduardo Noé
Starring: Paul Naschy, Narciso Ibañez Menta, Julia Saly, Silvia Aguilar, Azucena Hernández, Ricardo Palacios, Beatriz Elorrieta, Rafael Hernández, José Ruiz, Tito García and Pilar Alcán

Together with *La bestia y la espada mágica*, *El retorno del hombre lobo* is one of the cornerstones of the long running Waldemar Daninsky cycle, a visually stunning, wonderfully atmospheric film pervaded by a brooding air of menace and a fabulous Gothic castle shrouded in mystery and the stench of decay. Ulloa's color photography comes closer to Brueghel than ever, the shimmering light from flaming torches and candles deepening the gloom and casting dark shadows on the sinister surroundings. Once again Waldemar is pitted against his arch-rival Erzebeth Bathory de Nadasdy, the Bloody Countess, here transformed into a bloodthirsty vampiress. The film contains a number of incredibly beautiful and intensely Gothic scenes. The cast iron script makes for an iron-clad film.

Awards: Highly commended at Imagfic (Madrid, 1981) ; Highly commended at the 1982 International Fantastic Film Festival, Oporto, with a special mention for Paul Naschy's performance as Waldemar Daninsky.

LOS CANTABROS (1981)
Production Company: Monge Films S.A.; Director: Jacinto Molina; Story and Screenplay: Jacinto Molina; Director of Photography: Alejandro Ulloa; Music: Angel Arteaga; Makeup: Mariano Rey; Editor: Pedro del Rey
Starring: Paul Naschy, Verónica Miriel, Alfredo Mayo, Antonio Iranzo, Andrés Resino, Luis Ciges, Blanca Estrada, Vidal Molina, Frank Braña, José Ruiz, Paloma Hurtado, David Rocha, Jenny Llada and introducing Dan Barry

Another great Naschy film, this one is a cross between historical epic, fantasy and *peplum*, narrating the savage battles between the pre-Roman tribe and Caesar Augusto's legions in their attempts to conquer the indomitable region of Cantabria. The plot is a succession of bloody battles, gladiatorial combats, guerrilla warfare, adventure and intrigue until the Roman general Marco Vispiano Agripa (Paul Naschy) finally brings the territory under the Imperial yoke. Alejandro Ulloa's photography is superb, the complicated action scenes are well-handled and the film seems to have had the benefit of a fairly high budget. *Los cántabros* was a totally different type of film from anything that was being made in Spain but, unfortunately, it didn't get the distribution it deserved.

BUENAS NOCHES SEÑOR MONSTRUO (1982)
Production Company: José Frade; Director: Antonio Mercero; Screenplay: Antonio Mercero and José Angel Rodero; Director of Photography: Manuel Rojas; Makeup: Fernado Florido; Released December 18, 1982
Starring: Paul Naschy, Luis Escobar, Guillermo Montesinos, Andrés Mejuto, Fernando Bilbao and the teeny-bopper pop group Regaliz (Liquorice)
Luckily Paul Naschy doesn't play Waldemar Daninsky in this film but a character called H.L. [from hombre lobo, the initials being a jokey reference to J.R. from TV's *Dallas*—which was then all the rage in Spain].

H.L. pops up in the guise of a ferocious werewolf to throttle a bunch of snotty-nosed little brats seeking refuge from a storm. It's not true unfortunately, none of it really happens. This so-called homage to horror movies is nothing but a vehicle for the appalling kiddie pop group Regaliz. Apparently the original script was very different—the monsters' castle was visited by group of luscious, bed-worthy female tourists, but as the singing brats were á la mode. it wasn't to be.

LA BATALLA DEL PORRO (1982)
Production Company: Profilmar-Germinal Films- PC2; Director: Joan Minguell; Story and Screenplay: Francesc Bellmunt, Juanjo Puigcorbé, Miguel Sanz and Joan Minguell; Director of Photography: Tomás Pladeval; Music: Josep María Durán; Released March 3, 1982
Starring: Victoria Abril, Paul Naschy, Joan Borrás, Pepe Rubianes, Carlos Tristancho and Juan Armengol

The sequel to a minor box-office hit for Francesc Bellmunt, this zany comedy features a parody of the military in which Paul Naschy appears to be having a ball playing the blustering Captain Matarraña.

LATIDOS DE PANICO (1982)
Production Company: Acónito Films S.A.; Director: Jacinto Molina; Screenplay: Jacinto Molina; Director of Photography: Julio Burgos; Music: Moncho Alpuente and Servando Caballar; Makeup: Fernando Florido; Editor: Roberto Fandiño; Released May 20, 1983
Starring: Paul Naschy, Lola Gaos, Julia Saly, Pat Ondiviela, Manolo Zarzo and José Vivó

The third and final (so far) appearance of the Knight of Marnac. This appealing project was brought to life with aplomb. As usual the menacing shadow of the mace wielding warrior hangs over a claustrophobic old dark house while inside the basest passions—adultery, sex, murder—are given free rein, until the forces of Hell burst forth to exact the most horrifying vengeance. The armor clad ghost of the *Marshall from Hell* is up to his old tricks just as in the far distant first chapter. But this time the Hammers of Thor are not at hand to stem the tide of infernal horrors.

LA BESTIA Y LA ESPADA MÁGICA (1983)
Production Company: Amachi Films (Japan), Acónito Films S.A. (Spain); Director: Jacinto Molina; Story and Screenplay: Jacinto Molina; Director of Photography: Julio Burgos; Makeup: Fernando Florido and Seiti Arai; Executive Producers: Masurao Takeda and Julia Saly; Editor: Roberto Fandiño; Director 2nd Unit: Tatumi Fujita; Art Director: Félix Murcia and Hidemory Oyama; Wardrobe: Kyoto Isyo (Japan); Wardrobe: Peris Hermanos (Spain); Music: Angel Arteaga, Kenji Onuma and Sigheru Amachi; Chief Armourer: Masateru Motizuki (Japan); José Luis Chinchilla (Spain); Released November 24, 1983
Starring: Paul Naschy, Sigheru Amachi, Yoko Fuji, Junko Asahina, Yoshiro Kitamachi, Soburo Sauri, Beatriz Escudero, Gerard Tichy, Violeta Cela, Takemori Yamase, Makiko Kitashiro, Conrado San Martín and José Vivó

Filmed at Toshiro Mifune's Tokyo studios, this is the best Spanish fantasy adventure ever filmed, made on a fairly lavish budget and with a good deal of imagination. Waldemar goes from medieval Middle Europe to Renaissance Spain and from there to the Japan of the Shoguns. A fascinating rites of passage scenario combining the iconography of Arthurian legend with the most revealing aspects of traditional Japanese lore, *La bestia y la espada mágica* is a Katasongawa Showsko drawing brought to life as a backdrop for a werewolf story.

Awards: Grand Prix at the Brussels International Fantasy Film Festival (1983).

MI AMIGO EL VAGABUNDO (1984)
Production Company: Acónito Films S.A.; Director: Jacinto Molina; Story and Screenplay: Jacinto Molina; Director of Photography: Julio Burgos; Art Director: Enrique Alarcón; Music: Fernando García Morcillo; Makeup: Fernando Florido; Editor: Roberto Fandiño; Distributor: CIC; Released August 8, 1984
Starring: José Luis López Vázquez, Sergio Molina, José Bódalo, Alejandra Grepy, Julia Saly, Gracita Morales, Yolanda Farr, Pep Corominas, David Rocha, Jorge Nieto and guest starring Florinda Chico and Paul Naschy as Enrique Longoria

If Naschy's spirit was present in the marvelous *El caminante*, then this film carries his letter. The autobiographical childhood memories occasionally verge on the sweet but on the other hand the dreams involving the super hero are spot on. José Luis López Vázquez is superb, as is the great Bódalo and indeed the rest of the cast. The underlying critical humor serves to raise the tone of the film, resulting in a good, solid movie.

EL ULTIMO KAMIKAZE (1984)
Production Company: Acónito Films S.A.; Director: Jacinto Molina; Story and Screenplay: Jacinto Molina; Director of Photography: Julio Burgos; Executive Producers: Julia Saly and Masurao Takeda; Art Director: Enrique Alarcón; Music: Angel Arteaga; Makeup: Fernando Florido; Editor: Roberto Fandiño; Released August 7, 1984
Starring: Paul Naschy, José Bódalo, Manuel Tejada, Julia Saly, Leticia Marfil, Alejandra Grepy, Alberto Fernández, Guillermo Murray, Irán Eori, Pierrot, Mirta Miller, Lone Fleming, José Cela and Angeles Martín

Danton and Kamikaze are two top flight contract killers in the pay of rival crime syndicates, and each is intent upon liquidating the other. Their motto is "the end justifies the means" and "an eye for an eye." This harsh, gritty film includes a number of stunning set pieces such as a bomb explosion at a swimming pool and the machine gunning of the bathers until the water has turned completely red, the dynamiting of two petrol stations by Kamikaze and several cars blown to smithereens. In short, it's a well made action movie, with flesh and blood characters, which reflects the key traits of Naschy's personality, both on the aesthetic and ethical level—the ghost of the Nazi hydra returns to cast its iconographic shadow over Naschy's work.

OPERACION MANTIS (1984)
Production Company: Acónito Films S.A.; Director: Jacinto Molina; Story: Joaquín Oristrell; Story and Screenplay: Jacinto Molina and Joaquín Oristrell; Director of Photography: Julio Burgos; Music: Fernando García Morcillo; Makeup: Fernando Florido; Editor: Roberto Fandiño; Stunt Arranger: José Luis Chinchilla; Released February 25, 1985
Starring: Paul Naschy, José Luis López Vázquez, José "Saza" Sazatornil, Julia Saly, Antonio Gamero, Taida Urruzola, Paloma Cela, Yolanda Farr, Anne Karin and Fedra Lorente

This James Bond spoof has its share of laughs, being a zany comedy which, it could be argued, was ahead of its time, although the patchy script works against the jokey attempts to send up the author's proverbial misogyny. The box-office failure of *Operación Mantis* bankrupted Acónito Films S.A. This had been the company's costliest production to date and they were unable to get over such a blow. It was the end of a company which had managed, against all odds, to produce several of the most important films in the history of the Spanish horror fantasy genre.

MORDIENDO LA VIDA (1986)
Production Company: Dragones Cinematográficos; Director: Martín Garrido; Screenplay: Martín Garrido; Released September 17, 1990
Starring: Beatriz Barón, Martín Garrido, Eduardo Fajardo and guest starring Paul Naschy

In this unwholesome descent into the fetid depths of Mallorca's underworld, Naschy plays a natural-born killer, a gunman, known as El Murciano.

EL ULTIMO GUATEQUE II (1986)
Production Company: Doblejota Films; Director: Juan José Porto; Screenplay: Juan José Porto; Released June 16, 1988
Starring: Paul Naschy, Cristina Galbó, Miguel Ayones, José María Escuer, Ricardo Merino, Conrado San Martín and Miguel Arribas

This film casts an outdatedly caustic look back over the past 20 years through the story of a number of couples in which music is the linking leitmotif. The direction is ham-fisted and lackluster, although Paul Naschy gives a superb performance as a no-good newspaper boss.

EL AULLIDO DEL DIABLO (1988)
Production Company: Freemon Nash International; Director: Jacinto Molina; Story and Screenplay: Jacinto Molina; Director of Photography: Julio Burgos; Special Effects: Francisco Garcia; Music: Fernando García Morcillo; Makeup: Fernando Florido; Editor: José Antonio Rojo
Starring: Paul Naschy (Bluebeard, Quasimodo, Rasputin, Satan, Death, The Phantom of the Opera, Mr. Hyde, the Wolfman, Fu Manchu, Ghost, Alex Doriani, Héctor Doriani, the Frankenstein Monster), Caroline

Munro, Howard Vernon, Fernando Hillbeck, Cris Huerta, Isabel Prinz, Vidal Molina and Serge Mills (Sergio Molina)

The best cast Naschy has ever been able to assemble in his most way out film, a summary of his movie career, and a summary of his life seen as a bitter chronicle of the progressive ostracism to which Naschy and those around him have been subjected. A cameo appearance by Waldemar Daninsky constitutes a self-tribute. Extraordinary acting, in their respective roles, by Ms. Munro and Howard Vernon. Practically all of Naschy's obsessions, totems and icons make their way into this weird, amazing film; the things that scared him as a child (Bluebeard and ghosts), his sexual cravings and frustrations, incarnated in the shapely figure of a pretty housemaid dressed in red and black (we all know what a key role housemaids played in the sexual awakening of well-off kids in the post-war years). This may be Paul Naschy's nastiest film but it's also the most intimate and heartfelt, too. A psychologist could tell us a lot about the character's true personality, which at times is so transparent as to become overly complex. *El aullido del diablo* constitutes a homage to all his favorite monsters, from Frankenstein and Leatherface, to Fu Manchu and Mr. Hyde. The child in the film (could it be Naschy himself?) turns out to be the medium of violence and revenge. The great Caroline Munro, a horror movie favorite who could have been the Barbara Steele of the '80s, appears as a female succubus in the form of the voluptuous maid who gives herself to the local priest before using her charms in an attempt to wrest wealth and power from the owner of the house where time has stopped for ever. The butler, played by Boris Karloff lookalike Howard Vernon, is the recreation of the necrophiliac mortuary attendant at Zaragoza Faculty of Medicine who had sulfuric acid poured over his hand by the students. It's strange to reflect that Naschy's most way-out film also turns out to be his most coherent, and each and every one of the cameos are parts of himself, whether intentionally or not. The film is a many-faceted gem which, like good wine, improves with age. Just like Alaric de Marnac in *Latidos de pánico*, here we once again have an angel from hell who, through a child, makes the succubus-woman pay for her scheming ambition and promiscuity. In the final analysis, all of Naschy's most cherished icons, together with a major part of his own life, are conjured up in a setting which could be none other than—his own country house in Lozoya !

SHADOWS OF BLOOD (1989)
Production Company: Peney ASLB (Netherlands), Maeso (Spain); Director: Sidney Ling
Starring: Paul Naschy

Two serial killers meet up in Amsterdam and set out to prove which of the two can kill the most victims. A worthless production.

AQUI HUELE A MUERTO (1989)
Production Company: Impala-ASH Films; Director: Alvaro Sáenz de Heredia; Screenplay: Alvaro Sáenz de Heredia; Director of Photography: Mikel Malka; Music: José Tejeyra; Released January 25, 1990
Starring: Martes y Tres, Ana Alvarez and Paul Naschy

A painfully bad horror movie spoof including a self-mocking appearance by Paul Naschy. This comedy is just not funny. All the same it was one of the Spanish cinema's biggest ever box-office hits!

HORROR EN EL MUSEO DE CERA (1990)
Director: Jacinto Molina; Screenplay: Jacinto Molina
Starring: Paul Naschy, Loreto Valverde, Marta Valverde and Sergio Molina
Unreleased

STATE OF MIND (1992)
Production Company: Desert Productions/ Film Events (JBC Productions); Director: Reginald Adamson; Screenplay: Liam Bradley and Van Tongeren; Music: Jean Bruno Castelain
Starring: Lisa Gaye, Don Hanna, Manouk Van Der Meulen and guest starring Paul Naschy and Fred Williamson

Naschy plays the brutal warder of a women's prison where he rapes and abuses the inmates.

LA NOCHE DEL EJECUTOR (1993)
Production Company: Claqueta Films; Director: Jacinto Molina; Story and Screenplay: Jacinto Molina; Director of Photography: José Enrique Izquierdo; Music: Fernando García Morcillo

Starring: Paul Naschy, Manuel Zarzo, Loreto Valverde, Marta Valverde, José Alvarez, Luciana Adriana Vega and Sergio Molina as Roque

This film gives a new twist to the tired premise of midnight vigilantes taking the law into their own hands, as epitomized by the Michael Winner-Charles Bronson *Death Wish* pictures. This is one really angry and extremely violent movie in which a silent Paul Naschy moves through Madrid's underworld exterminating delinquent scum with explosive bullets or razor sharp knives thrown with deadly accuracy. The film's fast pace, competently handled set pieces and great special effects compensate for the obvious lack of resources, and José Enrique Izquierdo's cinematography adds another point of interest.

HAMBRE MORTAL (1996)
Production Company: Narnia Films (José María Aresté); Director: Toni Escalonilla; Screenplay: Javier M. Collantes and Toni Escalonilla; Music: José Miguel Nieto and Sergio Alcolea
Starring: Paul Naschy, Juan Calot and Sandra Toral

This film is a perverse joke which sends up Naschy's legendary career as a movie werewolf. Naschy plays the dreaded, ever furious Uncle Carlos, the particular nightmare of Rómulo who is the teenage co-star of this sarcastic picture. The surprise ending is bound to provoke a reaction among the countless fans of Waldemar Daninsky. The film exudes a love of movies from the very first frame and can be viewed as a heartfelt homage to the career of our most international horror fantasy film actor.

CIENTIFICAMENT PERFECTES (1996)
Production Company: Francesc Xavier Capell (FXC); Director: Francesc Xavier Capell; Screenplay: Francesc Xavier Capell; Director of Photography: Lluis Milara
Starring: Paul Naschy, Francesc Xavier Capell and Silvia Escuder

Ever ready to lend a hand to the new generation of fantastic filmmakers, despite himself being an established star, Paul Naschy guest stars in this feature film on the theme of genetic engineering and the manufacture of a superman. Director Francesc Xavier Capell was trained in the field of animation (at Disney and Cruz Delgado) and had previously directed another psychotronic opus titled *Electriman*. Here he embarks on a science fiction piece full of intrigue and dotted with disturbing moments. The elementary animation techniques provide some charming special effects.

LICÁNTROPO (EL ASESINO DE LA LUNA LLENA) (1996)
Production Company: Videokine / Primitivo Rodríguez; Director: Francisco Rodríguez Gordillo; Story and Screenplay: Jacinto Molina; Director of Photography: Manuel Mateos; Music: José Ignacio Cuenca and Tomky de la Peña; Makeup: Romana González
Starring: Paul Naschy, Amparo Muñoz, José María Cafarell, Javier Loyola, Eva Isanta

No other production had more media coverage in Spain in 1996 than *Licántropo*, a fact which raised expectations to unheard of levels. Two factors contributed to this high profile. On the one hand Waldemar Daninsky was making a return to the screen after an absence of several years, years filled with the memories of his excellent previous outings in such films as *La Noche de Walpurgis*, *El retorno del hombre lobo* and, above all, *La bestia y la espada mágica*. As if that weren't enough the super attractive actress Amparo Muñozwas making a comeback after several years away from movies, thus bringing an added appeal to the project. But enthusiasm started to wane after the producers sent out videos to the members of the Academy and organized screenings in several major cities. The dreaded word of mouth started sending out negative messages which obviously did the film no good at all. After seeing the movie what was happening is easily understood: everybody was expecting something else. Director Francisco R. Gordillo (brother of the film's producer Prmitivo Rodríguez Gordillo) avoids whenever possible, which is most of the time, the on screen appearance of Paul Naschy-Waldemar Daninsky, both man and wolf, thus neutralizing the film's most charismatic character and condemning the project from the outset. Amparo Muñoz doesn't fare much better, having to portray a cold character who doesn't arouse any audience empathy. To make matters worse, the supporting cast are feeble, the sound dubbing is atrocious, the editing is outmoded and the pacing is slow to the point of exasperation. Moreover, the script has obviously been doctored, the lack of resources and last minute improvisations are too evident (the scene at the press kiosk is a clear example) and it's just a good job that the great idea of having the mythological horror represented by the wolfman confront the real life modern horror of the serial killer has managed to survive intact. Far and away the best thing in the whole film is the menacing, wraith-like wolfman who manages to be impressive with very little any makeup. The trouble is that he has hardly any screen time. The photography and the music are merely passable while the direction is reasonably good. Francisco R. Gordillo had the chance to resurrect the Spanish horror fantasy genre in his hands and he blew it. Even so, *Licántropo* may yet become a cult movie—stranger things have been known to happen—and the film does contain a number of things which the fans value, starting with the presence of Paul Naschy-Waldemar Daninsky, and including the appealing ancient Gypsy legends and the innovation of the confrontation between ancestral terrors and real life horrors. In spite of everything, and although it doesn't carry "the mark of Naschy," *Licántropo* is the only truly fantastic film made in Spain in the last few years. The truth is, we feel it should have been so much better.

Awards: Paul Naschy took the popular jury's prize for Best Actor at the I Madrid International Film Festival 1997, and the Castillo de lágimas award went to Paul Naschy for *Licántropo* as "best film event of the year."

EL OJO DE LA MEDUSA (1997)
Production Company: SFK; Director: José M. Cabanach; Screenplay: Javier Morales and José M. Cabanach; Executive Producer: Pilar Blas; Art Director: José María Hernández; Production manager: Concha Parejo; Sound engineer: Ignacio Martín
Starring: Paul Naschy, Carlos Guglieri, Paloma Merino, David R. Arcos, Belén Martínez, Ignacion Martín, Julián Merino, Ricardo Luque and Pedro Merino

The flavor of old style film noir pervades this very modern thriller about a washed up detective who crosses the path of a ruthless gangster (Paul Naschy) by seducing his beautiful young mistress. The only way out—Russian roulette!

LOS RESUCITADOS (1997)
Director: Arturo Boadilla; Screenplay: Arturo Boadilla; Director of Photography: Miguel Mediavilla; Music: José Carlos Molina; Makeup: Juan Miguel Cataluña; Special Effects: RHK; Sound Recordist: Angel Alvarez
Starring: Paul Naschy, Tony Fuentes, Santiago Segura, Angélica Reverte and Antonio Mayans

A free adaptation of Becquer's *Miserre*, a swashbuckling period action-mystery story in which Captain Molina leads the Holy Guard in a confrontation with the Devil.

ÉRASE OTRA VEZ [Once again upon a time] (2000)
Production Company: Atlántico Films; Executive Producer: Pilar Sueiro; Director: Juan Pinzás; Story and Screenplay: Juan Pinzás; Director of Photography: Gerardo Moschioni; Music: Juan Sueiro; Editor: María Lara
Starring: Monti Castiñeiras, Pilar Saavedra, Vicente De Souza, Mara Sánchez, Victor Mosqueira, Isabel Vallejo, Marcos Orsi, Antón Reixa, Mimy Fuentes and guest starring Paul Naschy. Released: 31 / 03 / 2000

The first Spanish Dogma film tells the story of five friends who, 10 years after studying together at the faculty of journalism, decide to celebrate a reunion party at the luxurious home of the most succesful member of the group. During the get-together the best and the worst qualities of the old friends and their various partners come to the surface, resulting in tensions and conflicts which have to be dealt with before they each return to their daily lives. Naschy plays "the gardener, a sinister anarchist with echoes of the horrific characters the actor has specialised in playing for many years" (the quote is from Boquerini in *Imagenes* magazine, June 2000). The film concludes with a borderline fantasy twist ending.

MUCHA SANGRE (2000)
Production Company: Nostromo-Cinecito;Director: Pepe de las Heras; Screenplay: Ramón Heres and Pepe de las Heras; Director of Photography: Pablo Hernández; Music: Mariano Lozano; Make up: María Cañizares; Special Effects: Biefec
Starring: Paul Naschy, Rodolfo Sancho, Txema Sandoval, Isabel Vázquez, Julio Campos, Carlos Lucas

"A fantastic genre action comedy" is how the producers describe this film, which at the time of writing remains unfinished. Paul Naschy stars as a gangster named Vicuña. When two psychopaths escape from prison they head for Vicuña's hideout to settle a score. But Vicuña is really a lethal alien in human guise and the cons get more than they bargained for.

SHORT FILMS

PEZ [Fish] (1986)
Director: Luis Guridi; Screenplay: Luis Guridi
Starring: Paul Naschy, Popocho Ayestarán, Antonio Junco and Elena Huércanos.

The story of an M.D. who has to treat a patient who is turning into a fish!

SSS (1988)
Producer: Miguel Ángel Vidal; Director: Escuadra Cobra; Director of Photography: Flavio Martínez; Editor: Cristina Otero
Starring: Paul Naschy, Maru Valdevieso, Tomás Zori, Iñaqui Miramón, José María Cafarell and Carmelo Espinosa; Song "Big Girls Don't Cry" performed by The Four Seasons.

A film about a sect of deliquents who have the power to levitate. Naschy is their leader.

LA HIJA DE FU MANCHÚ [Daughter of Fu Manchu] (1990)
Production Company: Miguel Ángel Comas, La Cuadlilla Amalilla; Director: Luis Guridi; Screenplay: Luis Guridi; Director of Photography: Flavio Martínez; Editor: Cristina Otero
Starring: Paul Naschy (Fu-Manchú), Leonor Ramos and Antonio Junco

An amusing spoof of the famous Sax Rohmer character. Naschy brings a splendid sense of humor to his role.

EL NECRÓFAGO [The Ghoul] (1994)
Director, Screenplay and Music: Gonzalo J. Fuentes
Starring: Paul Naschy, Angeles and Alberto

Based on texts by Baudelaire.

EL ÁNGEL MÁS CAÍDO [The Most Fallen Angel](1995)
Director: Iván Bousas

MALA ESTRELLA [Bad Star] (1996)
Director: José María Gonzalez

RONDADORES NOCTURNOS II [Night Prowlers](1999)
Production Company: Runaway Train Productions (Spain); Director: Aure Roces; Screenplay: Alejandro de Bernardi, Paul Naschy, Aure Roces; Music: Paco Loco, Fran Fernandez, Igor Medio
Starring: Paul Naschy, Diana Sanchez, Hugo de Campos, Javier Cardena, Lorena Garcia, Silvia Gion, Jessica Cueto

Filmed in Asturias,this is a tale set in the 10th century about the Redeeming Spirit preparing his disciple to confront evil spirits named Apocalypse, Dominion and Slaughter.

DOCUMENTARIES

THE PRADO MUSEUM: GREAT SPANISH PAINTERS (1980) and GREAT UNIVERSAL PAINTERS (1980)
Production Company: Hori-Kikaku-Seisaku (Japan); Director: Jacinto Molina; Written by: Jacinto Molina; Director of Photography: Alejandro Ulloa; Music: Ángel Arteaga Based on Selections from Boccherini, Mussorsgky, Beethoven, César Frank, Mozart, Bruckner and Richard Wagner; Editor: Pedro del Rey
Narrator: Félix Acaso

This production won the Japanese Ministry Of Culture Award 1982, an accolade bestowed on the best cultural film of the year.

HISTORY OF SPAIN THROUGH THE ROYAL PALACE OF MADRID (1981)
Production Company: Diamond Films (Japan); Director: Jacinto Molina; Written by: Jacinto Molina
Starring: Paul Naschy (Napoleon, El Cid, Hernán Cortés, General Murat), Andrés Resino (the father), Bruno Molina (the son), Julia Saly, David Rocha, Eva Robin and Charlie Bravo

An eight hour docudrama on the history of Spain from Witiza to Juan Carlos I. It was shown both on TV and in cinemas. Later an edited down version was prepared. The period costumes, set construction, effects, extras etc., all contributed to making this a costly production.

EL ESCORIAL MONASTERY (1982)
Production Company: Diamond Films Ltd. (Japan); Director: Jacinto Molina; Written by: Jacinto Molina; Director of Photography: Alejandro Ulloa; Make Up: Ángel Luis de Diego
Starring: Paul Naschy (Felipe II), Julia Saly and Charlie Bravo

Docudrama about the famous monastery and the most relevant episodes in the life of King Felipe II.

PREHISTORY IN CANTABRIA (1982)
Production Company: Japanese TV Channel 9; Director: Jacinto Molina; Written by: Jacinto Molina; Director of Photography: Alejandro Ulloa; Make Up: Ángel Luis de Diego
Starring: Paul Naschy and Julia Saly

A docudrama made for Japanese TV about prehistoric life in the region of Cantabria in Northern Spain.

THE CAVES OF ALTAMIRA (1982)
Production Company: Japanese TV Channel 9; Director: Jacinto Molina; Written by: Jacinto Molina; Director of Photography: José Enrique Izquierdo

Three hour documentary about the celebrated prehistoric cave paintings, written and directed by Jacinto Molina for Japanese TV.

THE JUYO MASK (1982)
Production Company: Japanese TV Channel 9; Director: Jacinto Molina; Written by: Jacinto Molina

A docudrama of similar characteristics to those previously made by Jacinto Molina for Japanese TV.

HELL IN CAMBODIA (1983)
Production Company: Diamond Films Ltd. (Japan), Tomomori Yakamoto; Director: Jacinto Molina; Written by: Jacinto Molina; Director of Photography: Yoshiake Nishibe; Music: Masanori Yoshino; Editor: Jacinto Molina

THE HOUSE OF ALBA (1992)
As well as acting as production manager on this thirteen part documentary
series telling the history of the noble House of Alba, Jacinto Molina also directed some of the episodes. It was made for the Japanese State TV Channel NHK.

TELEVISION
I SPY (1966)
Starring: Boris Karloff, Robert Culp, Bill Cosby, Sancho Gracia and Jacinto Molina

The episode was titled "Mainly on the Plains."

EL AMOR BLANCO [White Love] (1980)
Production Company: Hori-Kikaku-Seisaku (Japan); Director: Kotami; Production Manager: Jacinto Molina

A Japanese melodrama filmed in Spain to mark the 25th anniversary of the Hori-Kikaku-Seisaku company.

DRAGÓN NEGRO [Black Dragon] (1981)
Production Company: Hori-Kikaku-Seisaku (Japan); Director: Nágano

Paul Naschy gives a fine performance as an Armenian gangster.

LA TERCERA MUJER [The Third Woman] (1982)
Production Company: Hori-Kikaku-Seisaku (Japan); Director: Nágano

Starring: Sigheru Amachi, Paul Naschy and Julia Saly
A 13-part action serial based on real events and shot in several countries. Paul Naschy plays an Interpol agent.

LA ESPADA DEL SAMURAI [Sword of the Samurai](1982)
Production company: Hori-Kikaku-Seisaku (Japan); Director: Nágano
Starring: Toshiro Mifune, Sigheru Amachi, and Paul Naschy

A 13-part serial about a Portuguese-Japanese renegade whose banditry brings him into conflict with the Shoguns.

LA MÁSCARA [The Mask] (1982)
"Una bala en el camino" (Episode 6 of this TVE series).
Director: José Antonio Páramo
Starring: Sancho Gracia, Paul Naschy, Ramiro Oliveros, Eva Robin, Miguel Palanzuela and Gabriel Llopart

In the 19th century El Ángel negro (Naschy), the inventor of a parabolic firing cannon, lays siege to the city of Zaragoza but is defeated by the swashbuckling champion of justice known as "La máscara negra."

BRIGADA CENTRAL [Central Brigade] (1990)
"Desde el pasado" ["Out of the Past"] (Episode 11 of this TVE series)
Director: Pedro Masó; Director of photography: Alejandro Ulloa; Music: Antón Garcia Abril
Starring: Imanol Arias, Assumpta Serna and Paul Naschy (as Chaves)

Naschy gives a superb performance as the cunning, cruel and ruthless cop-killer Chaves.

OLLA DE GRILLOS [Box of Bugs](1991)
A live children's program. In the first program Naschy played the Frankenstein monster, in the second the Mummy and in the third Count Dracula. His participation in the show was cut short by his sudden heart attack.

QUERIDO MAESTRO [Dear Teacher] (1999)
Paul Naschy played the sports master in this weekly drama series about life in an urban Spanish secondary school.

ANTIVICIO [Vice squad](2000)
In this series about the exploits of a special operations police outfit, Paul Naschy played a high ranking officer involved in selling the secret plans of the new Eurofighter attack aircraft. The series was taken off the air by TV Channel Antena 3 after just three episodes had been screened.

EL COMISARIO [The Superintendent] (2000)
Another cop show provides Naschy with his latest role for the small screen—an internal affairs officer looking into possible cases of corruption involving members of the Madrid city police force.